Sports Medicine

ELECTROCARDIOGRAPHY, HYPERTENSION AND OTHER ASPECTS OF EXERCISE

A collection of the formal papers presented at the *International Congress of Physical Activity Sciences* held in Quebec City, July 11-16, 1976, under the auspices of the CISAP-1976-ICPAS Corporation.

Médecine du sport

ELECTROCARDIOGRAPHIE, HYPERTENSION, ARTÉRIELLE ET AUTRES ASPECTS DE L'EXERCICE PHYSIQUE

Recueil des communications présentées dans le cadre du *Congrès international des sciences de l'activité physique* qui eut lieu à Québec, du 11 au 16 juillet 1976, sous les auspices de la Corporation du CISAP-1976-ICPAS.

Compiled and edited by

Recueilli et édité par

FERNAND LANDRY, Ph.D.
WILLIAM A. R. ORBAN, Ph.D.

Published by

Symposia Specialists
Inc.
Continuing Education in Sports Sciences

Publié par

Éditeur officiel
Québec

Released through
SYMPOSIA SPECIALISTS, INC. · 1460 N.E. 129th Street
Miami, Florida 33161, U.S.A.

JOINT PUBLICATION / COPRODUCTION

L'Editeur officiel du Québec

Le Haut-commissariat à la jeunesse,
aux loisirs et aux sports du Québec

Symposia Specialists Incorporated

Associate producers/Producteurs délégués
Michel Marquis
Miriam Hochberg

WORLDWIDE DISTRIBUTION / DISTRIBUTION MONDIALE

Symposia Specialists Incorporated
Miami, Florida 33161 U.S.A.

SOLE DISTRIBUTOR FOR QUEBEC
DISTRIBUTEUR UNIQUE AU QUÉBEC

Éditeur officiel
Québec

Copyright 1978
by
Symposia Specialists
Inc.

MIAMI, FLORIDA, 33161
Printed in the U.S.A.

Library of Congress Catalog
Card No. 78-56611
ISBN 0-88372-108-2

Table of Contents

Table des matières

CONTROVERSIES AND ADVANCES IN EXERCISE ELECTROCARDIOGRAPHY
L'électrocardiographie à l'effort: progrès et controverses

CHRONIC EFFECTS OF EXERCISE IN SUBJECTS WITH HYPERTENSION
Les effets thérapeutiques de l'entraînement physique chez l'hypertendu

INDIVIDUAL SCIENTIFIC CONTRIBUTIONS
Communications scientifiques individuelles

v

LA COMMISSION SCIENTIFIQUE
THE SCIENTIFIC COMMISSION

CONSEILLERS INTERNATIONAUX
INTERNATIONAL ADVISERS

Le Congrès international des sciences de l'activité physique, 1976
a été placé sous le distingué patronage de L'UNESCO, Organisation
des Nations Unies pour l'éducation, la science et la culture.

The International Congress of Physical Activity Sciences, 1976
has been placed under the distinguished sponsorship of UNESCO,
United Nations Educational, Scientific and Cultural Organization.

Acknowledgements

The *Scientific Commission* wishes to express its deepest appreciation to the Director General of UNESCO, Mr. AMADOU MAHTAR M'BOW, for having granted the official sponsorship of his organization to the *International Congress of Physical Activity Sciences — 1976.*

The *Scientific Commission* also wishes to express its sincere appreciation and thanks to the governments, as well as to the associations, committees and groups which have provided the financial, scientific and professional assistance necessary for the planning, organization and conduct of the *International Congress of Physical Activity Sciences — 1976.*

FINANCIAL AND ADMINISTRATIVE ASSISTANCE
— THE GOVERNMENT OF CANADA
  · Health and Welfare Canada
    Fitness and Amateur Sport Branch
  · Secretary of State
— THE QUEBEC GOVERNMENT
  · Haut-commissariat à la jeunesse, aux loisirs et aux sports
  · Le ministère des Affaires intergouvernementales
  · Le ministère des Affaires culturelles
  · Le ministère du Tourisme, de la chasse et de la pêche

— THE ORGANIZING COMMITTEE OF THE OLYMPIC GAMES OF MONTREAL

SCIENTIFIC AND PROFESSIONAL COOPERATION AND ASSISTANCE
— International Council for Sport and Physical Education
  · International Committee for Sociology of Sport
  · International Committee of History of Sport and Physical Education
  · International Work Group for the Construction of Sport and Leisure Facilities (IAKS)
  · Research Group on Biochemistry of Exercise
  · Working Group on Sport and Leisure
— International Council for Health, Physical Education and Recreation
— International Society for Sports Psychology
— International Society of Cardiology
— International Sports Press Association
— Association internationale des écoles supérieures d'éducation physique et de sport (AIESEP)
— International Society of Biomechanics
— American Alliance for Health, Physical Education and Recreation (AAHPER)
— American Academy of Physical Education
— American College of Sports Medicine
— National College Physical Education Association for Men (USA)
— Council for National Cooperation in Aquatics (USA)
— Canadian Association for Health, Physical Education and Recreation (CAHPER)
  · History of Sport and Physical Activity Committee
  · Sociology of Sport Committee
  · Philosophy Committee

Remerciements

La *Commission scientifique* exprime sa haute appréciation au Directeur général de l'UNESCO, M. AMADOU MAHTAR M'BOW, pour avoir bien voulu accorder le patronage de son organisme au *Congrès international des sciences de l'activité physique* — *1976.*

La *Commission scientifique* tient aussi à exprimer ses remerciements les plus sincères aux institutions gouvernementales, ainsi qu'aux organismes, associations et comités qui lui ont procuré les appuis financiers, scientifiques et professionnels nécessaires à la planification et au déroulement du congrès.

L'ASSISTANCE ADMINISTRATIVE ET FINANCIERE

— LE GOUVERNEMENT DU CANADA
  - Santé et bien-être social Canada
    Direction générale de la santé et du sport amateur
  - Secrétariat d'Etat

— LE GOUVERNEMENT DU QUEBEC
  - Haut-commissariat à la jeunesse, aux loisirs et aux sports
  - Le ministère des Affaires intergouvernementales
  - Le ministère des Affaires culturelles
  - Le ministère du Tourisme, de la chasse et de la pêche

— LE COMITE ORGANISATEUR DES JEUX OLYMPIQUES DE MONTREAL

COLLABORATION SCIENTIFIQUE ET PROFESSIONNELLE

— Le Conseil international pour l'éducation physique et le sport (CIEPS)
  - Le Comité international pour la sociologie du sport
  - Le Comité international de l'histoire de l'éducation physique et du sport
  - Le Groupe international de travail pour les équipements de sport et de loisir (IAKS)
  - Le Groupe de recherche sur la biochimie de l'effort
  - Le Groupe de travail Sport et loisirs

— Le Conseil international sur l'hygiène, l'éducation physique et la récréation (ICHPER)
— La Société internationale de psychologie du sport (ISSP)
— La Société internationale de cardiologie
— L'Association internationale de la presse sportive
— L'Association internationale des écoles supérieures d'éducation physique et de sport
— La Société internationale de biomécanique
— American Alliance for Health, Physical Education and Recreation (AAHPER)
— American Academy of Physical Education
— American College of Sports Medicine
— National College Physical Education Association for Men (USA)
— Council for National Cooperation in Aquatics (USA)
— Canadian Association for Health, Physical Education and Recreation (CAHPER)
  - History of Sport and Physical Activity Committee
  - Sociology of Sport Committee
  - Philosophy Committee

xi

ACKNOWLEDGEMENTS

- · Exercise Physiology Committee
- · Psycho-motor Learning and Sports Psychology Committee
- · Biomechanics Committee
- · Administrative Theory and Practice Committee

— Canadian Council for Cooperation in Aquatics
— Association des professionnels de l'activité physique du Québec (APAPQ)
— Canadian Association for Sports Sciences (CASS-ACSS)
— La Ville de Québec
— L'Université Laval

The Scientific Commission extends its deepest gratitude to all the individuals who, in the last three years, have worked behind the scenes in a most efficient and generous manner.

By formal resolution of the Scientific Commission at its meeting of April 28, 1977, Messrs. Fernand Landry and William A.R. Orban, respectively President and Vice-President of the Corporation were mandated to carry out the production of the official proceedings of the CISAP-1976-ICPAS (resolution CS 77-01-11).

NOTICE

By decision of the Scientific Commission, *French* and *English* were adopted as the two official languages of the International Congress of Physical Activity Sciences – 1976.

In these Proceedings, the communications appear *in the language in which they were presented* for French and English and *in English* as concerns the papers which were delivered in either German, Russian or Spanish. Abstracts in the two official languages accompany each paper included in Books 1 and 2 and the seminar presentations in the other books of the series.

REMERCIEMENTS

- · Exercise Physiology Committee
- · Psycho-motor Learning and Sports Psychology Committee
- · Biomechanics Committee
- · Administrative Theory and Practice Committee
— Le Conseil canadien de coopération en activités aquatiques
— L'Association des professionnels de l'activité physique du Québec
— L'Association canadienne des sciences du sport (CASS-ACSS)
— La Ville de Québec
— L'Université Laval

La gratitude de la Commission scientifique s'étend à toutes les personnes qui, au cours des trois dernières années, et trop souvent dans l'ombre, ont apporté leur efficace et généreuse collaboration.

Par résolution de la Commission scientifique à sa réunion du 28 avril 1977, MM. Fernand Landry et William A.R. Orban, respectivement président et vice-président de la Corporation, ont été mandatés pour effectuer la production des actes du CISAP-1976-ICPAS (résolution CS 77-01-11).

AVERTISSEMENT

Les langues *anglaise* et *française* furent adoptées par la Commission scientifique commes langues officielles du Congrès international des sciences de l'activité physique – 1976. De ce fait, les communications apparaissent au présent rapport officiel *dans la langue où elles ont été présentées* pour ce qui est de l'anglais et du français, et dans la langue *anglaise* pour ce qui est des communications qui furent faites dans les langues allemande, russe et espagnole.

Des résumés dans chacune des deux langues officielles accompagnent chacune des communications qui paraissent aux Volumes 1 et 2 ainsi que les présentations faites par les conférenciers invités dans les autres volumes de la série.

Preface

The staging of international scientific sessions on the occasion of the Olympic Games has become a well-established tradition.

The themes of the congresses held at the times of the Games celebrating the last five olympiads illustrate that the movement has indeed become multidisciplinary and international.

In choosing *Physical activity and human well-being* as the central theme of the Québec Congress, the Scientific Commission endeavored to offer to the eventual delegates from the entire world, on the eve of the Olympic Games of Montreal, a large and democratic platform for the sharing of knowledge and the exchange of viewpoints on the problems now confronting sport internationally. For each one of the *subthemes* retained in the program, four speakers of different disciplines and of international reputation were invited by the Scientific Commission to give their viewpoint or that of their discipline on the proposed subjects. Additionally, the Scientific Commission offered a series of twenty (20) seminars of monodisciplinary character, in which at least three specialists of international reknown were invited to express themselves on selected topics. One hundred and twenty-seven (127) speakers from all corners of the world thus accepted the invitation of the Scientific Commission and were present at the Québec Congress.

Over and above the thematic and disciplinary seminars which constituted the heart of its program, the Scientific Commission also reserved a large portion of the time to the presentation of individual scientific contributions in sixteen (16) different disciplines and in six (6) special events.

The work sessions, numbering more than eighty (80), made it possible for more than three hundred (300) authors from all corners of the world to present the results on their research and scholarly work.

The central objective of the whole Congress was to bring frontier knowledge pertaining to sport and physical activity in general to the attention of the maximum number of persons. To that effect, the invited speakers were urged to present — the results of the latest research or scholarly work on the subjects proposed — the most convincing facts or ideas — the disciplinary practices, questions or issues which were in greater debate or contention — whenever

Préface

La tenue de sessions scientifiques internationales à l'occasion des Jeux olympiques est une tradition maintenant bien établie. Les thèmes des congrès qui ont effectivement eu lieu aux temps de célébration des cinq dernières olympiades confirment certes la multidisciplinarité et l'internationalisme du mouvement.

En choisissant pour thème du Congrès *L'activité physique et le bien-être de l'homme*, la Commission scientifique canadienne souhaitait donner aux délégués éventuels du monde entier, à l'occasion des Jeux olympiques de Montréal, une plate-forme large et démocratique permettant un libre échange des points de vue sur les problèmes qui confrontent le sport partout. Pour chaque *sous-thème* retenu, quatre conférenciers de disciplines différentes et de réputation internationale furent invités par la Commission scientifique canadienne à venir donner leur point de vue ou celui de leur discipline d'appartenance sur le sujet proposé. En plus, la Commission scientifique avait prévu la tenue de séminaires à caractère monodisciplinaire, donnant l'occasion à au moins trois spécialistes, dans chacune des vingt (20) disciplines impliquées, de faire état des connaissances sur des sujets choisis. Un total de cent vingt-sept (127) conférenciers de tous les coins du monde répondirent ainsi à l'invitation de la Commission scientifique canadienne et furent présents à Québec.

Au delà des séminaires thématiques et disciplinaires constituant le coeur du programme, la Commission scientifique a voulu réserver une place importante du programme à la présentation de communications scientifiques individuelles dans l'éventail des disciplines impliquées.

Les sessions de travail, au nombre de plus de quatre-vingt (80), permirent à plus de trois cents (300) auteurs de livrer à leurs pairs de tous les coins du monde les résultats de leurs réflexions et de leurs recherches.

Le rapport scientifique que constitue la présente série de publications se veut donc un bilan général de ce que dit la recherche et de ce que sont les réalités de la pensée et de la pratique courante, à travers le monde, sur des sujets précis touchant l'activité physique en général. Notre Commission scientifique canadienne avait à cet effet incité tous les auteurs à faire ressortir — l'état des connaissances, des

possible, the various implications relative to the education, health, or well-being of the people.

It was judged acceptable at the Québec Congress that speakers addressing themselves to the same topics present complementary, differing or even opposed viewpoints on the subjects, questions or issues at stake. It was in the discussion periods, which were made an essential and integral part of all work sessions, that the data and the viewpoints were exposed to questions, commentaries and criticisms from the audience, in the full respect of democratic principles and of the basic regards due to each person.

The reports which constitute the present series of publications are in reality the responsibility of their authors; consequently, they should not be interpreted as necessarily reflecting the opinion of the editors or those of the members of the Canadian Scientific Commission.

We believe that in actual fact, the body of knowledge relative to the potential contribution of physical activity to human well-being will have progressed significantly at the time and as a result of the Québec session.

The series of volumes constituting the present scientific report illustrates, in our opinion, the fact that the Canadian Scientific Commission has endeavored to build a program which was consistent with the highest contemporary international standards. To that effect, the Scientific Commission had chosen to function on a democratic basis which it believes unprecedented in this type of international effort; both the quality and the representativity of the professional and scientific organizations which were invited to contribute to the total endeavor do indeed illustrate this fact.

The members of the Canadian Scientific Commission believe that they were correct in assuring that there would be place, within the framework of the CISAP-1976-ICPAS program, for contributions stemming from all the branches and sectors of human knowledge which may be interested, from one angle or the other, in physical activity and sports as contemporary phenomena.

The success of the Québec Congress is owed outright to the efforts of the members of the Scientific Commission, the International Advisors, the members of the Executive, the Executive Secretary and Treasurer as well as to those of the numerous collaborators who have in fact consecrated so much energy to the pursuit of the objectives. At the critical stages of our collective endeavor, the professional and scientific contributions of a large

travaux de recherche et des réflexions de pointe sur le sujet, — les faits et/ou les idées les plus convaincants, — les pratiques ou les questions en discussion et en contention, — le cas échéant, les implications diverses qui touchent l'éducation, le bien-être, la santé ou la qualité de vie des citoyens.

Il était bien sûr accepté au Congrès de Québec que des conférenciers différents présentent, sur un même sujet, des vues personnelles, complémentaires, divergentes, ou même carrément opposées. Ce fut à ce sujet dans les périodes de discussions, parties intégrantes de toutes les sessions de travail, que les données et les points de vue ont été exposés aux questions, aux commentaires et aux critiques, dans le plus grand respect cependant des principes démocratiques et des égards dus à la personne.

Les travaux qui paraissent à la présente série n'engagent donc en fait que leurs auteurs; ils ne doivent pas être interprétés comme reflétant nécessairement les opinions des éditeurs ou celles des membres de la Commission scientifique.

Nous croyons cependant que l'ensemble des connaissances relatives à la contribution potentielle de l'activité physique au bien-être de l'homme aura progressé de façon significative, au moment, et comme résultant de notre session de Québec.

Les divers volumes du présent rapport scientifique illustrent bien, croyons-nous, le fait que la Commission scientifique canadienne s'est appliquée à édifier un programme qui soit conforme aux standards les plus élevés de l'heure et a de plus choisi de fonctionner sur des bases démocratiques sans précédent dans ce genre d'effort international. Les qualités et la représentativité des organismes scientifiques et professionnels qui ont été mis à contribution dans l'ensemble du projet témoignent, entre autres, de cet état de choses.

Nous croyons avoir eu raison d'avoir voulu et d'avoir fait qu'il y ait place, dans le cadre des débats du CISAP-1976-ICPAS, pour des apports en provenance de toutes les branches du savoir humain qui s'intéressent à l'activité physique sous l'une ou l'autre de ses formes.

Le succès remporté par le Congrès de Québec ne saurait cependant que revenir de plein droit aux membres de la Commission scientifique, aux Conseillers internationaux, aux membres de l'Exécutif, au Secrétaire exécutif et trésorier, ainsi qu'aux nombreux autres collaborateurs, bref à tous ceux et celles qui, effectivement, ont mis la main à la pâte. Aux moments les plus importants de notre cheminement critique, les apports professionnels et scientifiques en

PREFACE

number of persons, foreigners as well as Canadians, have indeed been generous, efficient and noteworthy.

The co-editors

William A.R. Orban, Ph.D.
Vice-president of the
Scientific Commission

Fernand Landry, Ph.D.
President of the
Scientific Commission

provenance d'un grand nombre de personnes, étrangers et canadiens, ont été en effet on ne peut plus généreux, efficaces et marquants.

Les co-éditeurs

William A.R. Orban, Ph.D.
Vice-président de la
Commission scientifique

Fernand Landry, Ph.D.
Président de la
Commission scientifique

Controversies and Advances in Exercise Electrocardiography

L'électrocardiographie à l'effort: progrès et controverses

New Perspectives in Clinical Exercise Testing

Wayne Siegel

Maximal exercise testing is an important adjunct to clinical evaluation of patients with known or suspected coronary atherosclerotic heart disease. A variety of technological improvements including computer averaging of electrocardiograms and phonocardiograms, multiple lead acquisition of electrocardiographic data, maximal workload attainment, and real time online physician monitoring of the entire test procedure have all resulted in improved sensitivity and specificity of the test. The clinical utility of maximal exercise testing has now expanded to include the monitoring of potent medical and surgical therapy of life-threatening coronary atherosclerotic heart disease.

Introduction

The detection and treatment of coronary atherosclerotic heart disease is the greatest challenge of modern cardiology. With the expansion of facilities in multiple centers for the direct study of the anatomy and physiology of the coronary circulation in vivo [15] the potential for diagnosis has been markedly improved in the past two decades. The impetus of accurate diagnostic studies has been accelerated rapidly because of improved direct coronary arterial surgical revascularization techniques [7, 8, 10].

Because of the large number of patients with known or suspected coronary disease, the logistics for the development of diagnostic facilities has become a major problem. Graded maximal exercise tolerance testing provides an effective method for the detection of patients with asymptomatic as well as symptomatic coronary atherosclerotic heart disease. Objective evaluation of the reproducibility and production of symptoms, electrocardiographic abnormalities, arrhythmias and the production of abnormal cardiac physical

Wayne Siegel, Head, Cardiac Function Laboratory, Cardiology Training Program Director, Cleveland Clinic Foundation, Cleveland, Ohio, U.S.A.
Current address: Stewart Medical Group, Miami, Florida, U.S.A.

findings during stress are now available as indicators of significant life-threatening coronary atherosclerotic heart disease. The use of these stress-evoked indicators for the detection of coronary disease has become widespread. It is clear that a large number of patients who have abnormal responses to maximal exercise testing prove to have life-threatening coronary atherosclerotic lesions. Many of these patients are candidates for direct myocardial revascularization. A high suspicion of coronary disease based on an abnormal response to exercise stress forms the basis for detection of coronary athero-sclerotic heart disease in a sizable percentage of patients. Several factors which determine the diagnostic accuracy and yield of progressive or maximal exercise tests are listed in Table I.

The need for more accurate noninvasive but reliable techniques for accurate coronary disease detection is obvious. Present non-invasive diagnostic systems including exercise stress testing for detecting coronary disease are imperfect [9]. The utilization of maximal exercise testing [5], multiple lead exercise electrocardi-ography [3], exercise phonocardiography [2], exercise radioisotope myocardial perfusion studies [16], and a variety of new monitoring techniques including computer suppression of exercise-related noise artifact [4, 11] have all been recently introduced for improved coronary disease detection during exercise tests.

It is apparent that all of these methods and parameters currently require and will in the future require some form of exercise stress to provoke the coronary perfusion deficit which results in the abnormal response of the oxygen delivery system to the ventricular myo-cardium. This is related to the pathophysiology of coronary disease

Table I. Factors Affecting Diagnostic Accuracy of Exercise Tests for Separating Normal Subjects from ASHD Patients

1. Intensity of exercise stress
2. Degree of ST segment abnormality provoked (absolute changes)
3. Presence of exertional angina
4. Normality of resting ECG. Absence of conduction abnormality, ST−T changes, pre-excitation
5. Avoidance of vasodilators or digitalis
6. Absence of left ventricular hypertrophy
7. Number of leads recorded
8. ECG fidelity
9. Number of specific discriminating variables used in combination
10. Diagnostic acumen of tester

and the fundamental relationship between coronary oxygen delivery capacity and myocardial oxygen demand. Latent coronary disease rarely manifests itself until the myocardium is stressed and requires oxygen delivery which cannot be met by a coronary circulation which is inadequate. Thus, noninvasive detection of latent and overt coronary disease must incorporate stress of the coronary oxygen delivery system. It is the purpose of this paper to describe the clinical application of exercise testing and its utilization in coronary atherosclerotic heart disease detection by the use of an automated system and the application of this system for monitoring medical therapy and revascularization surgical procedures.

Effort-Induced Angina Pectoris

Angina pectoris is typically exertional discomfort or pain which may occur anywhere in the upper half of the body. Classic angina pectoris is provoked by walking or other types of physical exertion and it is usually relieved by rest particularly in the initial stages of the clinical presentation within five minutes [6]. The New York Heart Association functional classification is commonly known to most physicians. A more descriptive effort should be made to quantitate clinical functional assessment. The use of graded progressive maximal exercise testing allows for such a functional assessment with objective criteria relating to limitation of work capacity by quantitation of workload at the onset of angina, ST changes, arrhythmias, and gallop sound detection.

Exercise-Induced Changes in Cardiac Electrical Repolarization

Among the most important qualitative and quantitative criteria of the inability of the coronary circulation to meet myocardial oxygen demand is horizontal ST segmental depression of the electrocardiogram provoked by exercise stress. In coronary patients, myocardial ischemia occurs frequently without anginal pain and this can be manifested by the ischemic ST segmental response to stress. There is usually a pronounced depression of the entire ST segment beginning at the J point. The differentiation between so-called junctional ST segment depression and "ischemic" ST segment depression is occasionally difficult. Rapid heart rates in normal individuals, particularly in the older age group, are frequently accompanied by junctional ST segment depression without horizontal or downsloping changes in the ST segment. The "benign" junctional alteration alluded to is rapidly reversible during the postexercise recovery period. The true "ischemic" ST segment response of patients with coronary disease results in a horizontal depression carried beyond the initial J point area out to the initial portion of the T wave and this depression may last for many minutes during the recovery after exercise is completed. The "ischemic" response is not specific for coronary atherosclerotic heart disease and may occur in patients with hypertension or any lesion which imposes excessive ventricular myocardial work. Occasional "false abnormal" responses are also seen in otherwise healthy individuals. Current criteria for an abnormal ST segment response include a 0.1 mv depression of the ST segment at 80 msec after the J point in one or more recorded leads [3]. This change is measured as an absolute difference between the resting and maximal effort electrocardiographic ST segment. The baseline (PR segment) is used as a reference point. When lesser magnitude ST segment depression is included in the abnormal range, a higher incidence of "false positive" tests occur. When larger ST segment depression is required for inclusion as an abnormal response group, greater test specificity may be expected but an increasing number of "false negatives" will be encountered. The critical aspect of the exercise electrocardiographic interpretation, frequently not described in standard discussions of the subject, is the progressive horizontal flattening and ST segment depression observed as the patient continues through the exercise test. Minor J point depression and ST segment flattening which does not increase as the patient exercises continuously does not usually imply a significantly positive response. Difficulty is always encountered when the resting electrocardiogram is abnormal prior to the onset of exercise. At the present time, a thorough study of the meaningfulness of the ST segment changes over and above those seen at rest in the patient with an abnormal resting electrocardiogram has not been published with correlation studies of coronary anatomical findings. It seems unlikely that the ST segment must be absolutely flat or negative in slope to provide evidence of myocardial ischemia if there has been progressive horizontal flattening of the ST segment with progressive exercise [14]. It is apparent that physician monitoring of the exercise electrocardiogram is critical for appropriate evaluation of exercise testing. When ST segment depression disappears as the exercise becomes increasingly severe, a so-called normalization has occurred and this does not necessarily denote organic heart disease.

Current correlation studies are proceeding in our laboratory with coronary anatomical description obtained by direct cardiac catheterization techniques in patients who have achieved maximal stress test performance. Three hundred subjects with normal coronary arteriograms have been compared with 300 subjects with definite coronary perfusion deficits demonstrated by coronary arteriography requiring surgical treatment. The two patient groups form the basis for the examination of current criteria including the 0.1 mv ST depression at 80 msec after the J point as well as the normalized ST analysis described by Blomqvist [4]. Our recording system includes the Frank leads as well as the bipolar precordial lead with the positive electrode in the V_5 position and the negative electrode over the manubrium.

With recent approaches to electrocardiographic signal processing and electrocardiographic measurement utilizing computers, a significant improvement of the quality of electrocardiographic interpretation can be expected. In addition, multiple lead electrocardiography appears to offer advantages over single lead tracings obtained during exercise. A number of patients have been studied with abnormal responses in each of the four leads alone indicating that each lead offers relevant information in specific patients which would not be obtained if only one lead was recorded. It appears that the combination of four electrocardiographic leads obtained during exercise increases the incidence of abnormal exercise electrocardiograms by approximately 10% to 15% as compared to the single lead exercise electrocardiograms obtained with a bipolar lead. These findings appear to improve the specificity of the test.

The quantitative study of the Frank lead exercise electrocardiogram based on averaging technique in computer analysis by Blomqvist remains the classic study utilizing the techniques [4]. The use of computer assisted interpretation of exercise electrocardiograms by Simoons with discriminant function analysis has resulted in improved criteria [14]. The comparison of visual ST segment analysis with computer measured ST segment changes demonstrates computer superiority in improving specificity and sensitivity in a group of normal subjects and patients with defined coronary atherosclerotic heart disease [14]. Only patients with normal resting electrocardiogram were selected for the latter study. At higher heart rates the separation of patients and the control group gradually improved. However, at heart rates of over 160 beats per minute, the measurements from the normal subjects and the coronary disease group overlapped again. Thus, the few patients who reached these higher heart rates during exercise could not be distinguished from the normal subjects on the basis of the exercise electrocardiogram. It is likely that the discontinuation of the test in significant coronary disease is commonly occurring prior to achieving target maximal heart rates. The likelihood ratio of abnormal/normal = 25 to 1 if 0.1 mv criteria are used for measurements at 20 msec after the J point and 80 msec after the J point while the ratio of 3.7 to 1 is obtained when 0.05 mv ST segment depression is required for the same variables. It is of interest that in this same study polar-cardiographic techniques did not provide additional diagnostic information [14]. In general, a specificity of 90% with a sensitivity of 84% can be expected utilizing measurements which combine the ST segment amplitude at 20 msec after the J point and 80 msec after the J point in Frank lead X [14]. Detailed studies correlating the number of vessels involved and the severity of obstruction with the exercise electrocardiographic response are underway in our laboratory.

Exercise-Induced Cardiac Dysrhythmias

It has been known for a number of years that exercise stress may induce cardiac electrical irritability or cause alterations in intra-ventricular conduction. Most frequently these electrical phenomena are manifested as isolated ectopic ventricular beats and occasionally may result in runs of ventricular tachycardia. In addition, rate-related induction of the intraventricular conduction disturbances including right and/or left bundle branch block, Wolff-Parkinson-White pre-excitation syndrome and exercise-induced hemiblock have all been described. Most commonly, exercise-induced premature ventricular contractions disappear soon after the cessation of exercise once the heart rate drops below the level at which dysrhythmias were provoked.

The incidence of dysrhythmias occurring during exercise testing is usually increased as higher workloads are employed. More than twice the number of premature ventricular contractions were demonstrated utilizing treadmill exercise testing as opposed to the standard Master's two-step test [1]. While exercise-induced ventricu-lar premature beats may indicate the presence of significant coronary atherosclerotic heart disease, this is certainly not always the case. A good rule of thumb is that if exercise provokes additional dysrhythmias over and above those seen at rest and particularly if these become frequent or multifocal, there is high likelihood of the presence of organic heart disease. In addition, there is a higher incidence of cardiac dysrhythmias during heavy exercise when there appears to be an abnormality in the ST segment response to exercise.

The occasional patient is found without ST segment abnormalities but the precipitation of cardiac dysrhythmias is observed. Several of these patients have been shown to have significant and life-threatening narrowing of at least one coronary artery of greater than 75% narrowing. Unfortunately, the addition of dysrhythmias as criteria for an abnormal test does not appear to have predictive value greater than that of ST segment changes alone.

Exercise-provoked intraventricular conduction disturbances as well as the provocation of pre-excitation is frequently a benign finding in terms of the presence of coronary atherosclerotic heart disease. It must be stated that the appearance of exercise-induced conduction disturbances does not necessarily represent an abnormal test result. A definite diagnosis of heart disease, therefore, should be based on other information rather than the lone occurrence of brief transient cardiac conduction defects.

Gallop Sounds

A variety of stress tests have been devised for inducing abnormalities in ventricular function by inducing abnormalities in myocardial oxygen demand delivery capabilities. Isometric hand grip exercise may be employed for this purpose [13]. For dynamic exercise utilizing ergometry or treadmill stress the phonocardiogram may be recorded and averaged using techniques similar to those introduced by Blomqvist for the exercise electrocardiogram [11].

We are employing the full wave rectified phonocardiogram band passed at 25 Hz with analog to digital conversion of the full wave rectified signal every 5 milliseconds. Data analysis at the current stage of the development of this procedure indicates that it is of great utility as an associated finding in patients who have exercise-inducible coronary perfusion deficits. While the atrial gallop sound alone is not a specific indicator of coronary disease, the association of this finding with chest discomfort has great diagnostic importance. The presence of ST segment depression, atrial gallop sounds and angina pectoris provoked during exercise stress together imply an almost certain relationship to significant coronary atherosclerotic heart disease with greater than 99% specificity.

Use of Exercise Testing for Monitoring Medical Therapy and Revascularization Surgical Results

Perhaps the greatest potential for the use of exercise testing in patients with coronary atherosclerotic heart disease lies in the area of

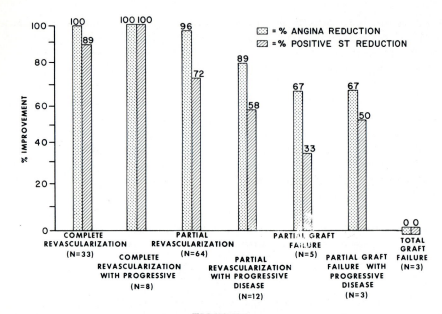

FIGURE 1.

monitoring both medical and surgical therapeutic interventions. The patient who has a clearly positive exercise tolerance test with angina pectoris, ST segmental changes and atrial gallop sound provoked during exercise is an ideal candidate for serial exercise testing during medical or surgical therapeutic intervention. The hemodynamic and clinical correlation of exercise test data as it relates to signs and symptoms of coronary underperfusion has been previously shown in graphic form. The control status of patients prior to therapeutic intervention is plotted as the product of heart rate and systolic blood pressure on the ordinate and is utilized as an index of myocardial oxygen consumption. External workload can be measured in ergometrically determined kilopond meters stage of treadmill stress or total body oxygen consumption. As the workload increases and the duration of the exercise level becomes prolonged, the rate pressure product reaches a level at which myocardial oxygen delivery is inappropriate to meet the demands of the heart muscle for oxygenation when segmental areas receive inadequate coronary perfusion. This results in the "threshold levels" at which angina pectoris, ST segmental changes, arrhythmias, or atrial gallop sounds appear. The pharmacological effect of beta-adrenergic blockade is demonstrated wherein the resting rate-pressure product is lowered because of lessened adrenergic activity in the cardiac system. As the patient exercises, the rate pressure product does not increase at the same level for a given workload as would be expected in the control state prior to beta-blockade. Thus, increasing workloads are experienced and the patient has an improved exercise tolerance despite a relatively constant threshold for inadequate myocardial oxygenation. In beta-blockade the threshold of inadequate oxygenation is reached at higher loads but the same signs and symptoms of coronary underperfusion will appear and exercise must be stopped.

It is clear from a large series of patients studied at the Cleveland Clinic utilizing angiography and maximal exercise testing before and after myocardial revascularization that a high correlation exists between the completeness of surgical revascularization and the reversal of exercise-inducible signs or symptoms related to coronary underperfusion [12]. Figure 1 demonstrates the relationship between these signs or symptoms of coronary perfusion deficits with the completeness of direct myocardial revascularization.

References

1. Anderson, M.T., Lee, G.B., Campion, B.C. et al: Cardiac dysrhythmias associated with exercise stress testing. Am. J. Cardiol. 30:763, 1972.
2. Aronow, W.S., Vyeyama, R.R., Cassidy, J. and Nebolon, J.: Resting and post-exercise phonocardiogram and electrocardiogram in patients with angina pectoris and in normal subjects. Circulation 43:273, 1971.
3. Blackburn, H.: The exercise electrocardiogram: Technological, procedural, and conceptional developments. In Blackburn, H. (ed.): Measurement in Exercise Electrocardiography. Springfield, Ill.:Charles C Thomas, 1968.
4. Blomqvist, G.: The Frank lead exercise electrocardiogram, a quantitative study based on averaging techniques and digital computer analysis. Acta Med. Scand. 178:suppl 440, 1965.
5. Ellestad, M.H., Allen, W., Wan, M.C.K., and Kemp, G.K.: Maximal treadmill stress testing for cardiovascular evaluation. Circulation 34:517, 1969.
6. Heberden, W.: Some account of a disorder of the breast. Med. Trans. R. Coll. Phys. 2:59, 1772.
7. Kouchoukos, N.T., Kirklin, J.W. and Oberman, A.: An appraisal of coronary bypass grafting. Circulation 50:11, 1974.
8. Loop, F.D., Spampinato, N., Siegel, W. and Effler, D.B.: Internal mammary artery grafts without optical assistance. Clinical and angiographic analysis of 175 consecutive cases. Circulation 48 (suppl. III):162, 1973.
9. Redwood, D.R. and Epstein, S.E.: Uses and limitations of stress testing in the evaluation of ischemic heart disease. Circulation 46:1115, 1972.
10. Sheldon, W.C., Rincon, G., Effler, D.B. et al: Vein graft surgery for coronary artery disease: Survival and angiographic results in 1000 patients. Circulation 48 (suppl. III):184, 1973.
11. Siegel, W. and Blomqvist, G.: A system for recording precordial motion during exercise. Clin. Res. 17:19, 1969.

12. Siegel, W., Lim, J.S., Proudfit, W.L. et al: The spectrum of exercise test and angiographic correlations in myocardial revascularization surgery. Circulation 51 (suppl. I):156, 1975.

13. Siegel, W., Nutter, D.O., Schlant, R.C. and Hurst, J.W.: The use of isometric exercise as a diagnostic maneuver in patients with heart disease. Ann. Int. Med. 74:822, 1971.

14. Simoons, M.L.: Computer Assisted Interpretation of Exercise Electrocardiograms. Rotterdam: Bronder-Offset B.V., 1976.

15. Sones, F.M., Jr. and Shirey, E.K.: Cine coronary arteriography. Mod. Concepts Cardiovasc. Dis. 31:735, 1962.

16. Zaret, B.L., Strauss, H.W., Martin, N.D. et al: Non-invasive evaluation of myocardial perfusion with potassium 43: Study of patients at rest, exercise and during angina pectoris. N. Engl. J. Med. 288:809, 1973.

Le diagnostique clinique à l'effort; nouvelles perspectives

L'auteur se dit d'avis que l'évaluation clinique à l'effort maximum peut être d'une grande utilité dans l'évaluation de patients que l'on soupçonne être affectés de maladie coronarienne. Il traite des diverses catégories d'améliorations techniques qu'a connues la méthode, ces derniers temps, et qui ont toutes contribué à la précision et à la spécificité des tests. L'utilité clinique de la méthode s'étend heureusement maintenant aux affections athérosclérotiques les plus menaçantes.

Resolve That the Exercise Electrocardiogram Is of Limited Diagnostic Value

Gordon R. Cumming

The XECG at present is an imprecise tool and less accurate than a medical history. False positive tests are very frequent and are so frequent in women so as to make it useless. False negative tests in subjects with obvious disease occur. Despite these shortcomings the XECG provides some factual data and establishes a rapport with the patient since it has good public and professional acceptance. Nevertheless, it should be used with caution as an adjunct to diagnosis and management, rather than a major determinant of medical decisions.

Introduction

Can anyone seriously question the validity of the exercise ECG (XECG)? Are not thousands of cardiologists throughout the world earning a living by doing exercise stress tests? Have not the majority of hospitals and medical clinics dealing with cardiac patients established stress testing stations and in recent years purchased treadmills, ergometers, special lead systems, etc.? Have not commercial firms marketing treadmills and ergometers sold more units in the 1970s than in all prior years put together? Has not the exercise ECG reached the ultimate in scientific credibility by being interpreted and coded by computer and paid for by government insurance programs?

Negative reports are seldom published, and many budding investigator authors consider negative investigations a failed experiment not suitable for publication, a feeling shared by journal editors. As a result, most publications deal with new diagnostic procedures, or with results affirming the diagnostic accuracy and validity of existing tests. Newer techniques and modifications are usually always

Gordon R. Cumming, Department of Pediatrics, University of Manitoba and Department of Cardiology, Health Sciences Children's Centre, Winnipeg, Manitoba, Canada.

13

presented as being an improvement on the old. The electrocardiogram is a particular case in point. Ernst Simonson made an
interesting observation on the vectorcardiogram (VCG) [41].
Thirty-three papers were collected comparing the diagnostic efficacy
of the VCG and ECG with the VCG being called superior to the ECG
in 79% of the reports. Simonson then assembled a series of ECG and
VCG from 40 patients and submitted these to ten VCG experts.
Based on the diagnoses confirmed in a variety of ways, the VCG
interpretation was labeled correct 49% of the time and the ECG 54%
of the time, the difference not being significant. So much for the
clearcut reports in the literature on the superiority of the VCG when
it comes to practical usage.

Important as the contributions of the innovators and champions
of various diagnostic tests are, it must be apparent that limitations of
diagnostic tests tend to be overlooked either knowingly or unknow-
ingly, and exercise electrocardiography provides a glowing example.
As late as 1972 one of the pioneers of exercise electrocardiography,
Arthur Master, made the following statement: "The augmented
two-step test when negative completely excludes the presence of
coronary artery disease" [34].

Even the most ardent enthusiasts of the XECG admit that it is
negative in at least 25% of patients with definite angina having
angiographically proven coronary artery narrowings. We also know
that XECGs, including XECGs following more strenuous exercise
than provided by the augmented Master's test, are negative in up to
50% of patients with proven previous myocardial infarctions. Why
did journal editors not question this statement by Master, and why
did Master make this claim after having 30 years of experience with
the XECG?

The main medical use of the XECG is in the diagnosis of chest
pain, and the XECG pattern is now used by many physicians as one
of the major criteria as to whether a patient's chest pain is due to
coronary heart disease. In this day of laboratory tests we tend to
ignore the value of the careful clinical history. Table I indicates that
the XECG is likely inferior to the simple tool of careful medical
history when it comes to making a diagnosis of coronary heart
disease or absence of coronary heart disease. The values given are
estimates based on several reports reviewed by Redwood and
Epstein [39]. The diagnosis was independently made by coronary
angiography, realizing angiograms are not foolproof either, tending
to underestimate the severity of coronary disease.

When the clinician decided that the history is typical for angina
pectoris in a male patient, significant coronary narrowings are

Table I. Accuracy of Diagnosis by History and Exercise Electrocardiogram

Type of Pain	% of Correct Diagnoses Based on Coronary Angiography	
	History	Exercise ECG
Typical angina	90-95	70-75
Previous myocardial infarction	70-80	50
Atypical angina	60	50-70
Noncoronary chest pain	95	80

present over 90% of the time on the angiograms [40]. In the same group of patients the XECG is positive in only 70% of patients [13, 31, 36]. When the chest pain by history clearly does not satisfy any of the criteria for angina, significant coronary narrowings are absent over 90% of the time [40]. Even in the 5% to 10% of these subjects who have arteriographic evidence of narrowings, the narrowings may not be producing coronary insufficiency and are not necessarily responsible for the symptoms. Because of the occurrence of false positive XECGs, the XECG in this situation will be less reliable than history.

When the history is equivocal for angina, and it is in these patients where a definitive laboratory test is urgently needed, one cannot expect the exercise test to be any better than it was for patients who had clearcut histories for either angina or no angina, i.e., there will likely be at least 30% false negative and 10% to 20% false positive results. It should be noted that exercise tests are frequently negative in Prinzmetal's variant angina [23].

The literature contains many reports correlating the results of exercise tests with coronary angiography, but most of those undergoing the angiography are potential candidates for coronary artery surgery on the basis of their symptoms. These symptoms alone indicate that most of these patients should demonstrate angiographic evidence of obstructive coronary disease and the overloading of these angiographic series by patients with obvious coronary disease gives a false impression of the efficacy of the XECG. A more critical test of the value of the XECG would be a large series of patients where the history was *truly* equivocal, but such series are not easily obtained and no satisfactory published series making this comparison is available.

When a person has angina walking down the hall to the exercise laboratory, the exercise test is hardly needed for diagnosis. Series with 200 or 2,000 exercise tests correlated with coronary angiograms on patients in whom a definite clinical diagnosis of angina is possible are meaningless to indicate the diagnostic power of the XECG in patients in whom it is really required for diagnosis. When a test result merely confirms a definite clinical diagnosis, it becomes a psychological crutch for the physician rather than a useful diagnostic aid.

Table II lists some of the questions that should be asked of a diagnostic test. When evaluating the frequency of false positive XECGs should the evaluation be done in a series of patients undergoing coronary arteriography for angina so that only few false positives are likely? Or should this evaluation be done in asymptomatic persons whose only abnormality was an XECG change? In the latter situation the false positive rate may be higher than 50% [9, 28].

The rate of false negative tests in patients with known CHD has been reasonably well documented, and in patients with angina averages 25% to 30% [13, 31, 36, 40] and in patients without angina but having a prior myocardial infarction is about 50% [43].

In normal subjects having submaximal exercise tests considerable information is available on the prognostic importance of XECG changes. Despite various exercise test protocols and various criteria for positive tests and varying methods of selection of subjects, it is clear that when an ischemic ST change occurs in an asymptomatic male during submaximal exercise, that person has three to ten times the risk of developing clinical coronary heart disease over the next five years compared to someone not showing this change [1, 4, 10, 11, 19, 25, 27, 30, 35].

However, how many of these "normal" subjects who went on to get clinically manifest coronary heart disease (CHD) actually had mild unrecognized clinical angina at the time of the initial testing in

Table II. Evaluation of a Diagnostic Test

Does the test have many false positive results?

Does the test have many false negative results?

Do we have enough information on this test in normal subjects over a long period of time?

Are the results of this test of critical importance in arriving at a diagnosis?

Are the results of this test only needed to confirm what is already almost a certainty?

If not in agreement with the working diagnosis based on history, exam and other tests, will the results of this test be ignored?

Can we assess the cost benefit of this test? Is the test more effective in ruling out or detecting disease?

which the ECG change was shown. I have been impressed that many patients who have definite angina admit on careful questioning that in retrospect mild symptoms typical for angina were present for several years before they paid any attention to them. It is only when the pain becomes very obvious and somewhat severe that the patient is able to retrospectively recognize the prior milder symptoms. In the published series there is no record that the patients who subsequently went on to develop clinical angina were questioned carefully enough concerning the chest discomfort that they had in the past after clinical CHD had developed.

In asymptomatic populations there is the possibility that the XECG provides no predictive information not already provided by well-known CHD risk factors. Subjects with XECG changes have a definite increase in the frequency of risk factors above that shown by subjects who have normal XECGs in the general population [16]. The only study in which the predictive value of the XECG apart from other major risk factors has been examined did not clearly solve the issue. In this major epidemiologic study under the chairmanship of Keys involving over 5,000 subjects, only 28 patients with coronary events were observed in five years in subjects with positive XECGs. This is a rather small number of subjects on which to base any firm conclusions. When age and other major risk factors were factored out, the XECG was of borderline predictive value only in American railroad workers (p < .05) and was of no additional predictive value at all in men from other countries [7].

With the Master's test, Mattingly [35], Brody [10] and Bellet [4] after 3 to 15 years of observation identified 32 out of 102 initially asymptomatic subjects who developed CHD out of a total population of 2,172 men. Maximal or near-maximal tests have replaced the Master's test in the hopes of improving sensitivity. Table III reviews six of the available series. The sensitivity ranged from a low of 19 to a high of 100% (mean 53%). Eighty-two percent of the men remained free of CHD at follow-up, i.e., a man with an ECG change had a 4-5:1 chance of not getting any clinical manifestations of CHD. All of these are not false positive tests. Some of these men undoubtedly have coronary narrowings that have not progressed to the point of clinical symptoms, while some are true false positives in patients with no anatomic coronary disease.

In a population study is the extra sensitivity worth the added problems of maximal exercise? What about the 80% of subjects that would be warned about impending CHD yet nothing developed? Some of those with maximal exercise ST changes do not have these

Table III. Prediction of CHD from Near-Maximal Tests

First Author	No. of Subjects	Average Follow-up Years	No. of Subjects CHD	% Identified by XECG (Sensitivity)	% False Positive
Bruce [11]	221	5	5	60	86
Aronow [1]	100	2.5	4	75	77
Kattus [30]	313	2.5	10	100	67
Cumming [19]	510	3	26	58	75
Froelicher [27]	710	6	7	19	90
Bruce [12]	1339	7	24	29	91
Totals and Means	3193	4	76	53	82

changes on repeat testing (18% in an unpublished series [15] and 58% in the Chinese men tested by Bruce et al [12]). Bruce has not emphasized this point.

There is a growing interest in objectively evaluating the actual usefulness of all laboratory tests in terms such as sensitivity, specificity, true and false negative and positive ratios. These terms are specifically defined in Table IV [37].

To assess the value of XECG we need to have sufficient data to construct decision matrixes as in Table V.

Populations similar to B have been well studied and were reviewed by Redwood and Epstein [39]. There are no studies in populations similar to A, since coronary angiograms are seldom done on asymptomatic persons without some specific indication. From two studies we know that about 50% of subjects whose only abnormality was an XECG change had negative angiograms [9, 28]. It is also known that 25% of men aged 50 to 60 will have a positive exercise test [16], so that (a) and (c) of part A can be recorded. It is necessary to estimate (b) and (d).

The contribution of a test toward a diagnosis may be indicated as a numerical probability by utilizing the theorem of the 18th century mathematician, Bayes. The information content of a test (XECG) is related to the probability of CHD (or nondisease) before the laboratory test is obtained and from values assigned for the frequency of true and false positive tests. The probability formulae are:

$$\text{Post test probability CHD XECG positive} = \frac{\text{TPR} \times \text{expected frequency CHD}}{\text{TPR} \times \text{expected frequency CHD} + \text{FPR} \times \text{expected frequency no CHD}}$$

Post test probability CHD XECG negative $=$ $$\frac{FNR \times \text{expected frequency CHD}}{FNR \times \text{expected frequency CHD} + TNR \times \text{expected frequency no CHD}}$$

A 50-year-old male complaining of typical anginal chest pain has a 95% chance of having angiographic narrowings. As noted in Table V the true positive ratio for the exercise test is .74, and the false positive ratio in the general population of the 50-year-old men would be .20. If a positive exercise test is obtained in this subject, the probability of CHD using the Bayes' theorem would be 0.99. The test has increased the likelihood of diagnosis from 95% to 99%, a gain of only 4%.

On the other hand, if the anginal history was atypical and based on experience, the clinician estimated that there was a 60% chance that the patient had true CHD. What might be the contribution of the XECG to a diagnosis? If a positive exercise test was obtained

Table IV.

True Positive Ratio (TP)	=	number of positive tests in those with CHD / total number of patients with CHD
	=	probability that a patient with disease will have a positive test
	=	sensitivity of the test in detecting the disease
False Positive Ratio (FP)	=	number of positive tests in those without CHD / total number of patients without CHD
	=	probability that a normal patient will have a positive test
True Negative Ratio (TN)	=	number of negative tests in those without CHD / total number of patients without CHD
	=	probability that a normal subject will have a normal test
	=	specificity of the test
False Negative Ratio (FN)	=	number of negative tests in those with CHD / total number of patients with CHD
	=	probability that patients with CHD will have a negative test

Table V. Exercise ECG and Angio Changes in 2 Male Populations

Exercise Test Result	A. 100 Asymptomatic Men 50-60 Years		B. 100 Men with Typical Anginal Pain	
	Angio +	Angio –	Angio +	Angio –
Positive	(a) 13	(c) 12	(a) 70	(c) 1
Negative	(b) ? 15	(d) ? 60	(b) 25	(d) 4
TPR $\frac{a}{a+b}$	.46		.74	
FPR $\frac{c}{c+d}$	.17		.20	
TNR = 1–FPR	FNR = 1–TPR			

using Bayes' theorem the new probability of CHD would be 0.82. There is a gain in information of 22% based on the exercise test, and the contribution of the test to a diagnosis is considerable. Supposing that the new exercise test was negative rather than positive in this patient. The new probability based on Bayes' theorem of the subject having coronary disease would be 0.42. The test allows us to say there is a 58% chance that the subject has no coronary disease when before the test was done we knew that there was only a 40% chance, and the gain is 18%. Positive and negative tests were of similar diagnostic value.

Bayes' theorem may be also applied to the general population of men aged 50, or to men with chest pain that is clinically not angina, estimating that a man aged 50 has a 15% chance of having asymptomatic coronary artery narrowings. Based on the estimates in Table V the true positive ratio for the exercise test is .46 and the false positive ratio is .17. A positive exercise test using the Bayes' theorem makes the probability of coronary disease 32%. If the test were negative the likelihood of coronary narrowing decreases to 10%, a decrease of only 5%. The cost benefit of doing the test to exclude CHD can clearly be questioned.

Jellife [29] applied the Bayes' rule to the diagnostic accuracy for the ECG criteria of LVH. The Allenstein criteria have a false negative rate of 29% and a false positive rate of 17%. Using, for example, the incidence of LVH in a teaching hospital of 25%, in a community hospital of 5%, and in a screening clinic of 1%, the effects of the incidence on the errors of interpretation are shown in Table VI.

The accuracy was likely to be best for a negative test and best in a screening situation. The accuracy was poor for a positive test which could be wrong 96% of the time in a screening situation.

Table VI. Accuracy of the ECG Diagnosis of LVH

Place	% Incidence of Actual LVH	% of False Positive ECGs if Positive	% of False Negative ECGs if Negative
Teaching hospital	25	42	10
Community hospital	5	82	2
Screening clinic	1	96	0.4

From Jeliffe [29].

A similar analysis can be carried out with the XECG, arbitrarily assigning an overall false negative rate of 30% and a false positive rate of 30% (Table VII).

The accuracy is likely to be highest when the test is negative in a screening situation or in the patient with noncoronary chest pain. A positive test in a patient with typical angina is likely to be correct 88% of the time. A positive test in a screening situation is likely to be in error 98% of the time! Even the disbelievers of the XECG think it is better than this, but the figures give an indication of the application of probability manipulations to the appraisal of the XECG, and how imperfect it is.

There are further problems that throw doubt on the value of the XECG including the selection of lead systems, criteria of a positive test, the nonspecificity of the ST changes, interobserver variation and the high frequency of positive tests in women.

Lead Systems and Criteria of a Positive Test

In the resting ECG reference has already been made of the argument as to what lead system is best, the standard 12-lead or the Frank vector system. At least at rest there is enough consensus to reduce the argument down to a two-lead system, but the situation is not so simple for exercise. Of the 50 or more lead systems advocated

Table VII. Probable Accuracy of the XECG Diagnosis
of CHD in Different Clinical Situations

Situation	Expected Frequency of CHD (%)	% of False Positive Tests if Positive	% of False Negative Tests if Negative
Male with typical angina	95	12	58
Male with possible angina	50	30	30
Male with ? muscular chest pain	5	88	2
Screening test	1	98	0.4

for exercise, Rautaharju and Wolf made the comment that if all lead systems were used in a normal subject at least one would show a typical ischemic change [38].

Some authors [21] have erroneously concluded that Blackburn et al [8] settled the issue of what lead system to use for exercise. A study was made of multiple resting leads in 22 men with resting ST changes, and the highest frequency of ST depressions occurred in lead CM5. There was a reasonable correlation between R wave amplitude and the level of ST depression. Since Blackburn's conclusions were not based on exercise records, this investigation was but a preliminary one in selecting a potential lead system for exercise.

Blackburn also reviewed 100 consecutive XECGs in which positive tests were obtained after submaximal exercise [6]. Lead V5 alone detected 89% of the abnormalities; leads II, aVF, V3 and V6 covered the other 11%. This investigation concerns submaximal exercise. The recording started 45 seconds after exercise and a positive test included ECGs showing .05 to .09 mv ST depression. Furthermore, V5 is not quite the same as lead CM5 which is slightly distorted and augments both the R wave voltage and the ST change [8]. In addition, most exercise laboratories are now conducting near-maximal tests. The ECG is recorded during and immediately after strenuous exercise. Despite this the criteria for a positive test remain almost the same as those used for the milder exercise with post exercise ECGs using standard leads starting 30 seconds or more after the exercise was completed.

The shift of the ST segment with exercise likely forms a continuum between normal and abnormal. Valid statistical studies [20] are badly needed to select criteria taking into consideration exercise intensity, heart rate and other parameters (including systolic product) and fitness levels. These considerations might better define criteria that should be used rather than just picking a convenient number such as 1 mm.

Interobserver Variation

Another well-known problem with the XECG is interobserver variation. This question was also reported on by Blackburn [5] and a technical group study involving 14 experts. Thirty-eight exercise records were submitted; the number recorded as abnormal varied from 5% to 58%. This is hardly the record of a precise laboratory tool.

Nonspecificity

The fact that the XECG changes called ischemic may be produced in some patients with rheumatic heart disease, myocardial disease, late systolic murmur syndrome, hypertensive heart disease, congenital heart disease, hypertrophic cardiomyopathy, pericarditis and almost every other type of heart disease does not seem to bother some exercise electrocardiographers. ST depressions are not specific for ischemia. Other conditions associated with XECG ST changes similar to ischemia include hypokalemia, hypocalcemia, digitalis and quinidine therapy, WPW syndrome and left bundle branch block. In some susceptible persons, ST changes are produced by the upright posture, or any activity including exercise that increases sympathetic activity [21].

The underlying changes in the clinical diagnosis in those with other cardiac diseases may not always be apparent, thus giving rise to confusion with ischemic heart disease. The selection of those with vasoregulatory asthenia [24] or excess sympathetic activity from those that are produced by ischemia may not be all that simple.

XECG Changes in Women

Another problem with the XECG is the frequency of positive tests in women. The results of four surveys [2, 17, 32, 37] in normal women without chest pain, without known cardiovascular disease, is shown in Table VIII. Forty-two percent of clinically normal women aged 50 to 59 have a positive XECG. Of what possible value is the XECG in deciding whether a woman with chest pain has angina? Sketch et al [42] correlated the XECGs of 58 women (with chest pain) with angiographic findings and reported a true positive ratio of 0.50 and a false positive ratio of 0.22.

Using Bayes' theorem a positive XECG in a woman with a 50% chance of having CHD increases that chance to only 69%. If the test

Table VIII. Frequency of Positive Exercise ECG Changes in Women

| Reference | % of Positive Records | | | | |
	20-29	30-39	40-49	50-59	60+
I. Astrand [2]	0	17	20	30	50
Lepeshkin [32]	5	29	22	53	–
Profant [37]	–	14	31	50	100
Cumming [17]	14	14	34	36	33
Means	6	19	27	42	61

is positive in a population study for the detection of CHD and the frequency of disease is estimated at 5%, the positive test increases the probability of CHD to only 11%, and 89% of positive tests are likely false positives. The XECG is clearly of little value in women.

One report supports the use of the XECG in women [33]. In 98 women having angiography and an XECG, the TPR was .70 and the FPR was .22, and most false positives were eliminated when subjects with abnormal resting ECGs and any drug therapy (including diazepam) were excluded. If these results were true for the general population, it would mean that over 30% of women aged 50 to 60 would have significant coronary narrowings, an unlikely figure.

Arrhythmia Detection by XECG

The exercise test has potential benefit for producing rhythm changes (usually ventricular ectopic activity [VEA]) that might be of prognostic value, that might be of diagnostic import in patients with exercise-induced symptoms, and the observation of the arrhythmia might allow appropriate drug therapy. There are several drawbacks to this logic.

Exercise test-induced ectopic activity has not been shown to be of prognostic importance [7]. The reproducibility of VEA is very poor [22]. Continuous monitoring by the Holter method is far superior to exercise testing in revealing patients with potentially serious VEA, and therapy for exercise test-induced VEA is not too satisfactory [14].

Prediction of Fitness From Exercise Tests

That indefinable thing we call physical fitness is said to be a side benefit of doing the XECG. Fitness in recent years has unfortunately become simplified into meaning $\dot{V}O_2$/kg body weight, which if nothing else is a good index of obesity. Froelicher et al [26] measured the consistency of the direct determination of $\dot{V}O_2$ max on the treadmill in fit young volunteers and found a mean coefficient of variation of 5%, a value similar to that found in 15-year-old athletes [18]. This is the variation in motivated subjects studied under research conditions willing to push themselves. The prediction of fitness with direct measurements in clinical patients would have a much larger variation. Not only that, but the $\dot{V}O_2$ for different tests varies. The max $\dot{V}O_2$ for the Taylor treadmill test gave $\dot{V}O_2$ max values 7% greater than the Bruce method in the hands of Froelicher et al [26], so that not only does the treadmill give different values than the bicycle, but different treadmill tests give different values. When these tests are used clinically, oxygen uptake is usually predicted rather than measured, and the limitations of these predictions are not fully appreciated.

The Bruce treadmill time improved two minutes from trial 1 to trial 3 in the study of Froelicher et al [26] and yet $\dot{V}O_2$ max did not change at all. The 95% confidence limits of all predictive measures for $\dot{V}O_2$ max are at least ±15 ml/kg/min. This was the average 95% confidence range found by Froelicher et al for the Bruce and Balke treadmill test, while the 95% confidence range found by the Åstrands for their nomogram on the subjects in whom it was developed was ±10 ml/kg/min [3], and for subjects other than those in whom it was developed the limits are at least ±15 ml/kg/min. If we take a man of 40 and predict $\dot{V}O_2$ max to be 30 ml/kg/min, it could actually be 20 ml/kg/min which is very low, or 40 ml/kg/min which is quite a respectable value. Our own work indicates that the Åstrand nomogram underpredicts $\dot{V}O_2$ max in sedentary 40- to 65-year-old Canadians by 18%.

The prediction of $\dot{V}O_2$ max from these various tests is so imprecise that we are perhaps much better off leaving the fitness data in raw scores rather than the actual work done, i.e., fitness should be presented as being able to last 11.5 minutes on the Bruce test or 18 minutes on the Balke test, or being able to push 18 kpm/kg/min on the ergometer in a multistage test. We should not delude ourselves that we can actually predict $\dot{V}O_2$ max with enough precision to make the conversion worthwhile.

Decision Making

There is little point to a diagnostic test (save for paper writing and data collection) unless the test result influences not only the diagnosis but the management decisions.

Only a few centers consider an XECG change alone in an asymptomatic person to be an indication for coronary angiography. The decision for bypass surgery seldom depends upon an XECG. All exercise programs for the coronary prone patient or the patient with clinical coronary disease should start with low intensity exercise, have gradually increasing loads and should be individualized according to the subjective response, regardless of the XECG result. The documentation with a laboratory test of the safe heart rate (maximal rate before any ST change) is pseudoscientific because there is little danger of associated ST change per se. The heart rate ST change relationship may not be the same for different exercises, or from one situation to another because of climate, emotion, isometric components and other factors. Exercise can be dangerous in patients with no ST change.

Most decisions can be made without the XECG result; and that result does not alter decisions made on a careful history and clinical evaluation. For example: A 45-year-old man who has severe angina walking from the parking lot to his work area and is unable to earn a living because of the disability will have coronary angiography carried out regardless of any XECG. A 37-year-old typist who experiences sharp pains under the left breast, particularly when rushed at work, becomes concerned about her heart. An exercise test is performed and is positive. The clinician has already decided the pain is musculoskeletal and ignores the test result. A 54-year-old man had a myocardial infarction four months ago. There were no sequelae, and he was put on a very gradual walking program starting six weeks after the infarction. He now walks two to three miles daily at a pace of 16 minutes to the mile. If he pushes a little harder he gets slight tightness in the chest. Is an exercise test needed for a diagnosis? Is the exercise test really needed to prescribe an exercise program, or can he continue to walk at a pace that is close to but not producing angina?

Comparison With Other Laboratory Tests

Some laboratory tests provide a diagnosis by definition, an example being a blood hemoglobin concentration. A hemoglobin concentration of 5 gm/100 ml means that the patient has anemia, and while borderline values exist the tests' limitations are well defined. The diagnosis of mild to moderately severe diabetes mellitus is easily made from the fasting blood sugar with a well-defined value for normal. In borderline cases diagnosis may be less clear and a form of stress test is obtained by following the levels of blood glucose after a standard glucose challenge. This test is used to pick out subjects with "prediabetes" or those with reduced glucose tolerance.

Ask clinicians if they would bother with blood glucose or glucose tolerance curves if: there were over 40 different chemical methods (i.e., XECG systems); 50 different glucose tolerance protocols (i.e., exercise protocols); ten chemists disagreeing about the results in 40% of the subjects; ten different criteria for abnormality; positive tests in ten unrelated diseases; 30% to 50% of the subjects with positive tests turn out to be normal while 30% of the patients with diabetes have a normal test; a test costing in excess of $50 requiring 30 minutes of a physician's time along with that of a technician committed to nothing else; a test requiring costly space and equipment; a test producing some discomfort and definite danger to the subject; a test requiring a permission form and even with this the threat of legal action remains in the background; and a test that usually is not needed as clinical diagnosis is possible 90% of the time.

References

1. Aronow, W.S.: Thirty month follow-up of maximal treadmill stress test and double Master's test in normal subjects. Circulation 47:287, 1973.
2. Astrand, I.: Exercise electrocardiograms recorded twice with an 8-year interval in a group of 204 women and men 48-63 years old. Acta Med. Scand. 178:27, 1965.
3. Astrand, I.: Aerobic work capacity in men and women with special reference to age. Acta Physiol. Scand. 49, Suppl. 169, 1960.
4. Bellet, S., Roman, L., Nichols, G. and Muller, O.: Detection of coronary prone subjects in a normal population by radioelectrocardiographic exercise test: Follow-up studies. Am. J. Cardiol. 19:783, 1967.
5. Blackburn, H. et al: The exercise electrocardiogram: Differences in interpretation. Am. J. Cardiol. 21:871, 1968.
6. Blackburn, H. and Katigbak, R.: What electrocardiographic lead to take after exercise. Am. Heart J. 67:184, 1964.
7. Blackburn, H., Taylor, H.L. and Keys, A.: CHD in seven countries: The electrocardiographic prediction of 5 year CHD incidence among men aged 40-59. Circulation 41 (suppl. 1):154, 1970.
8. Blackburn, H., Taylor, H.L., Okamoto, N. et al: Standardization of the exercise electrocardiogram. A systematic comparison of chest lead configurations employed for monitoring during exercise. In Karvonen, M.J. and Barry, A.J. (eds.): Physical Activity and the Heart. Springfield:Charles C Thomas, 1967.
9. Borer, J.S., Brensike, J.F., Redwood, D.R. et al: Limitations of the electrocardiographic response to exercise in predicting coronary artery disease. N. Engl. J. Med. 293:367, 1975.
10. Brody, A.J.: Master two-step exercise test in clinically unselected patients. JAMA 171:1195, 1959.
11. Bruce, R.A. and McDonough, J.R.: Stress testing in screening for cardiovascular disease. Bull. N.Y. Acad. Med. 45:1288, 1969.
12. Bruce, R.A., Pao, Y.L., Ting, N. et al: Seven year follow up of cardiovascular study and maximal exercise of Chinese men. Circulation 51:890, 1975.
13. Cohn, P.F., Vokonas, P.S., Herman, M.V. and Gorlin, R.: Post exercise electrocardiogram in patients with abnormal resting electrocardiograms. Circulation 43:648, 1971.
14. Crawford, M., O'Rourke, R., Ramskrishna, N. et al: Comparative effectiveness of exercise testing and continuous monitoring for detecting arrhythmias in patients with previous myocardial infarction. Circulation 50:301, 1974.
15. Cumming, G.R.: 5 year follow-up of asymptomatic men having maximal exercise electrocardiograms (in preparation).

16. Cumming, G.R., Borysyk, L. and Dufresne, C.: The maximal exercise ECG in asymptomatic men. Can. Med. Assoc. J. 106:649, 1972.

17. Cumming, G.R., Dufresne, C., Kich, L. and Samm, J.: Exercise electrocardiogram patterns in normal women. Br. Heart J. 35:1055, 1973.

18. Cumming, G.R., Goodwin, A., Baggley, G. and Antel, J.: Repeated measurements of aerobic capacity during a week of intensive training at a youths' track camp. Can. J. Physiol. Pharmacol. 45:805, 1967.

19. Cumming, G.R., Samm, J., Borysyk, L. and Kich, L.: Electrocardiographic changes during exercise in asymptomatic men: 3-year follow-up. Can. Med. Assoc. J. 112:578, 1975.

20. Davies, C.T.M., Kitchin, A.H., Knibbs, A.V. and Neilson, J.M.: Computer quantitation of ST segment response to graded exercise in untrained and trained normal subjects. Cardiovasc. Res. 5:201, 1971.

21. Ellestad, M.H.: Stress testing. Principles and Practise. Philadelphia:Davis, 1975, p. 27.

22. Faris, J.V., McHenry, P.L., Jordan, J.W. and Morris, S.N.: Prevalence and reproducibility of exercise-induced ventricular arrhythmias during maximal exercise testing in normal men. Am. J. Cardiol. 37:617, 1976.

23. Fernandez, D., Rosenthal, J.E., Cohen, L.S. et al: Alcohol-induced Prinzmetal variant angina. Am. J. Cardiol. 32:238, 1973.

24. Friesinger, G.C., Biern, R.O., Likar, I. and Mason, R.E.: Exercise electrocardiography and vasoregulatory abnormalities. Am. J. Cardiol. 30:733, 1972.

25. Froelicher, F.F.: The application of electrocardiographic screening and exercise testing to preventive cardiology. Prev. Med. 2:592, 1973.

26. Froelicher, V.F., Brammell, H., Davis, G. et al: A comparison of the reproducibility and physiologic response to three maximal treadmill exercise protocols. Chest 65:512, 1974.

27. Froelicher, V.F., Thomas, M.M., Pillow, C. and Lancaster, M.C.: Epidemiologic study of asymptomatic men screened by maximal treadmill testing for latent coronary artery disease. Am. J. Cardiol. 34:770, 1974.

28. Froelicher, V.F., Yanowitz, F.G., Thompson, A.J. and Lancaster, M.C.: The correlation of coronary angiography and the electrocardiographic response to maximal treadmill testing in 76 asymptomatic men. Circulation 48:597, 1973.

29. Jeliffe, R.W.: Quantitative aspects of clinical judgement. Am. J. Med. 55:431, 1973.

30. Kattus, A.A., Jorgensen, C., Worden, R. and Alvaro, A.: ST segment depression with near-maximal exercise in the detection of preclinical coronary heart disease. Circulation 44:585, 1971.

31. Kelemen, M.H., Gillilan, R.E., Bouchard, R.J. et al: Diagnosis of obstructive coronary disease by maximal exercise and atrial pacing. Circulation 48:1227, 1973.

32. Lepeshkin, E.: In Discussion following Irma Astrand's chapter on Electrocardiographic changes in relation to the type of exercise, the work load, age and sex on pp. 309-322. In Blackburn, H. (ed.): Measurement in Exercise Electrocardiography, Springfield, Ill.:Charles C Thomas, 1958.

33. Linhart, J.W., Laws, J.G. and Satinsky, J.D.: Maximum treadmill exercise electrocardiography in female patients. Circulation 50:1173, 1974.

34. Master, A.M.: Exercise testing for evaluation of cardiac performance. Am. J. Cardiol. 30:718, 1972.

35. Mattingly, T.W.: The post exercise electrocardiogram. Its value in the diagnosis and prognosis of coronary arterial disease. Am. J. Cardiol. 9:395, 1962.

36. McConahay, D.R., McCallister, B.D. and Smith, R.E.: Post exercise electrocardiography: Correlations with coronary arteriography and left ventricular hemodynamics. Am. J. Cardiol. 28:1, 1971.

37. Profant, G.R., Early, R.G., Nilson, K.L. et al: Responses to maximal exercise in healthy middle-aged women. J. Appl. Physiol. 33:595, 1972.

38. Rautaharju, P.M. and Wolf, H.K.: In Hoffman, I. (ed.): Proceedings of the XIth International Symposium on Vectorcardiography, New York City 1970. Amsterdam:North Holland, 1971.

39. Redwood, D.R. and Epstein, S.E.: Uses and limitations of stress testing in the evaluation of ischemic heart disease. Circulation 46:1115, 1972.

40. Ross, R.S. and Friesenger, G.C.: Coronary arteriography. Am. Heart J. 72:437, 1966.

41. Simonson, E., Tuna, N., Okamato, N. et al: Diagnostic accuracy of the vectorcardiogram and electrocardiogram. A cooperative study. Am. J. Cardiol. 17:829, 1966.

42. Sketch, M.H., Mohiuddin, S.M., Lynch, J.D. et al: Significant sex differences in the correlation of electrocardiographic exercise testing and coronary arteriograms. Am. J. Cardiol. 36:169, 1975.

43. Weeda, H.W.H.: ECG changes during and after maximal exercise test in patients with myocardial infarction. Malatt. Cardiovasc. 10:61, 1969.

Faiblesse de l'ECG à l'effort comme moyen de diagnostique clinique

L'auteur affirme que l'électrocardiographie à l'effort est une technique relativement imprécise moins sûre que l'histoire médicale d'un sujet. Les faux résultats positifs sont très fréquents, tout particulièrement chez les femmes. Des résultats négatifs s'obtiennent également souvent chez des sujets qui de toute évidence ont des affections. Malgré ses faiblesses, l'ECG à l'effort procure certaines données intéressantes et permet d'établir un rapport avec le patient, en raison principalement de la faveur dont la technique jouit auprès du public. A tout événement l'auteur se dit d'avis que l'ECG à l'effort doit être utilisé avec toute la prudence qui s'impose, et plutôt comme aide que comme base d'une évaluation et d'une décision d'ordre clinique.

The Diagnostic Value of Exercise Electrocardiogram: A Five-Year Experience

Gilles R. Dagenais and Fauzia Irshad

Exercise ECG with the present routine criteria is useful as one of the diagnostic aids for clinical evaluation. However like most other techniques the limitations of exercise ECG must be fully understood and the findings correlated with available clinical data. With these guidelines, exercise testing is a useful clinical tool complementary to clinical evaluation and coronary arteriography.

Introduction

Exercise electrocardiogram is one of the diagnostic approaches of routine exercise cardiovascular testing. Table I depicts the possible utilizations of electrocardiogram during exercise testing. Although this classification is given to reveal the possible uses of electro-

Table I. Utilization of Electrocardiogram During Exercise Test

For monitoring in:
1. Assessing functional capacity
2. Detecting symptoms related to exercise
3. Detecting abnormal physical findings related to exercise
4. Association with other techniques used to assess hemodynamic, metabolic or perfusion abnormalities
5. Assessment of therapeutic interventions

For diagnosis of:
1. Dysrhythmia
2. Ischemia

For prognostic assessment

Gilles R. Dagenais and Fauzia Irshad, Institut de Cardiologie de Québec, Hôpital Laval et Université Laval, Québec, Canada.
Supported in part by the Canadian and Quebec Heart Foundations.

31

cardiogram during exercise testing, it is obvious that the three main items are closely related. For example, electrocardiographic monitoring for assessment of functional capacity may be used also as a diagnostic procedure for detecting dysrhythmia or ischemia with their prognostic implications. Although the exercise electrocardiogram has been found useful in these situations, its diagnostic value by itself in predicting the presence of coronary artery disease has generated enormous controversies. The criticisms result mainly from studies [6, 13] which revealed that exercise electrocardiogram had a low specificity due to a high rate of "false positive" and a low sensitivity due to a high rate of "false negative" tests. In this presentation, we will attempt to illustrate the controversies by discussing these limitations and the usefulness of exercise electrocardiogram mostly from observations made at the Quebec Heart Institute. However, before embarking on this subject the natural course of coronary artery disease and its means of detection will be discussed.

Coronary Artery Disease and its Manifestations

Coronary atherosclerosis may be present even in the young adult without any symptoms. However, manifestations of the disease characterized by angina pectoris, myocardial infarction or sudden death may become apparent some years later. In the asymptomatic and symptomatic phase, the best approach to detect coronary artery disease is coronary arteriographic studies. However, this invasive technique cannot be used as a screening procedure to detect coronary atherosclerosis in all hospital patients and in population studies. The other approaches to detect coronary atherosclerosis are based upon the possible repercussions of this disease characterized by myocardial ischemia. One of the best and most natural ways to induce myocardial ischemia is the utilization of exercise. Exercise is used mainly to assess if myocardial oxygen supply satisfies myocardial oxygen demand. If an increase in myocardial oxygen demand due to a higher heart rate, systolic pressure and contractility cannot be satisfied, myocardial ischemia ensues and may be indicated by clinical, electrocardiographic, hemodynamic and metabolic abnormalities. In the absence of valvular or myocardial disease or hematological and biochemical disorders, the abnormalities are due to coronary artery disease until proven otherwise.

Exercise electrocardiogram has been used to detect myocardial ischemia for more than 40 years. ST-segment depression flat or downsloping of 1.0 mm or more for a duration of 0.08 second in comparison to resting control tracing is accepted as the best indicator of myocardial ischemia. ST elevation of 1.0 mm flat or upsloping has the same value. Using these criteria let us now review our data to assess their diagnostic power.

Exercise Electrocardiogram in Predicting Angiographically Documented Coronary Artery Disease

The exercise test observations were derived from 523 consecutive patients who had undergone coronary arteriograms. The Bruce treadmill test with CM5 electrocardiographic recording was used for our routine tests and has been described [8]. The patients exercised to fatigue or to onset of anginal pain severe enough to require nitroglycerin usually. If the patients did not develop angina or a positive electrocardiogram they had to reach at least 90% of their maximal heart rate for their age for their test to be considered valid. Figure 1 illustrates our results according to the coronary arteriographic findings. The presence of coronary disease is defined as a narrowing of at least 50% on one, two or three vessels. Eighteen percent of patients (19/104) with no significant coronary artery disease had a positive electrocardiogram giving a specificity of 82%. This relatively low specificity contrasts with the 92% specificity

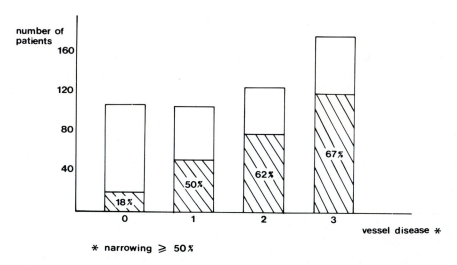

FIG. 1. Prevalence of positive electrocardiogram during graded exercise test in 523 consecutive patients in regard to their coronary arteriographic findings (see text).

reported by Bartel and his group using the same technical approaches in a similar hospitalized population [3]. However, it should be pointed out that among the 19 of 104 patients with normal coronary arteriograms 2 had anemia and 6 had hypertension (160/110 mm Hg at rest) achieving systolic blood pressure greater than 220 mm Hg. It is possible that these factors may have contributed to the apparition of "ischemic changes" on exercise electrocardiogram.

The exercise electrocardiogram detected 61% (256/419) of the patients with coronary artery disease. Thus 39% of these patients with coronary artery disease who were "adequately" stressed had a negative electrocardiogram. If we had used multiple electrodes, as we did in a subgroup, about 25% of the patients would still have had a negative electrocardiogram. Although the exercise electrocardiogram had in general low sensitivity, it was found to have a better sensitivity as regards detecting crucial coronary lesions. In 60 patients who had main left stem coronary artery disease or its equivalent (proximal stenoses on both left anterior descending and left circumflex) the electrocardiogram was positive in 55 cases (Fig. 2). On the other hand, in patients with triple vessel disease with no main stem disease, 36% had a negative electrocardiogram during exercise. However, it should be realized that more than half of these patients did not experience angina and were able to reach 90% of their maximal heart rate. We believe and it is supported by others [16] that these patients who achieved excellent performance have a good prognosis. In summary, the prevalence of positive electrocardiogram is related to the typical symptomatology of angina and the extent and severity of coronary artery disease. On the other hand, the exercise electrocardiogram with the criteria used failed to predict the presence of coronary artery disease in 39% of our patient population. These results are similar to reported studies [3].

Exercise Electrocardiogram in Predicting Documented Ischemic Heart Disease

The low diagnostic power of the exercise electrocardiogram may be due to the different facets of myocardial ischemia and coronary artery disease. For example, it is possible that myocardial ischemia occurred in some patients without angiographic evidence of coronary artery disease, thus giving some so-called false positives to explain our specificity of 82%. On the other hand, in some patients with coronary artery disease, exercise may not have been strenuous enough to induce myocardial ischemia. If this was the case, this would explain the low sensitivity.

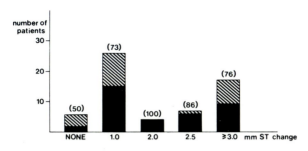

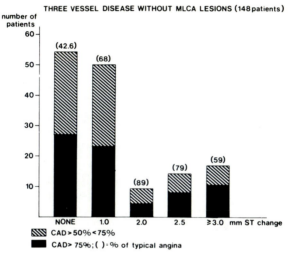

FIG. 2. Amount of ST segment depression in 60 patients with main left coronary artery (MLCA) or its equivalent, proximal left anterior descending artery (LAD) plus proximal left circumflex artery (LCA) stenosis. The same correlation is shown for 148 patients with triple vessel disease.

To verify these possibilities, the exercise electrocardiographic findings of 141 consecutive patients were correlated with their coronary arteriographic observations and with their myocardial lactate balance obtained during a standardized pacing test. In this study, coronary artery disease was defined as a narrowing equal to or greater than 75% of at least one of the three main vessels. Myocardial ischemia during atrial pacing was defined as an arteriocoronary sinus difference in lactate equal to or inferior to zero as described previously by our laboratory [7]. Table II summarizes the findings. In these 141 patients, 110 had significant coronary artery disease while 31 had either normal arteriograms or narrowing of less than

Table II. Correlations Between Positive ECG During Exercise and
Myocardial Lactate Production During Atrial Pacing in 141 Patients

	Positive ECG	Lactate Production	Positive ECG/ Lactate Production
Coronary artery disease*	70/110	60/110	47/60
No coronary artery disease†	3/31	4/31	1/4
Sensitivity	64%	55%	
Specificity	90%	87%	
Sensitivity of exercise ECG in relation to lactate production: 75%			

*Coronary narrowing ≥ 75%
†Coronary narrowing ≤ 50%

50%. Two points should be noted from this study. First, the sensitivity of exercise electrocardiogram to predict the presence of angiographically documented coronary artery disease was 64% with a specificity of 90%. Second, myocardial lactate production during pacing was detected in 60 patients and 47 of them had a positive electrocardiogram. Although a higher sensitivity of exercise electrocardiogram was observed when related to documented ischemia (75%) than to coronary artery disease (64%), exercise electrocardiogram failed to detect 25% of patients with evidence of ischemic heart disease. This failure was not due to a higher cardiac work during pacing, since there was no significant difference in maximal heart rates achieved during pacing and during exercise. Thus it seems unlikely that the major limitation of exercise electrocardiogram results in the high prevalence of myocardial ischemia without angiographically documented coronary artery disease or to a high prevalence of patients with coronary artery disease who failed to develop exercise-induced ischemia.

Solution to Improve the Diagnostic Power
of Exercise Electrocardiogram

Another hypothesis to explain the diagnostic limitations of exercise electrocardiogram to detect ischemia is based on the inadequacy of the present criteria used as an indicator of ischemia, that is, the established ST segment change. In an attempt to define better criteria, a collaborative study between the Quebec Heart

Institute and Dalhousie University Computer Center directed by Dr. P. M. Rautaharju was undertaken. A comprehensive multivariate vector analysis was made to identify the best discriminators of Frank lead electrocardiogram waveforms at rest and during exercise test between 375 clinically normal men previously reported [17] and 105 patients with angina pectoris associated with coronary narrowing greater than 75% on angiograms. Analysis of X Y Z vector leads was performed using a Bayesian type statistical multivariate two-group differential diagnosis program. A total of six best discriminating variables chosen from 20 possible ST and T waveform parameters were permitted to be used for the differential diagnostic procedure. The procedure used and the preliminary results have been reported [9]. In multivariate analysis the exercise electrocardiogram was classified as abnormal in 96% of the patients with angina. The same multivariate statistical analysis of Frank lead electrocardiogram was done for the resting tracings. Ninety-two percent of the ST-T of rest electrocardiogram was classified as abnormal. In view of the high prevalence of rest ST-T abnormalities, we decided to evaluate whether ST-T changes elicited by exercise would yield an adequate sensitivity for exercise electrocardiographic test. Indeed the change from rest to exercise produced a sensitivity of 90%. This value contrasts with the sensitivity of 64% using the previously defined criteria in the same patients. We observed that T waveform changes contributed heavily to diagnostic discrimination between the normal and patient group. When analysis was limited to ST segment alone without T wave variables, the sensitivity dropped to 68%, a reduction of 22%. The six best discriminators in multivariate analysis include mean values of the ST segment of X Y and Z leads, the slope of the ST segment of the Z lead and, in addition, two higher order waveform parameters which can be related to changes in the symmetry of the T wave, specifically the so-called triphasic component of the T waveform. These features are not easily extracted by visual analysis of X Y Z leads; however, their detection by computer analysis is quite simple. Thus, in this population, the multivariate statistical program improves the diagnostic accuracy of the exercise test. It has to be emphasized that the relatively high sensitivity achieved for exercise electrocardiogram by multiple variate analysis was obtained in two relatively small groups chosen from the extreme ends of coronary artery disease spectrum. It is evident that further evaluation with a larger independent test group is required to validate our new criteria. Similar studies to define better criteria have been reported by other centers [2, 5, 10, 14, 15, 19].

The Place of Exercise Electrocardiogram
in Regard to Coronary Artery Disease

Considering the present state of the art of exercise electrocardiogram with its important limitations for the detection of coronary heart disease, should this diagnostic procedure be abandoned until better criteria are defined? Even with the present routine criteria used in different centers, exercise electrocardiogram is useful as an assessment tool of future manifestations of coronary heart disease. Several studies indicate that exercise electrocardiogram has a predictive value for coronary artery disease [1, 4, 11, 12, 18]. However, its value as an independent prognosticator index still remains to be determined.

Exercise electrocardiogram with the present routine criteria is useful as one of the diagnostic aids for clinical evaluation. It should be realized that the diagnosis of ischemic heart disease is not as simple as the diagnosis of anemia. During diagnostic exercise test, all possible indicators of ischemia should be looked for. During or immediately following exercise, the appearance of angina, abnormal left ventricular function evaluated during physical examination and ST segment depression or elevation which may be associated with dysrhythmia should be assessed. Like most other techniques the limitations of exercise electrocardiogram must be fully understood and the findings correlated with available clinical data. Along these guidelines, exercise testing proves a useful clinical tool complementary to clinical evaluation and coronary arteriography. Finally, it has to be realized that further research is needed to define better electrocardiographic criteria of myocardial ischemia.

References

1. Aronow, W.S. and Cassidy, J.: Five years follow-up of double Master's test, maximal treadmill stress test, and resting and postexercise apexcardiogram in asymptomatic persons. Circulation 52:616, 1975.
2. Ascoop, C.A., Distelbrink, C.A., De Lang, P. and Van Bemmel, J.H.: Quantitative comparison of exercise vectocardiograms and findings at selective coronary arteriography. J. Electrocardiol. 7:9, 1974.
3. Bartel, A.G., Behar, V.S., Peter, R.H. et al: Graded exercise stress tests in angiographically documented coronary artery disease. Circulation 49:348, 1974.
4. Bellet, S., Roman, L.R. and Nichols: Detection of coronary-prone subjects in a normal population by radio-electrocardiographic exercise test: Follow-up studies. Am. J. Cardiol. 19:783, 1967.
5. Blomqvist, C.G.: The Frank lead exercise electrocardiogram: Quantitative study based on averaging technic and digital computer analysis. Acta Med. Scand. 178 (suppl. 440), 1965.

6. Borer, J.S., Brensike, J.F., Redwood, D.R. et al: Limitations of the electrocardiographic response to exercise in predicting coronary artery disease. N. Engl. J. Med. 293:367, 1975.
7. Dagenais, G.R., Marquis, Y. and Moisan, A.: Valeurs du glucose, potassium et phosphate inorganique comme indicateurs métaboliques d'ischémie myocardique chez l'humain. Arch. Mal. Coeur 68:169, 1975.
8. Dagenais, G.R., Moisan, A., Marquis, Y. et al: Effects of practolol on exercise tolerance, cardiac hemodynamics, and metabolism in patients with coronary artery disease. Cardiovasc. Res. 10:25, 1976.
9. Dagenais, G.R., Villadiego, R.B. and Rautaharju, P.M.: Characteristics of normal and ischemic VCG response to exercise, quantified by means of waveform vector analysis. In Hoffman, I. and Hamby, R.I. (eds.): Vectocardiography 3. Amsterdam:North-Holland Publishing Company, 1976, p. 209.
10. Dower, G.E., Bruce, R.A., Poll, J. et al: Ischemic polarcardiographic changes induced by exercise. A new criterion. Circulation 48:725, 1973.
11. Doyle, J.T. and Kinch, S.H.: The prognosis of an abnormal electrocardiographic stress test. Circulation 41:545, 1970.
12. Ellestad, M.H. and Wan, M.K.C.: Predictive implications of stress testing. Circulation 51:363, 1975.
13. Froelicher, V.F. Jr., Yanovitz, F.G., Thompson, A.J. and Lancaster, M.C.: The correlation of coronary arteriography and the electrocardiographic response to maximal treadmill testing in 76 asymptomatic men. Circulation 48:597, 1973.
14. Horsten, T.R. and Bruce, R.A.: Compared ST forces of Frank and bipolar exercise electrocardiograms. Am. Heart J. 78:346, 1969.
15. Kornreich, F., Block, P. and Brismee, D.: The missing waveform information in the orthogonal electrocardiogram (Frank Leads). III. Computer diagnosis of angina pectoris from "maximal" QRS surface waveform information at rest. Circulation 49:1212, 1974.
16. Margolis, J.R.: Treadmill stage as a predictor of medical and surgical survival in coronary artery disease. Circulation 52, IV:108, 1975.
17. Rautaharju, P.M., Punsar, S., Blackburn, H. et al: Waveform patterns in Frank-Lead rest and exercise electrocardiograms of healthy elderly men. Circulation 48:541, 1973.
18. Robb, G.P. and Seltzer, F.: Appraisal of the double two-step exercise test. A long-term follow-up study of 3,325 men. JAMA 234:722, 1975.
19. Simoons, M.L. and Hugenholtz, P.G.: Gradual changes of ECG waveform during and after exercise in normal subjects. Circulation 52:570, 1975.

L'électrocardiogramme à l'effort et son utilité clinique; résultats d'une expérience portant sur cinq années

L'électrocardiogramme à l'effort, effectué selon les critères de l'heure, peut être utile dans l'évaluation clinique de patients ou sujets. En raison de ses limitations cependant, l'ECG à l'effort doit être bien maîtrisé par ceux qui l'utilisent et les résultats toujours comparés aux autres données cliniques disponibles. Sur la base d'une expérience portant sur plus de 500 sujets, l'auteur se dit d'avis que l'électrocardiogramme peut s'avérer tout particulièrement utile en tant qu'instrument d'évaluation clinique complémentaire à la corono-angiographie.

Chronic Effects of Exercise in Subjects With Hypertension

Les effets thérapeutiques de l'entraînement physique chez l'hypertendu

Central Hemodynamics in Normal, Well-Trained and Hypertensive Subjects

W. Kindermann and H. Reindell

The relationships between end-diastolic and end-systolic volumes are discussed. The causes and effects of cardiac hypertrophy (physiologic hypertrophy and regulative dilatation) and its relationship to cardiac output at rest and during exercise are presented. Some implications of a concentric and eccentric hypertrophy are examined. The significance of such heart enlargement to training, physical performance and aging is suggested.

The classic laws of the heart established by Frank [8], Starling [22] and Straub [23] are based on experiments on isolated hearts and heart-lung preparations. For a long time they have been regarded as the basis for understanding the normal and pathological functions of the human heart as well. According to these laws, in the healthy heart in situ there exists a dependence of cardiac work on preload and afterload. It has been assumed by Starling [22] that at rest the total blood volume contained in the left ventricle is ejected as stroke volume. During physical work, an increased cardiac performance would be achieved only by an increased end-diastolic volume [22] and thus by the development of a higher tension of the myocardial fibers at end-diastole [23]. An increase in heart volume as a result of a chronically increased physiological workload [22] was considered to be due to myocardial damage. On the basis of research on hemodynamics in the human heart in vivo [7, 9, 13], as well as of X-ray investigations on the athlete's heart [18] and of anatomic-pathological examinations on pressure- and volume-overloaded hearts [15, 16], the importance of Starling's law of the heart under healthy conditions and for the pressure- and volume-overloaded heart

W. Kindermann and H. Reindell, Abteilung und Lehrstuhl für Leistungs- und Sportmedizin und Lehrstuhl für Klinische Kardiologie am Zentrum Innere Medizin der Universität Freiburg, Federal Republic of Germany.

with a healthy myocardium has been considerably modified. However, the function of the healthy human heart is regulated by additional laws.

A definite relationship exists between end-diastolic volume, stroke volume and end-systolic volume, which is also called residual blood volume (Fig. 1). The angiocardiographically measured end-diastolic volume of the left ventricle in man is on the average 70 ± 20 ml/m^2 body surface. Of this, a stroke volume of 45 to 55 ml/m^2 is ejected during the ejection phase. There remains a residual blood volume of 20 to 25 ml/m^2. The ejection fraction (ratio of stroke volume to end-diastolic volume) determined angiographically is 60% to 75%. Using the dye dilution or the thermodilution technique, this value is about 50%. Cardiac output at rest is about 6 to 7 l/min at a heart rate of 70 beats/min, mean cardiac index about 3.5 l/min/m^2 (range 2.5 to 4.5).

Physical exercise requires an increased oxygen uptake by an individual to meet the energy demand. Thus, cardiac output will rise.

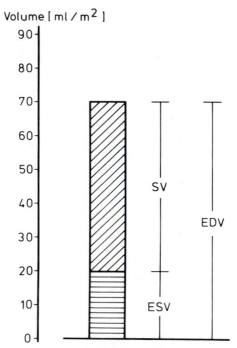

FIG. 1. Relationship between end-diastolic volume (EDV), stroke volume (SV) and end-systolic volume (ESV) of left ventricle [5].

There is a linear relationship between oxygen consumption and cardiac output up to 70% of the maximal oxygen uptake (Fig. 2; review on this problem in Rowell [21]). The cardiac output increases by about 6 l/min with an increase in oxygen consumption of 1 l/min. The cardiac output during supine exercise is increased mainly by a rise in the heart rate. The stroke volume increases only slightly. In sitting position, the stroke volume is at rest significantly lower because of the orthostatic venous pooling of blood in the lower limbs. There are almost no differences during exercise in comparison with the supine position. The heart rate may increase to values of more than 200 beats/min in young individuals. There is a linear correlation with the oxygen uptake up to about 70% of the maximal oxygen uptake. Concomitant with the increase in cardiac output, the arteriovenous oxygen difference rises from 4 to 5 ml/100 ml at rest to about 15 ml/100 ml at maximal workload. In female subjects the increase in cardiac output at a given workload is higher than in males. This is because of a lower arteriovenous oxygen difference in females which is due to a lower hemoglobin content. In aged subjects the increase in cardiac output is lower than in young adults at the same

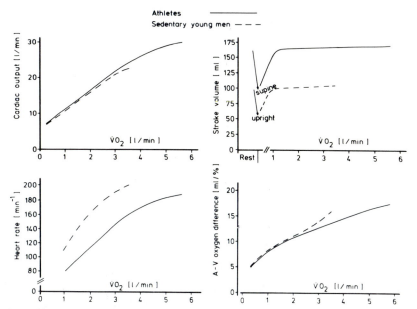

FIG. 2. Cardiac output, stroke volume, heart rate and arteriovenous oxygen difference in relation to oxygen uptake at rest and during exercise in normal subjects and athletes [21].

workload (Fig. 3). This is almost compensated by a more elevated arteriovenous oxygen difference.

Figure 4 demonstrates the pressure changes in the systemic and in the pulmonic circulation in healthy subjects at rest and during exercise. Regarding the functional evaluation of the heart the pulmonary capillary pressure and the diastolic pulmonary artery pressure are of particular importance. These pressures correlate with the filling pressures of the left ventricle when the pulmonary resistance is normal [12]. The end-diastolic ventricular pressure is determined by the contractility and the compliance of the heart muscle as well as by the strength of the atrial contraction. During exercise, healthy subjects show only a moderate rise of the filling pressure and thus of the diastolic pulmonary artery pressure or the pulmonary capillary pressure. Systolic and mean pulmonary artery pressure increase to a somewhat higher extent. The change in arterial pressure is similar. There is only a moderate increase in diastolic pressure. The rise of mean and particularly of peak systolic pressure is pronounced. Peripheral resistance, elastic resistance of the central arteries and cardiac output are the determinants of pressure changes in the systemic circulation. The most pronounced drop of the arterial pressure takes place at the level of the arterioles. At rest, the resistance of the vessels is about 1300 to 1400 dyn $\times$ sec $\times$ cm^{-5}; during exercise this value declines to about one third. The situation in the pulmonary circulation is similar.

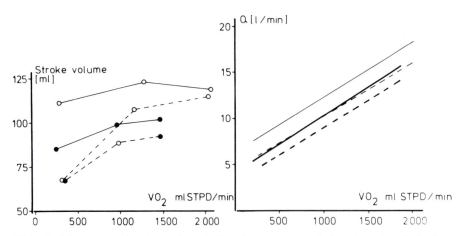

FIG. 3. Mean stroke volume in relation to oxygen uptake at rest and during exercise in old (closed circles) and young (open circles) men (*left*) and regression lines for cardiac output and oxygen uptake in old (heavy lines) and young (thin lines) men (*right*) in supine (full lines) and sitting (broken lines) position [9].

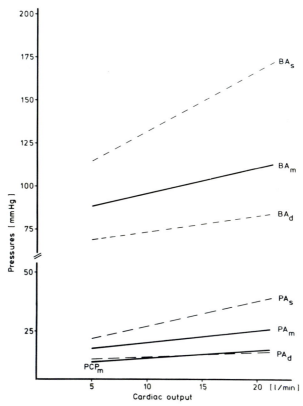

FIG. 4. Mean values for systolic, mean and diastolic pressure in systemic and pulmonary circulation and mean pulmonary capillary pressure (PCP_m) in normal subjects [7].

When aging there is a rise of pressure in the various heart chambers and the vessels (Fig. 5). At rest, only small differences can be seen in this respect; the pulmonary capillary pressure is even somewhat lower in aged subjects. A similar tendency is observed in the diastolic and mean pulmonary artery pressure. During physical exercise the pressure in the pulmonary capillaries, the diastolic pulmonary artery pressure and the end-diastolic pressure in the right ventricle are 6 to 7 mm Hg higher in aged persons as compared to young subjects [9]. Systolic and mean pulmonary artery pressure are also elevated. Similar differences due to age can be demonstrated in the systemic circulation (Fig. 6). Systolic and mean pressure in the brachial artery are 30 and 20 mm Hg higher during maximal physical workload in comparison with young subjects [9]. The increase in pressure during exercise takes place at a steeper rate in aged persons.

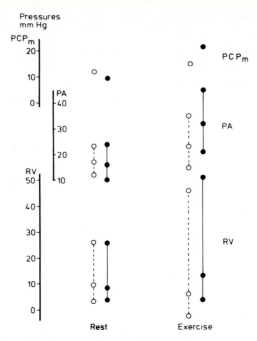

FIG. 5. Mean values for intracardiac and intrapulmonary pressure at rest and during exercise (about 100 w) in sitting position in old (closed circles) and young men (open circles). PCP$_m$ = mean pulmonary capillary pressure; PA = pulmonal artery; and RV = right ventricle [9].

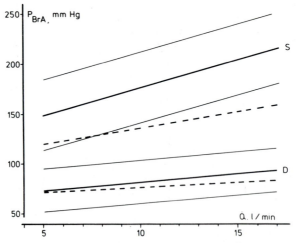

FIG. 6. Systolic (S) and diastolic pressures (D) in the brachial artery in relation to cardiac output (Q̇) at rest and during exercise in supine position in old men. Regression lines (heavy lines) ± 95% confidence interval for single observations (thin lines). Broken lines denote regression lines in young men [9].

In this group, the diastolic arterial pressure increases only slightly during exercise. Vascular resistance in the systemic and pulmonary circulation is higher in elderly than in young subjects at rest and during exercise; the decrease in vascular resistance during exercise is less pronounced in old subjects [9]. Structural changes of heart and vessels are considered to be the main causes for the pressure rise with age. They are probably due to an increase in fibrous tissue content which is accompanied by a decrease in elastic properties. These phenomena cause a diminution of the compliance of the heart [9, 14].

A chronically increased physiological volume load increases the heart size. This is due to a "physiologic hypertrophy" of muscle mass [15, 16] and to a "regulative dilatation" of all heart chambers [17, 18]. It is accompanied by an increase in the performance of the heart. The upper limit of an increased heart size following endurance training is a relative heart volume of 19.6 ml/kg body weight (normal value 11.3). This value was observed by our group in a German 5,000 m record holder, winner of the silver medal at the Olympic Games in Tokyo. A strikingly similar relationship between heart size and physical activity is known from Zoology. Thus, roes have much higher relative heart volumes than all other animals [1]. The roe's heart is almost double in size compared with the untrained human heart.

The hemodynamics of an athlete's heart is not markedly different from an untrained person (Table I). According to the review of Rowell [21], the increase in cardiac output with increased oxygen consumption is approximately the same in trained and untrained persons (Fig. 2). Maximal cardiac output of 40 l/min and more has been reported in highly trained endurance athletes [6]. There is only a minor increase in stroke volume during supine exercise in athletes which is similar to nonathletes. Absolute values for the stroke volume are markedly higher in trained subjects at rest and during exercise [2, 6, 18]. They correlate significantly with the heart volume [18]. The maximal stroke volume may be higher than 200 ml [6] (Table I). Similar arteriovenous oxygen differences are seen in trained and untrained subjects when working at the same load. However, maximal arteriovenous oxygen difference is noticeably augmented in trained subjects. In contrast, according to longitudinal investigations there is an improved outscooping of oxygen from blood after training resulting from an improved capillarization and from a higher enzymatic capacity of muscle [3, 4]. To date, this problem is not yet solved. The maximal heart rate is

Table I. Hemodynamics at Rest and During Exercise in 11 Subjects with Athlete's Hearts

Subjects Sports	Heart volume (ml) Heart-volume (ml/kg)	Watt	$\dot{V}O_2$ (ml STPD/ min)	$(A-V)O_2$ ml/%	Heart rate (beats/ min)	Cardiac output (1/min)	Stroke volume (ml)	Pressures (mm Hg)			
								PA_s	PA_d	PA_m	PCP_m
1. W.M., 24 years Running (3000 m steeple chase)	1320 18,2	Rest 100 200 300	241 1559 2684 4090	6,60 10,58	40 88 119 162	3,7 14,8	91 168	18 32 34 35	8 16 15 13	13 25 26 26	10 16 16 14
2. G.N., 25 years Running (400 m)	1150 15,7	Rest 100 200 300	312 1387 2595 3497	3,11 8,95 11,02 14,14	48 98 132 170	10,0 15,5 23,5 24,7	204 158 178 145	20 33 28 30	9 13 10 10	14 26 19 20	10 6 7
3. W.M., 18 years Running (400 m)	1110 14,5	Rest 100 200 225	331 1452 2616 2947	3,70 7,37 11,73 14,56	56 112 152 165	9,0 19,7 22,2 20,2	160 176 146 122	31 30 26 28	10 14 10 8	19 23 21 21	12 14 10 10
4. G.B., 17 years Bicycling	1165 14,6	Rest 100 200 300 375	495 1335 2303 3566 4350	3,76 7,31 9,92 11,12 13,04	55 91 118 150 170	13,2 21,0 23,6 32,0 33,3	240 230 200 213 196	27 36 38 36 38	13 14 18 16 19	19 26 26 26 28	18 17
5. V.N., 20 years Rowing	1410 16,8	Rest 100 200 300	331 1452 2616 3749	3,16 7,33 9,27 12,61	50 90 139 172	10,5 19,8 28,1 30,4	205 210 201 177	26 30 32 43	11 12 11 13	18 22 24 28	
6. H.L., 24 years Bicycling	1050 13,7	Rest 100 200 300 325	406 1662 2814 4108 4441	3,69 8,46 10,39 14,09 14,47	52 93 135 169 176	11,0 19,2 25,4 29,2 30,7	206 196 191 173 174	17 21 23 23 24	5 11 12 12 11	11 17 18 18 18	8 11
7. A.R., 19 years Running (800-1500 m)	1060 14,9	Rest 100 200 300	331 1452 2616 3749	3,28 7,95 10,69 12,72	48 89 142 170	10,1 18,3 24,4 29,4	205 203 172 173	17 29 26 29	8 14 12 13	12 21 20 23	9
8. P.K., 16 years Skiing	945 14,3	Rest 100 200 275	300 1731 2827 3556	3,79 10,24 13,41 14,59	49 110 157 180	7,9 16,9 21,1 24,4	161 154 134 136	23 34 40 39	10 11 16 16	16 24 30 30	8 9 8 9
9. F.H., 25 years Rowing	1120 12,9	Rest 100 200 300	2000 2995 4104	9,28 12,35 16,45	128 167 190	21,6 24,2 25,0	168 145 131	27 26 31 34	11 16 13 14	20 21 23 26	14
10. G.F., 21 years Speed skating	1080 14,4	Rest 100 200 250	331 1452 2616	4,33 11,24 14,18	55 105 145 172	7,7 12,9 18,5	140 123 127	26 37 32	13 18 14	20 27 25	13 17 10
11. O.H., 19 years Running (1500-5000 m)	890 14,5	Rest 100 200 250	303 1590 2718 3538	3,49 9,24 13,09 15,11	66 112 158 184	8,7 17,2 20,8 23,4	131 154 132 127	26 32 30 38	11 10 17 15	18 21 24 27	

not significantly different in the trained and untrained condition. Submaximal exercise is performed at a lower heart rate by trained subjects compared to untrained ones.

The higher oxygen transport capacity of athletes is thus explained mainly by a greater stroke volume at rest and during exercise, as well as by an elevated arteriovenous oxygen difference. There is a good correlation between maximal stroke volume and heart volume; however, in consequence of training an increase in stroke volume without a corresponding rise in heart size is also possible which has been observed particularly in elderly subjects [10, 20].

The pressures in the systemic and in the pulmonary circulation do not considerably differ in trained and untrained persons at rest and during work (Table I). Because of the higher stroke volume it may be possible that systolic pressure becomes higher in relation to heart rate in trained persons [2]. The arterial peripheral and pulmonary resistance do not show differences due to physical training. At low and moderate workload it is possible that trained subjects may develop a more marked increase in the end-diastolic filling pressure of the left ventricle which is evident from the pulmonary capillary pressure and the diastolic pressure in the pulmonary artery (Table I). According to results from our group, the contractility of an athlete's heart increases to a lower extent during exercise compared to the untrained heart [26]. At rest, there are no such differences. This may be due to a diminished sympathetic activity during exercise in consequence of training. The reduced contractility also could help to explain the higher filling pressure during low and moderate workload in trained subjects. The decreased heart rate and contractility of the trained heart during submaximal workloads decrease also the myocardial oxygen consumption. Results obtained recently by our group suggest that physical training may reduce the oxygen consumption of the heart even if hemo-dynamic parameters are at the same level compared to untrained individuals [11].

Particularly in young athletes, one occasionally may find hypertonic disturbances in regulation (Fig. 7). These subjects show an exaggerately high cardiac output with insufficient oxygen utilization of the skeletal muscle during physical work. Since the resistance of the peripheral vessels remains generally within normal limits, the observed increased blood pressure values are solely due to the higher cardiac output. The athlete with the hypertonic disturb-ance in regulation in Figure 7 is a 17-year-old cyclist who gained the

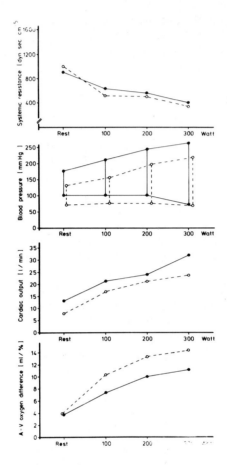

FIG. 7. Arteriovenous oxygen difference, cardiac output, blood pressure and systemic resistance in two athletes with increased heart size. 0----0---- normal hemodynamics; ●——●—— hypertonic disturbance in regulation.

world championship two years later in the 4,000 m pursuit race. Disorders such as that just described can frequently be positively influenced in a favorable manner particularly by augmenting the endurance-type exercise in the general training program. This type of exercise has regulatory influences on the vegetative nervous system.

Compensated chronic pressure load causes a concentric hypertrophy. The ejection fraction even may be slightly increased. The heart may remain similar to a normal one in cases of left or right pressure overload [19]. In case of chronic volume overload the heart size increases in both end-systole and end-diastole if the loading of the ventricle accounts to more than one third of stroke volume. The ejection fraction does not change. Thus, the dynamic of the sufficient human heart during both pressure and volume overload is fundamentally different than it could have been anticipated by the classic laws of the heart.

On the basis of these laws the chronically pressure-overloaded human heart increases in size because of the rise in residual blood volume [25]. The diastolic filling pressure increases, too. This augmentation in size was considered to be a physiological adaptive process. Accordingly, an insufficiency should occur when heart size and diastolic filling pressure further increase and systolic blood pressure decreases. However, data obtained in the human heart in situ by invasive techniques demonstrate a fundamentally different reaction. As mentioned above, during chronic pressure overload cardiac hypertrophy develops with a decrease in residual blood volume. Heart size decreases in end-systole and end-diastole. The heart size is not increased despite the increase in wall thickness. Heart size is independent from pressure load [19]. The mean diastolic filling pressure is not elevated [24]. Merely, the end-diastolic filling pressure in the left or in the right ventricle is somewhat elevated in correlation to the magnitude of the systolic pressure increase because of the stronger atrial contraction.

Hypertrophy represents a compensatory mechanism to meet an increased workload of the heart. An increase of the *mean* diastolic pressure in hearts of normal size already points to a disturbed myocardial function. An incipient dilatation of the left ventricle shows that instead of the concentric hypertrophy an eccentric hypertrophy has developed. Thus, the myocardial function is disturbed. In X-ray the heart is asymmetric because of an enlarged left ventricle. The heart size still may be in the normal range (Fig. 8). Cardiac output at rest usually is normal, whereas a decrease in cardiac output may already be seen during exercise (Table II). With progressing dilatation of the left ventricle the heart size is above the normal range. In this condition the functional capacity of the left ventricle is markedly reduced. Then, heart failure is observed during exercise or even at rest. The ejection fraction of the left ventricle is considerably lowered, whereas the filling pressures are markedly elevated. Finally, the myocardial insufficiency due to chronic pressure overload may even increase the filling pressure in the right ventricle. Radiologically one can demonstrate a heart configuration which is undistinguishable from mitral valve defects.

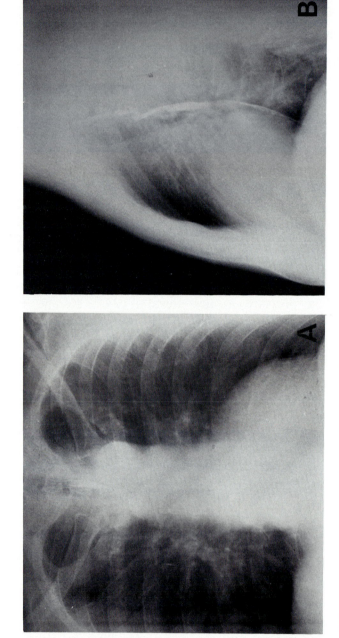

FIG. 8. Chest X-ray in a patient with hypertension and normal heart size. (A) X-ray posterior-anterior: enlarged left ventricle and (B) X-ray lateral: normal finding.

**Table II. Hemodynamics at Rest and During Exercise
in One Patient with Hypertension**

Watt	$\dot{V}_{O_2}$ [ml/min] STPD	$A-V_{O_2}$ [ml/%]	$\dot{Q}$ [l/min]	SV [ml]	HR [beats/ min]	Pressures [mm Hg] PA$_s$	PA$_d$	PA$_m$	PCP$_m$	Vd$_{end}$	Ad_m	BA	Syst Resist dyn sec cm 5
Rest	262	4,9	5,3	92	58	25	10	18	11	8	5	230/110	2520
25	600	8,2	7,3	77	93	45	29	40	30			220/120	1860
50	890	9,7	9,2	81	113	48	28	40	30	6	8	250/120	1610

Heart volume : 800 ml
                  10,0 ml/kg

Age :   54 years
Height : 176 cm
Weight : 80 kg

ECG   ST depression
       left bundle branch block
       during exercise

References

1. Bergmann, J.: Uber die Grösse des Herzens bei Menschen und Tieren. Dissertation. München, 1884.
2. Bevegard, S., Holmgren, A. and Jonsson, B.: Circulatory studies in well trained athletes at rest and during heavy exercise, with special reference to stroke volume and the influence of body position. Acta Physiol. Scand. 57:26, 1963.
3. Caesar, K. and Jeschke, D.: Trainingseinflüsse auf die Kreislaufperipherie. Internist 11:283, 1970.
4. Clausen, J.P. and Trap-Jensen, J.: Effects of training on the distribution of cardiac output in patients with coronary disease. Circulation 42:611, 1970.
5. Dodge, H.T. and Baxley, W.A.: Hemodynamic aspects of heart failure. Am. J. Cardiol. 22:24, 1968.
6. Ekblom, B. and Hermansen, L.: Cardiac output in athletes. J. Appl. Physiol. 25:619, 1968.
7. Ekelund, L.G. and Holmgren, A.: Central hemodynamics during exercise. Circulation Res. 20/21(suppl. 1), 1967.
8. Frank, O.: Isometrie und Isotonie des Herzmuskels. Z. Biol. 41:14, 1901.
9. Granath, A., Jonsson, B. and Strandell, T.: Circulation in healthy old men, studied by right heart catheterization at rest and during exercise in supine and sitting position. Acta Med. Scand. 176:425, 1964.
10. Hartley, H.L., Grimby, G., Kihlbom, A. et al: Cardiac output during submaximal and maximal exercise in middle aged before and after physical conditioning. Scand. J. Clin. Lab. Invest. 24:335, 1969.
11. Heiss, H.W., Barmeyer, J., Wink, K., et al: Durchblutung und Substratumsatz des gesunden menschlichen Herzens in Abhängigkeit vom Trainingszustand. Verh. Dtsch. Ges. Kreislaufforsch. 41:247, 1975.

12. Kaltman, A.J., Herbert, W.H., Conroy, R.J. and Kossmann, C.E.: The gradient in pressure across the pulmonary vascular bed during diastole. Circulation 34:377, 1966.
13. Kindermann, W., Keul, J. and Reindell, H.: Grundlagen zur Bewertung leistungsphysiologischer Anpassungsvorgänge. Dtsch. Med. Wschr. 99:1372, 1974.
14. Kohn, R.R. and Rollerson, E.: Studies on the mechanism of the age-related changes in swelling ability of human myocardium. Circ. Res. 7:740, 1959.
15. Linzbach, A.J.: Herzhypertrophie und kritisches Herzgewicht. Klin. Wschr. 26:459, 1948.
16. Linzbach, A.J.: In Die Funktionsdiagnostik des Herzens. Berlin-Göttingen-Heidelberg:Springer Verlag, 1958.
17. Reindell, H. and Delius, L.: Klinische Beobachtungen über die Herzdynamik beim gesunden Menschen. Dtsch. Arch. Klin. Med. 193:639, 1948.
18. Reindell, H., Klepzig, H., Steim, H. et al: Herz, Kreislauferkrankungen und Sport. München:Johann Ambrosius Barth Verlag, 1960.
19. Reindell, H., König, K. and Roskamm, H.: Funktionsdiagnostik des gesunden und kranken Herzens. Stuttgart:Thieme Verlag, 1967.
20. Rost, R. and Dreisbach, W.: Zur wissenschaftlichen Begründung körperlichen Trainings als Mittel der Prävention und Rehabilitation bei älteren Menschen. II. Veränderungen im Bereich der zentralen Hämodynamik durch körperliches Training. Sportarzt Sportmed. 26:32, 1975.
21. Rowell, L.B.: Circulation. Med. Sci. Sports 1:15, 1969.
22. Starling, E.H.: Das Gesetz der Herzarbeit. Linacre-Vortrag 1915, Berlin u. Leipzig 1920.
23. Straub, H.: Die Dynamik des Herzens. Die Arbeitsweise des Herzens in ihrer Abhängigkeit von Spannung und Länge unter verschiedenen Arbeitsbedingungen. In Handbuch der normalen und pathologischen Physiologie. Bd. VII. Berlin:Springer Verlag, 1926.
24. Strauer, B.E.: Anderungen der Kontraktilität bei Druck- und Volumenbelastungen des Herzens. Verh. Dtsch. Ges. Kreislaufforsch. 42, 1976, im Druck.
25. Thurn, P.: Hämodynamik des Herzens im Röntgenbild. Stuttgart:Thieme Verlag, 1956.
26. Wink, K., Roskamm, H., Schweikhart, S. and Reindell, H.: Der Einfluss körperlicher Belastung auf die Kontraktilität des hypertrophierten linken Ventrikels bei Hochleistungssportlern. Z. Kardiol. 62:366, 1973.

Données d'hémodynamie centrale chez des sujets normaux, bien entraînés et hypertendus

L'auteur discute des relations qui existent entre les volumes télésystoliques et télédiastoliques. Il traite ensuite des causes et des effets de la forme de cardiomégalie qu'il qualifie d'hypertrophie physiologique et de dilatation régulative, et il en montre les liens avec le débit cardiaque au repos et à l'effort. Sur la base des variables classiques d'hémodynamie, l'auteur examine aussi les diverses implications de l'hypertrophie en fonction de l'entraînement, de la performance et du processus du vieillissement.

Acute Effects of Exercise in Subjects With Hypertension as a Function of Drug Administration

Per Lund-Johansen

Hemodynamic changes at rest and during exercise as a function of drug therapy are discussed. A survey of the long-term effects of thiazide diuretics, alpha-methyldopa, clonidine, beta-blockers, prazosin and prazosin plus tolamolol is given. The results demonstrate that the mechanism behind the pressure drop clearly differs. The possible clinical significance of the changes is discussed.

Arterial Hypertension: A Vicious Circle

About 20 years ago the well-known physiologist Sarnoff demonstrated that an *acute* increase in the systemic arterial pressure represents a much greater workload on the myocardium of the left venticle than the same relative increase in the volume load [23]. According to this, one should perhaps expect that *chronic elevation* of the systemic pressure — arterial hypertension — would result in breakdown of the heart pump function relatively soon, and that the ability to perform hard physical exercise would be restricted in hypertensive subjects early in the course of their disorder.

However, as we all know, most hypertensive subjects live for many years, or even decades, without overt clinical signs of heart failure. This is due to compensatory mechanisms which enable the heart to perform its pump function against the increased pressure load. These changes have been extensively studied in animals in recent years — parallel with the alterations in the resistance vessels. These fascinating studies have shown that hypertension, when first established, remarkably quickly changes the metabolism and structure of the myocardium and the resistance vessels [4, 5, 9, 22, 25]. In the beginning these changes look useful and may be reversible if

P. Lund-Johansen, Medical Department A, Haukeland Hospital, Bergen, Norway.

the blood pressure is reduced [4, 9, 25]. However, usually they represent the start of a vicious circle leading to permanent structural narrowing of the resistance vessels and muscular hypertrophy and reduced compliance of the left ventricle [4, 5, 25].

I would particularly draw attention to the studies in the spontaneously hypertensive rat (SHR). In this animal the functional and morphological changes from birth to death can be followed over a period of about two years [4, 5, 22, 25, 27].

Long-Term Hemodynamic Changes in Hypertensive Man

Our knowledge about the morphology and pathophysiology of the circulatory system in hypertensive man is far more fragmentary. The changes occurring in the end-stage of the process are relatively well described, but the functional and morphological changes in the early phase of hypertension are less well known. Hoping to contribute to elucidation of these problems, we have studied the central hemodynamics at rest and during acute exercise loads in males with essential hypertension in various stages and compared them with aged-matched normotensive controls [11]. The results demonstrated that the hemodynamic mechanisms behind the increased pressure differed. In the subjects in their 20s a high cardiac pump function at rest, due to tachycardia, was common, but during severe exercise the pump function was subnormal due to reduced stroke volume. The total peripheral resistance — falling within "normal" limits in most subjects at rest — was clearly increased during exercise. Thus, alterations both in the heart pump function and the peripheral resistance vessels were seen in subjects with uncomplicated essential hypertension in their 20s. In subjects in their 40s and 50s the cardiac pump function was subnormal both at rest and during exercise and the resistance clearly increased also at rest.

These results from cross-sectional samples seemed to indicate a change in the central hemodynamics with time. No systematic longitudinal studies in untreated subjects with essential hypertension had been carried out.

Recently, we got the chance to restudy nearly all our untreated patients who were less than 35 years old when first studied ten years ago [21]. The results demonstrated that despite the fact that the blood pressure had not changed significantly and that no signs or clinical symptoms of heart failure were present, the cardiac output had decreased at rest as well as during exercise due to reduction in the stroke volume and the total peripheral resistance had increased

(Fig. 1A, B). Thus, the hemodynamic changes in man with mild essential hypertension over a decade seem to resemble what is found

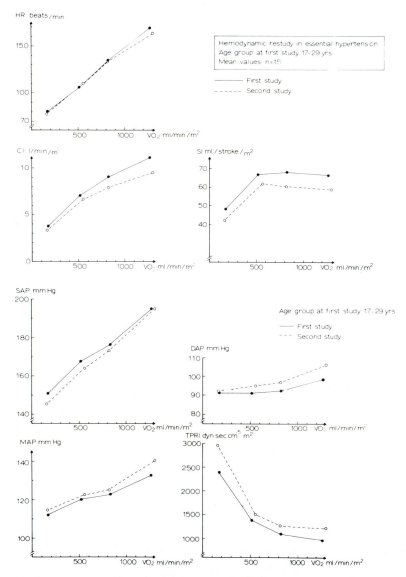

FIG. 1A,B. Central hemodynamics at rest and during exercise at first study (————) and at restudy (- - - - -) after ten years without therapy. Mean values. CI = Cardiac index, SI = Stroke index, HR = Heart rate, SAP = Systolic arterial pressure, DAP = Diastolic arterial pressure, MAP = Mean arterial pressure, TPRI = Toral peripheral resistance index.

in the SHR over a period of a few months [22, 25]. It would seem very likely that the functional disorders in man will be due to the same structural changes as those which have been found in the rat. Thus, the vicious circle seems to operate in man, but at a much slower speed, and therefore is so hard to study. Over a period of one year almost no changes can be detected in man with untreated mild hypertension [12].

Regression of Hypertensive Changes by Drug Therapy

I have wanted to present these results as a background for the following discussion about how the hemodynamics at rest and the hemodynamic response to exercise may be changed by our anti-hypertensive drugs. I think the *most interesting problem is if by long-term use of the antihypertensive drugs it is possible to stop or reverse the vicious circle, or more simply, change the hemodynamic alterations toward normal.* Studies in SHR seem to indicate that this is possible with some of our antihypertensive drugs [5, 25].

Time does not permit a discussion of all types of drugs available today nor of the drug effects on various types of static and dynamic exercise in various types and stages of hypertension. Therefore, I will restrict the discussion to the most commonly used drugs — thiazide diuretics, alpha-methyldopa, clonidine, beta-blockers, vasodilators and a combination of a vasodilator and a beta-blocker. Main emphasis will be put on the long-term changes (which often differ from the immediate effects).

Our method has involved measurement of oxygen consumption, heart rate, cardiac output (by Cardiogreen) and intra-arterial brachial pressure at rest supine and sitting and during steady state exercise on bicycle at 300, 600 and 900 kpm/min. After the first hemodynamic study the patients — who have all been males with previously untreated essential hypertension in WHO stage I or II — have been treated by the drug or drugs under study for one year. The hemodynamic study has then been repeated. Table I shows a survey of the number of patients and variety of drugs studied so far.

Thiazide Diuretics

Acute and Semi-acute Effects

After *intravenous administration* or *oral thiazide therapy for a few days* the blood pressure at rest and during exercise decreases due to a reduction in the cardiac output. This is caused by a drop in the stroke volume, the heart rate being unchanged [7]. The mechanism

Table I. Follow-up Studies in Essential Hypertension (Males)

Untreated		31
1 year	7	
10 years	24	
Treated (1 year)		129
Diuretics	31	
Symp. N.S. Inhibitors	26	
Beta-blockers	51	
Peripheral vasodilators	10	
Vasodil. + Beta-blocker	11	
Total		160

responsible for the immediate drop in the cardiac output after *injection* of thiazides is not known [7]. A few hours after administration, when diuresis has been produced, the plasma volume drops and this is probably the mechanism behind the decrease in the stroke volume at this stage. Thus, the *acute* effects of thiazide diuretics do not lead to a normalization of the central hemodynamics at rest or during exercise. The cardinal hemodynamic disturbance in most types of hypertension — the increase in the total peripheral resistance — is not corrected.

Long-Term Effects

It was quite a sensation when Conway and Lauwers in 1960 were able to demonstrate that by *continuous* administration of thiazide diuretics a readjustment of the circulatory system seemed to take place [2]. When subjects were restudied hemodynamically *at rest supine* after one year on treatment, the cardiac output was no longer reduced and the persistent drop in arterial pressure was caused by reduction in the total peripheral resistance. Thus, the circulatory system had been changed in a normal direction. The alterations in the hemodynamics during *exercise* were unknown and were therefore studied in our laboratory [12]. The results are seen on Figure 2. The mean arterial pressure was reduced about 15% at rest and during exercise. The heart rate was unchanged. There was a small decrease in the stroke volume at rest sitting, but not during exercise, and the cardiac output — being slightly reduced at rest sitting — was equal to pretreatment level during exercise. The drop in blood pressure was caused by a significant decrease in the total peripheral resistance. Thus, these results confirmed Conway and Lauwers' findings at rest [2]. In addition, they show that during muscular exercise the central hemodynamics had been changed in a normal direction.

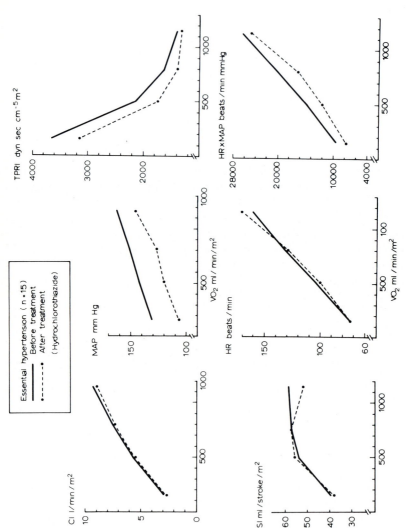

FIG. 2. Central hemodynamics at rest and during exercise before and after hydrochlorothiazide therapy. Mean values. Symbols as in Figure 1.

Other Diuretics

Studies on other diuretics like chlorthalidone [12] and mefrusid [3] are more scanty and will not be discussed here.

Sympathetic Inhibitors

Alpha-methyldopa and Clonidine

Studies of the long-term effects of these drugs have shown that the drop in pressure was mainly caused by a reduction in heart rate and cardiac output with little effect upon total peripheral resistance [13, 14]. An interesting feature with clonidine was that during submaximal muscular exercise this drug has very little effect upon the central hemodynamics, indicating that this drug — which probably has its most prominent effect on the central part of the nervous system [10] — has little effect on the blood pressure control during severe exercise. It is likely that the clonidine effect is then overridden by other mechanisms controlling the circulation during severe muscular exercise.

Beta-blockers

The beta-blockers have been widely used in therapy of hypertension in Europe and Australia, but have so far not been accepted for use in hypertension by the Food and Drug Administration in the United States. The beta-blockers may be divided into cardioselective and noncardioselective compounds with two subtypes within each of these main groups, based on whether or not intrinsic sympathicomimetic activity is present.

In long-term use in hypertension the major changes induced by the different types seem to be largely the same, although minor changes in the effect upon stroke volume and peripheral resistance seem to exist [15, 17-19].

Acute Effects

When beta-blockers are given *intravenously* or *orally* for one to two days, the mean arterial pressure at rest and during exercise is usually little affected. The cardiac output drops due to a marked decrease in the heart rate without any compensatory increase in the stroke volume. The drop in the cardiac output is associated by an increase in the total peripheral resistance, thus leaving the blood pressure almost unchanged [6, 8]. The marked decrease in the cardiac output at rest and during exercise is associated with an increase in the arteriovenous oxygen difference.

Long-Term Effects

Since the main immediate effect of beta-blockade is a decrease in the blood flow without any decrease in the blood pressure, it is somewhat surprising that the beta-blockers should become one of the leading types of drugs in treatment of hypertension [6]. This is due to a readjustment phenomenon. After a period of days or weeks the blood pressure in most hypertensive subjects drops due to a decrease in total peripheral resistance [8]. However, in contrast to the situation in subjects treated with thiazide diuretics, the blood flow *remains reduced* at least over a period of one year (probably permanently) due to the persistent decrease in the heart rate.

In our laboratory we have studied the hemodynamic long-term effects of four beta-blockers in a group of 51 hypertensive subjects. Figure 3 shows results obtained by *alprenolol* [15]. The heart rate was still markedly reduced after one year on therapy. The stroke volume during exercise was higher than before treatment, resulting in less reduction in cardiac output than corresponding to the reduction in heart rate. The pressure reduction during exercise was relatively modest. The peripheral resistance was not decreased compared to pretreatment levels.

A recent follow-up study of these patients treated with alprenolol as the sole drug for three years demonstrated that the heart rate was still reduced and so was the cardiac output. There had been no further decrease in the total peripheral resistance as a consequence of prolonged treatment. The "break" on the heart was still present.

Figure 4 shows the results in the groups treated with *timolol* and *atenolol* [17, 18]. The reduction in heart rate was very marked, about 25%. In the timolol group there was no compensatory increase in the stroke volume and, as a consequence, the cardiac output was reduced about 25% at rest and during exercise. The total peripheral resistance was significantly higher after therapy at rest as well as during exercise. This is not unexpected since a noncardioselective beta-blocker like timolol will also block the $beta_2$-receptors in the arterioles, thus leaving the alpha-receptors unopposed to the increased content of catecholamines occurring during muscular exercises resulting in unopposed vasoconstriction.

In the atenolol group there was a compensatory increase in the stroke volume, resulting in less reduction in cardiac output than on timolol. The peripheral resistance during exercise was not significantly changed.

The hemodynamic results obtained by *metoprolol* [19] were relatively similar to those seen in the atenolol group.

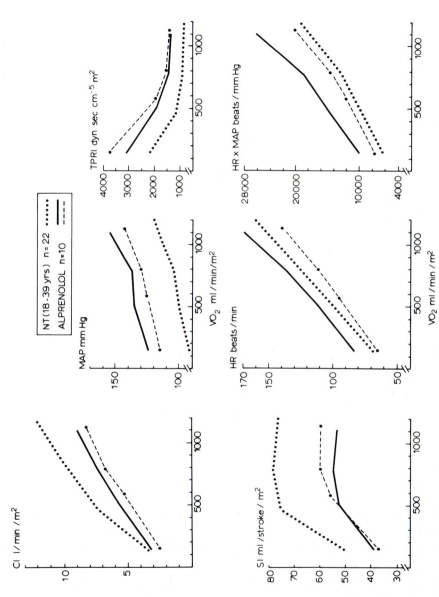

FIG. 3. Central hemodynamics at rest and during exercise before and after alprenolol therapy. Mean values. (·····) shows mean values in normotensive subjects 18 to 39 years old. Symbols as in Figure 1.

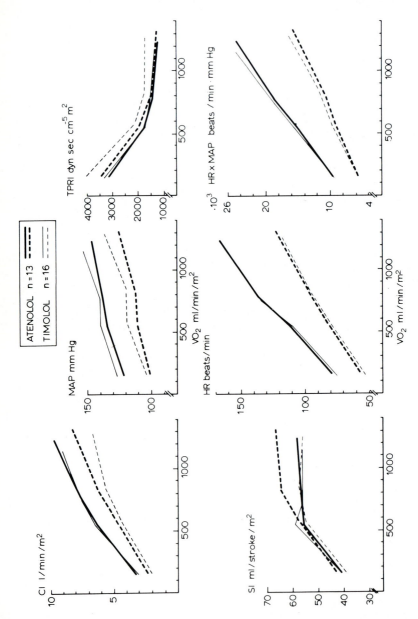

FIG. 4. Central hemodynamics at rest and during exercise before and after atenolol and timolol therapy. Symbols as in Figure 1.

Thus, although some sort of circulatory readjustment takes place on long-term therapy with beta-blockers, still after one year of treatment the blood flow is clearly hypokinetic due to the marked decrease in the heart rate. On some beta-blockers there is a compensatory increase in the stroke volume, but not high enough to compensate completely for the marked reduction in the heart rate. As an end-result we achieve a large reduction in the pressure/heart rate product and consequently in the workload on the heart. This has to be "paid" by a decrease in the blood flow. As the oxygen consumption is not changed, the A-VO$_2$ difference has to be increased. It is puzzling that these alterations were so well tolerated. The majority of the patients were able to carry out even quite demanding physical exercise like walking in the mountains and cross-country skiing without any symptoms. At the hemodynamic restudy no subjects had greater difficulties performing the 900 kpm/min load than at the first study.

In hypertensive patients with a markedly decreased pretreatment cardiac output, it is likely that the beta-blockers may precipitate heart failure. That is probably one of the main reasons why the Food and Drug Administration has been withholding this type of drug in hypertension.

Vasodilators

The most widely used vasodilator has been *hydralazine*. However, used alone, this drug leaves the beta-adrenoreceptors unblocked and a compensatory tachycardia takes place resulting in little effect on the blood pressure.

A relatively new promising vasodilator is *prazosin*. This compound has an additional effect which seems to prevent the tachycardia which should be expected from the vasodilating effect [1].

Short-Term Hemodynamic Studies

Blood pressure reduction is caused by a significant decrease in the total peripheral resistance in the presence of an unchanged cardiac output [24].

Long-Term Studies

The hemodynamic long-term effects at rest and during exercise of this interesting drug are shown on Figure 5. The hemodynamic long-term response clearly differed from what was seen by the use of thiazide diuretics and beta-blockers. The drop in pressure was caused

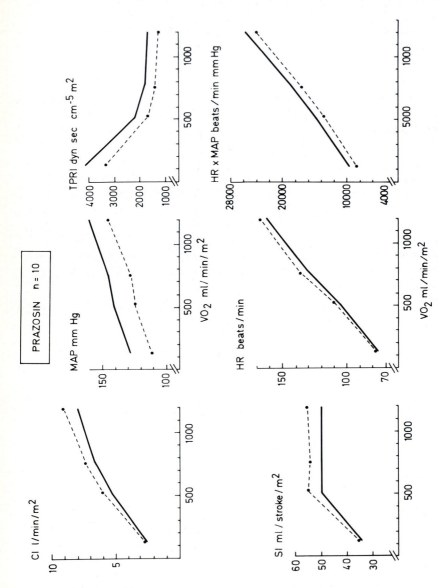

FIG. 5. Central hemodynamics at rest and during exercise before and after prazosin therapy. Symbols as in Figure 1.

by a significant reduction in the total peripheral resistance at rest and during exercise. The cardiac index tended to be higher than before treatment and was significantly increased during exercise. The increase in blood flow was mainly caused by increase in stroke volume [16].

From a pathophysiological point of view prazosin has resulted in a marked decrease in total peripheral resistance and the blood flow is not decreased. The heart rate, which tends to be abnormally high in essential hypertension, was still increased. The reduction in the pressure-heart rate product was relatively modest in contrast to the situation with the beta-blockers.

Combination of Vasodilator and Beta-blocker

If the beta-adrenoreceptors are blocked by a beta-blocker, the tendency to tachycardia induced by vasodilators should be prevented and the blood pressure reduction augmented. This expected response was found in a group of patients on long-term treatment with prazosin plus a beta-blocker, tolamolol (unfortunately tolamolol had to be taken out of clinical investigations due to suspicion of carcinogenic effect in high-dose long-term studies in animals) [20]. The results demonstrated that the blood pressure drop was caused by a combination of reduction in cardiac output and total peripheral resistance. During exercise, however, the reduction in cardiac output was modest and the blood pressure reduction was then mainly caused by reduction in total peripheral resistance. The heart rate was decreased due to the beta-blockade, but the decrease was less than what was seen by the use of beta-blockers alone. On this regimen the subjects were able to retain the ability to produce a high cardiac output during submaximal muscular exercise.

Conclusion

This brief survey has shown that the hemodynamic mechanism behind the drop in blood pressure induced by various antihypertensive drugs differs markedly between the various types. Knowledge of these results might have practical implication for the choice of treatment in various types of hypertensive subjects. A few examples will be mentioned. Patients with incipient cardiac insufficiency should primarily be treated with diuretics (in addition to digitalization). They should avoid beta-blockers and probably also vasodilators.

On the other hand, patients with tendency to tachycardia, palpitations, arrhythmias or angina pectoris will usually benefit from treatment with beta-blockers (provided contraindications do not exist). Third, patients with low cardiac output, very marked hypertension and reduced renal perfusion will probably benefit from a combination of vasodilators and beta-blockers.

What should be the drug of choice in patients with mild and moderate hypertension? Is it possible to restore the circulatory system back to normal? So far this question cannot be answered on the basis of the existing data. If it is assumed that a normal blood flow and a decreased resistance would carry the best prognosis, then the thiazide diuretics or prazosin should be preferred — provided no side effects will appear. On the other hand, the beta-blockers have a greater ability to relieve the strain on the heart and may also possibly protect against fatal arrhythmias. Recent studies in animals on the effect of various antihypertensive drugs have indicated that it is not unimportant whether the blood pressure is reduced by one mechanism or the other [25]. It is possible that future studies of the hemodynamic effects of the various antihypertensive drugs in animals and man might contribute to an answer to this key question.

References

1. Constantine, J.W.: Analysis of the hypotensive action of prazosin. *In* Cotton, D.W.K. (ed.): Prazosin — Evaluation of a New Anti-hypertensive Agent. Amsterdam:Excerpta Medica, 1974, p. 16.
2. Conway, J. and Lauwers, P.: Hemodynamic and hypotensive effects of long-term therapy with chlorothiazide. Circulation 21:21, 1960.
3. Danielsson, M., Bevegard, S. and Castenfors, J.: Effekt pa central hemodynamik under mefrusid terapi. *In* Hypertonisymposium/Saltsjobaden, Ed.: Bayer (Sverige) AB. Uppsala:Centraltryckeriet, 1975, p. 31.
4. Folkow, B.: Vascular changes in hypertension — review and recent animal studies. *In* Berglund, G., Hansson, L. and Werkö, L. (eds.): Pathophysiology and Management of Arterial Hypertension. Göteborg: Lindgren & Söner A.B., 1975, p. 95.
5. Folkow, B., Hallbäck, M., Lundgren, Y. et al: The importance of adaptive changes in vascular design for the establishment and maintenance of primary hypertension, as studied in man and in spontaneously hypertensive rat. *In* Okamoto, K. (ed.): Spontaneous Hypertension — Its Pathogenesis and Complications. Tokyo:Igaku Shoin Ltd, 1972, p. 103.
6. Frohlich, E.D., Tarazi, R.C., Dustan, H.P. et al: The paradox of beta-adrenergic blockade in hypertension. Circulation 37:417, 1968.
7. Greene, M.A., Boltax, A.J. and Scherr, E.S.: Acute effects of intravenous chlorothiazide upon cardiovascular hemodynamics. Am. Heart J. 62:659, 1961.
8. Hansson, L.: Beta-adrenergic blockade in essential hypertension. Acta Med. Scand. Suppl. 550:7, 1973.
9. Henry, J.P., Stephens, P.M. and Santisteban, G.A.: A model of psychosocial hypertension showing reversibility and progression of cardiovascular complications. Circ. Res. 36:156, 1975.

10. Kobinger, W.: Pharmacologic basis of the cardiovascular actions of clonidine. *In* Onesti, G., Kim, K.E. and Moyer, J.H. (eds.): Hypertension: Mechanisms and Management. New York and London, 1973, p. 369.
11. Lund-Johansen, P.: Hemodynamics in early essential hypertension. Acta. Med. Scand. Suppl. 482, 1967.
12. Lund-Johansen, P.: Hemodynamic changes in long-term diuretic therapy of essential hypertension. Acta Med. Scand. 187:509, 1970.
13. Lund-Johansen, P.: Hemodynamic changes in long-term alpha-methyldopa therapy of essential hypertension. Acta Med. Scand. 192:221, 1972.
14. Lund-Johansen, P.: Hemodynamic changes at rest and during exercise in long-term clonidine therapy of essential hypertension. Acta Med. Scand. 195:111, 1974.
15. Lund-Johansen, P.: Hemodynamic changes at rest and during exercise in long-term beta-blocker therapy of essential hypertension. Acta Med. Scand. 195:117, 1974.
16. Lund-Johansen, P.: Hemodynamic changes at rest and during exercise in long-term prazosin therapy of essential hypertension. *In* Cotton, D.W.K. (ed.): Prazosin — Evaluation of a New Anti-hypertensive Agent. Excerpta Medica, 1974, p. 43.
17. Lund-Johansen, P.: Hemodynamic long-term effects of timolol at rest and during exercise in essential hypertension. Acta Med. Scand. 199:263, 1976.
18. Lund-Johansen, P.: Hemodynamic long-term effects of a new beta-adrenoceptor blocking drug, atenolol (ICI 66082), in essential hypertension. Br. J. Clin. Pharmacol. 1976. (In press.)
19. Lund-Johansen, P. and Ohm, O.J.: Hemodynamic long-term effects of metoprolol at rest and during exercise in essential hypertension. 1976. In preparation.
20. Lund-Johansen, P.: Hemodynamic long-term effects of prazosin plus tolamolol in essential hypertension. 1976. In preparation.
21. Lund-Johansen, P.: Long-term hemodynamic trends in untreated essential hypertension — a 10 year follow-up study. Third International Workshop on the Relationship between Cardiac Output and Hypertension. Puerto Rico, April 9, 1976.
22. Pfeffer, M.A. and Frohlich, E.D.: Hemodynamic and myocardial function in young and old normotensive and spontaneously hypertensive rats. Circulation Res. suppl I, 28, 1973.
23. Sarnoff, S.J., Braunwald, E., Welch, G.H. et al: Hemodynamic determinants of the oxygen consumption of the heart with special reference to the tension-time index. *In* Rosenbaum, F.F. and Belknap, E.L. (eds.): Work and the Heart. New York, 1959.
24. Smith, I.S., Fernandes, M., Kim, K.E. et al: A three-phase clinical evaluation of prazosin. *In* Prazosin — Clinical Symposium Proceedings. Postgraduate Medicine. Special Issue. McGraw-Hill, 1975, p. 53.
25. Tarazi, R.C.: The heart in hypertension: Its load and its role. Hosp. Practice 10:31, 1975.
26. Tarazi, R.C.: Long-term hemodynamic effects of beta-adrenergic blockade in hypertension. *In* Onesti, G., Kim, K.E. and Moyer, J.H. (eds.): Hypertension: Mechanisms and Management. New York and London, 1973, p. 343.
27. Yamori, Y. and Okamoto, K.: Spontaneous hypertension in rats versus essential hypertension in man. Singapore Med. J. 14:393, 1973.

Les effets aigus de l'activité physique chez des sujets hypertendus, en fonction de l'administration de certains médicaments

L'auteur traite des effets que produisent certaines drogues sur la circulation sanguine, en situation de repos et au cours de l'effort physique. Il traite spécifiquement des effets chroniques de l'administration des drogues diurétiques et des agents beta-bloqueurs. Les données montrent que les mécanismes par lesquels la tension artérielle peut diminuer varient considérablement; l'auteur discute de la signification clinique des changements observés.

The Chronic Effects of Exercise in Subjects With Hypertension

Rune Sannerstedt

Results based on the circulatory findings in arterial hypertension of various stages reveal different hemodynamic group patterns at rest. Chronic effects of training on hemodynamic changes of a magnitude that will substantially and permanently lower the systemic blood pressure appear possible in patients with early, latent arterial hypertension but improbable in individuals with established hypertension.

Since the use of physical training as an approach to treating coronary patients was introduced among others by Varnauskas et al [12] at the Sahlgrenska University Hospital in Göteborg considerable interest has been devoted to physical conditioning as a tool to benefit not only patients with coronary artery disease, but also those with other cardiovascular disorders, including hypertensive cardiovascular disease.

In comparison to coronary heart disease, however, experience of physical conditioning in patients with arterial hypertension is limited. As may be seen from the survey of the available literature presented in Tables I and II, a wide variety of training procedures of varying lengths has been used, making comparisons between results from the various studies difficult. Moreover, published data have not always been reported in a form that allows critical evaluation of the findings.

In our own study we have applied the principle of what may be called interval training, using a stationary bicycle ergometer on which the subjects exercise continuously for one full hour three times a week (Fig. 1). Each session of one hour is subdivided into five periods of 12 minutes, with three incremental workloads during each of them, aiming at a heart rate of 150 to 160 beats per minute during the highest level of exercise.

Rune Sannerstedt, Department of Medicine I, Sahlgrenska University Hospital, Göteborg, Sweden.

Table I. Latent Arterial Hypertension

Authors	Diagnosis	No. of Patients	Training	Results
Hanson and Nedde [4]	Labile hyp.	2	Various ex. 3 times/ wk for 7 mo.	More marked BP drop than in establ. hyp.
Choquette and Ferguson [3]	Borderline hyp.	37	Calisthenics, jogging, volleyball once week- ly for 7 mo.	Lower syst. and diast. BP at rest and after submax. ex.
Sannerstedt et al [11]	Latent hyp.	5	Bicycling 3 times/wk for 6 wk	Tendencies to lower BP, HR and CO

Table II. Established Arterial Hypertension

Authors	Diagnosis	No. of Patients	Training	Results
Johnson and Grover [6]	Sustained ess. hyp.	4	Treadmill ex. 3 times/ wk for 10 wk	No influence on BP
Boyer and Kasch [2]	Ess. hyp.	23	Walk-jog training twice a week for 6 mo.	Drop in syst. and diast. BP
Hanson and Nedde [4]	Establ. ess. hyp.	4	Various ex. 3 times/ wk for 7 mo.	Drop in BP at rest and during ex.
Kiveloff and Huber [7]	High blood pressure	22	Max. isometric ex. for 6 sec tid for 5-8 wk	Drop in syst. and diast. BP with unchanged HR
Sannerstedt et al [11]	Establ. hyp.	2	Bicycling 3 times/wk for 6 wk	No influence on BP

Considering the varying hemodynamic background in different stages of arterial hypertension, it seems rather self-evident to subdivide hypertensive patients into those with latent and those with established arterial hypertension when discussing the circulatory effects of chronic exercise and the tentative therapeutic value of physical conditioning. Further, it has been considered appropriate in this context to omit advanced hypertension with signs of cardio-vascular damage, even though physical conditioning may also be indicated in such cases. However, it then has to be assumed that this is undertaken mainly for general rehabilitation purposes and not specifically to achieve a blood pressure reduction.

In accordance with this, the following presentation will be based on the circulatory findings in arterial hypertension of various stages as seen in our own studies at the Sahlgrenska University Hospital in

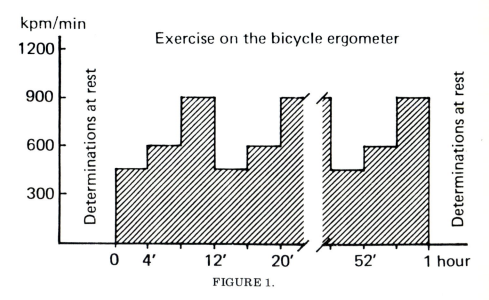

FIGURE 1.

Göteborg [8-10]. Such studies in untreated men with essential arterial hypertension of varying severity have revealed different hemodynamic group patterns at rest (Fig. 2). Using the system proposed by WHO in 1962 to classify the various stages of arterial

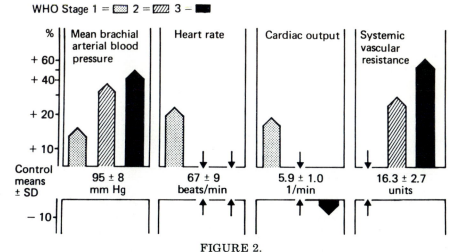

FIGURE 2.

hypertension, the following hemodynamic group characteristics emerge:

WHO Stage 1: A hyperkinetic circulation at rest with increased heart rate and cardiac output;

WHO Stage 2: A normokinetic circulation at rest with normal cardiac output, but with an increased calculated systemic vascular resistance;

WHO Stage 3: A hypokinetic circulation with decreased cardiac output at rest together with an increased calculated systemic vascular resistance.

Differences between healthy controls and hypertensive patients, and between the various hypertensive groups, can also be noted with respect to the acute responses to physical exercise on a bicycle ergometer. Thus, the group of men with arterial hypertension WHO Stage 1, for example, react with smaller increases in heart rate and cardiac output than both the control group and the two other hypertensive groups (Fig. 3). On the other hand, it should be pointed out that the average percentage increase in the mean systemic blood pressure is identical in healthy controls and all three WHO groups of hypertensive men.

How, then, may chronic exercise and training procedures in hypertensive individuals influence their circulatory system?

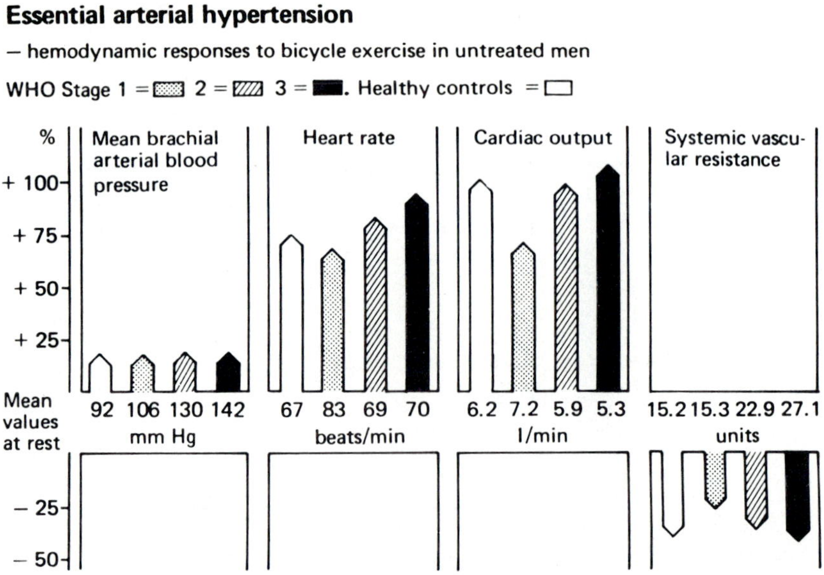

Essential arterial hypertension

— hemodynamic responses to bicycle exercise in untreated men

WHO Stage 1 = ▨ 2 = ▨ 3 = ■. Healthy controls = ☐

FIGURE 3.

Looking first at established arterial hypertension corresponding to WHO Stage 2, it has been pointed out that the hemodynamic group characteristic is a normokinetic circulation during physical rest and that the main hemodynamic abnormality in the systemic circulation is an elevation of the calculated systemic vascular resistance (Fig. 4). The logical therapeutic approach would be to lower the systemic vascular resistance, and some theoretical possibilities for achieving this are indicated in the figure.

Can this be achieved through physical conditioning? The sparse data in the literature do not give an unequivocal answer. Pooling the detailed hemodynamic findings from the studies by Johnson and Grover [6] and Sannerstedt et al [11] even indicates that, if anything, the blood pressure tends to be somewhat higher after the training period, both at rest and during exercise (Fig. 5). Considering the theoretical possibilities for induction of a lasting blood pressure reduction it also seems rather improbable that physical conditioning alone would induce hemodynamic changes of a magnitude that will substantially lower the systemic blood pressure.

Quite another situation is met with when turning to patients with early, latent arterial hypertension, where a predominant hemodynamic group feature is the hyperkinetic circulation at rest with

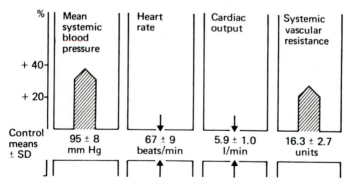

FIGURE 4.

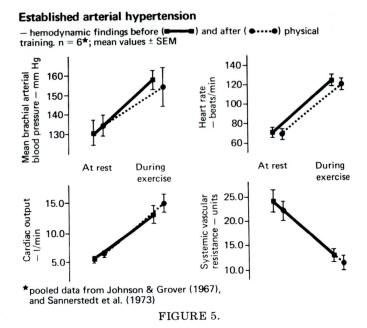

Established arterial hypertension
— hemodynamic findings before (■———■) and after (●····●) physical
training. n = 6★; mean values ± SEM

★pooled data from Johnson & Grover (1967),
and Sannerstedt et al. (1973)

FIGURE 5.

increased heart rate and cardiac output (Fig. 6). Logically, the treatment of choice would aim at lowering the heart rate and cardiac output, for example, through reduction of sympathetic tone and/or increase of vagal tone as indicated in the figure.

Knowing that decreases in heart rate and cardiac output are generally observed in connection with physical training in healthy individuals [5], physical conditioning might be expected to benefit subjects with early, latent arterial hypertension. Our own results from a small group of men with latent hypertension support this hypothesis, the heart rate and cardiac output tending to be lower after the training period both at rest and during exercise, as also was the mean brachial arterial blood pressure (Fig. 7).

Further studies are needed before definitive conclusions can be drawn as to whether physical training of individuals with latent hypertension will result in hemodynamic changes of sufficient magnitude to keep the blood pressure permanently at a lower level, thereby postponing the start of drug treatment, making previous drug treatment superfluous, or at least lessening the dose of antihypertensive drugs needed. Our own data, scanty as they are, indicate that this may not infrequently be the case.

An opposite facet of the problem is whether chronic exercise and physical training may have any deleterious effects on patients with

Latent hypertension WHO stage 1

Hemodynamic pattern at rest in untreated men

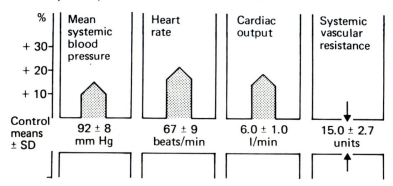

Ways to reduce the cardiac output

1 reduction of sympathetic tone
2 increase of vagal tone
3 reduction of venous return

4 diminished myocardial
   contractility
5 combinations of 1 − 4

FIGURE 6.

Latent arterial hypertension

— hemodynamic findings before (■━━■) and after (●····●) physical training. n = 5; mean values ± SEM

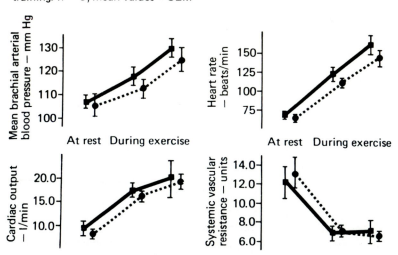

FIGURE 7.

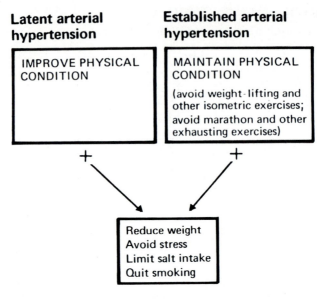

FIGURE 8.

arterial hypertension. Very little is known about this, but in the light of the fact that various procedures encompassing either static or dynamic exercises may lead to heavy blood pressure increases in hypertensive patients, with peaks well above 300 mm Hg, the risk of acute cardiovascular disasters should not be ignored, especially in patients with high blood pressure levels initially and signs of cardiovascular engagement. Generally speaking, patients with established arterial hypertension, even though urged to maintain their level of physical fitness, should therefore be advised to avoid weightlifting and other strenuous isometric exercises and also marathon runnning and similar exhausting activities.

In summary, then, actively improving the level of physical fitness through physical training may turn out to be worthwhile in patients with early, latent arterial hypertension (Fig. 8). Although available data do not convincingly favor such an approach in patients with established arterial hypertension, this patient category should nevertheless be encouraged to maintain their level of physical fitness.

Finally, it has to be emphatically pointed out that any recommendations to hypertensive patients about physical activity should always include advice on general measures like weight reduction and combating stress.

References

1. Arterial Hypertension and Ischaemic Heart Disease. Preventive Aspects. Report of an Expert Committee. World Health Organization Technical Report Series No. 231, 1962.
2. Boyer, J.L. and Kasch, F.W.: Exercise therapy in hypertensive men. JAMA 211:1668-1671, 1970.
3. Choquette, G. and Ferguson, R.J.: Blood pressure reduction in "borderline" hypertensives following physical training. Can. Med. Assoc. J. 108:699-703, 1973.
4. Hanson, J.S. and Nedde, W.H.: Preliminary observations on physical training for hypertensive males. Circ. Res. 27 (suppl. 1):49-53, 1970.
5. Hanson, J.S., Tabakin, B.S., Levy, A.M. and Nedde, W.: Long-term physical training and cardiovascular dynamics in middle-aged men. Circulation 38:783-799, 1968.
6. Johnson, W.P. and Grover, J.A.: Hemodynamic and metabolic effects of physical training in four patients with essential hypertension. Can. Med. Assoc. J. 96:842-847, 1967.
7. Kiveloff, B. and Huber, O.: Brief maximal isometric exercise in hypertension. J. Am. Geriat. Soc. 19:1006-1012, 1971.
8. Sannerstedt, R.: Differences in haemodynamic pattern in various types of hypertension. Triangle 9:293-299, 1970.
9. Sannerstedt, R.: Hemodynamic findings at rest and during exercise in mild arterial hypertension. Am. J. Med. Sci. 258:70-79, 1969.
10. Sannerstedt, R.: Hemodynamic response to exercise in patients with arterial hypertension. Acta Med. Scand. 180(suppl. 458), 1966.
11. Sannerstedt, R., Wasir, H., Henning, R. and Werkö, L.: Systemic haemodynamics in mild arterial hypertension before and after physical training. Clin. Sci. Molec. Med. 45:145s-149s, 1973.
12. Varnauskas, E., Bergman, H., Houk, P. and Björntorp, P.: Haemodynamic effects of physical training in coronary patients. Lancet 2:8-12, 1966.

Les effets à long terme de l'exercice physique chez des hypertendus

Les données circulatoires obtenues chez des hypertendus à différents degrés montrent des caractéristiques hémodynamiques spécifiques à l'état de repos. En se basant sur les résultats de la recherche, l'auteur montre que l'entraînement physique peut produire des changements appréciables et durables de la tension artérielle chez des sujets qui en sont à la phase initiale de l'état d'hypertension; il se dit par ailleurs d'avis que ces changements bénéfiques apparaissent malheureusement peu probables chez des sujets ou des patients chez lesquels l'hypertension artérielle est confirmée.

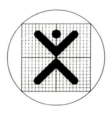

Individual Scientific Contributions

Communications scientifiques individuelles

Myocardial Function as Influenced by Age and Habitual Leisure Time Physical Activity: A Cross-Sectional Study

Paul S. Fardy, Carl M. Maresh,
Robert D. Abbott and Trygve Kristiansen

Introduction

The duration of left ventricular systolic time intervals (STIs) provides a relatively simple noninvasive and atraumatic measurement of myocardial function [1, 13]. Application of these measurements includes their ability to discern acute cardiac stress [7, 9], to evaluate functional changes from intervention programs [3, 4, 8] and to differentiate between normal and abnormal cardiac functioning [15, 17]. The purpose of this paper is to focus attention on the effects of aging and current leisure time physical activity upon the duration of STIs.

Methodology

Five hundred and six healthy males, aged 27 to 74, participated in this investigation. Information on current leisure time physical activity was determined from their response to a written questionnaire. Left ventricular time components, including total electromechanical systole (Q-S_2), left ventricular ejection time (LVET), pre-ejection period (PEP) and total cycle time converted to heart rate (HR), were obtained from simultaneous recordings of the carotid

Paul S. Fardy, Department of Medicine, Case Western Reserve University, Cleveland, Ohio; Carl M. Maresh, Physical Education Department, University of Pittsburgh, Pittsburgh, Pa.; Robert D. Abbott, Educational Psychology Department, University of Washington, Seattle, Wash.; and Trygve Kristiansen, Duke University Medical Center, Durham, North Carolina, U.S.A.

The study was conducted at California State University at Fullerton and was supported by NSF Institutional Grants, and by the Department of Biometry, School of Medicine, Case Western Reserve University, Cleveland, Ohio.

pulse wave, electrocardiogram and phonocardiogram at a paper speed of 50 mm/sec. Measurements were made during supine rest and at one minute following a submaximal two-minute step test, 24 steps per minute on a 30.5 cm bench. Mean values were determined from averaging five consecutive cardiac cycles. Linear regression technique was utilized to calculate STIs corrected for HR. Data analysis was facilitated with a PDP 11/45 computer. A complete discussion of research methodology utilized in this investigation is described elsewhere [5].

Aging

In order to assess the usefulness of STIs for evaluating myo-cardial performance it is essential that data be available on normal healthy populations over a cross section of ages. Unfortunately, few such studies have been undertaken [11, 12]. In the present investigation the study sample was divided into age categories 25-34, 35-44, 45-54 and 55-74. Physical characteristics of each age category as well as overall ages are presented in Table I.

Correlations between age and STIs are presented in Table II. The correlations were low or of zero order substantiating the results of previous findings [12]. Although some of the correlations are

Table I. Physical Characteristics of 506 Male Subjects Age 25 to 74
(Mean ± SD)

Age Groups	Height	Weight	Age	N
All ages	178.9 ± 6.7	80.6 ± 10.1	42.7 ± 9.0	506
25-34	179.4 ± 6.4	80.8 ± 10.9	32.1 ± 1.7	106
35-44	179.0 ± 7.3	81.2 ± 10.3	39.4 ± 2.7	212
45-54	179.1 ± 6.0	80.6 ± 9.3	49.1 ± 2.7	130
55-74*	176.9 ± 6.0	77.5 ± 8.8	59.7 ± 4.2	58

*The 55-64 and 65-74 age groups were combined due to the small number in the 65-74 age group.

Table II. Correlations Between Age
and Left Ventricle Cardiac Cycle Time Components

Condition	HR	Q-S$_2$	LVET	PEP
Resting	.101*	.104*	.048	.116†
One minute postexercise	.198†	−.088*	−.031	−.072

*p < 0.05
†p < 0.01

significant, it is obvious that none are strong and at best account for less than 4% of the between test variance.

Significance testing of regression coefficients between HR and STIs was employed in each of the age categories. Q-S_2 and LVET coefficients were significant (P <0.001) at rest and one minute after exercise for all age groups. Regression coefficients for PEP were significant (between 0.01 and 0.05) in age groups 25-54. In the 55-74 age group the regression coefficient was nonsignificant at rest although significant following exercise (P <0.01). If the F value is significant then adjustment for HR is indicated. Mean comparisons of STIs according to age categories are presented in Table III. These results replicate a prior study of men in the same approximate age range [10]. The effects of aging were more apparent at one minute postexercise than at rest. Increased age was associated with higher HR and shortened Q-S_2, LVET and PEP. Considering that maximal HR declines with age at a rate of about one beat a year [2] the stress imposed by exercise was even greater relative to maximal HR. These findings indicate that increased age results in a declining ability to adapt to exercise stress. STIs which best reflect the effect of aging, Q-S_2 and LVET, had been identified previously as the best discriminants between "excellent" and "poor" cardiovascular fitness [6].

Habitual Leisure Time Physical Activity

The relationship between leisure time physical activity and cardiovascular function and coronary artery disease [16, 18] is of

Table III. Comparisons Among Age Classification
for Systolic Time Intervals (Mean ± SD)

| | Age Classifications | | | |
Variable	25-34 (n = 106)	35-44 (n = 212)	45-54 (n = 130)	55-74 (n = 112)
Resting				
HR (bt/min)	63 ± 9.1	65 ± 9.9	66 ± 11.2	66 ± 9.9
Q-S_2 (msec)	396.7 ± 19.0	397.9 ± 17.5	400.4 ± 17.5	406.4 ± 20.2
LVET (msec)	301.1 ± 14.8	303.3 ± 16.0	302.4 ± 15.5	306.2 ± 18.5
PEP (msec)	94.4 ± 18.3	95.4 ± 16.3	98.1 ± 15.8	100.1 ± 14.2
One minute postexercise				
HR	78 ± 14.3	81 ± 15.4	85 ± 16.5	87 ± 18.1
Q-S_2	346.2 ± 20.6	343.4 ± 17.7	338.6 ± 19.8	340.1 ± 15.1
LVET	269.2 ± 14.9	267.7 ± 13.9	263.1 ± 15.9	264.2 ± 17.5
PEP	77.0 ± 16.2	75.7 ± 12.7	75.6 ± 14.4	75.9 ± 15.5

considerable interest to the health professional. Considering the declining energy requirements of most occupational activities, further contributions of exercise to public health are more likely to be influenced by an increase in leisure activity. At present it is estimated that 55% of the general population participates in little or no physical activity during their leisure time [14]. Moreover, half of those that do participate with some regularity are not active more than twice a week [14]. In this study leisure time physical activity was classified as light, less than 30 METS hr/wk; moderate, 30-60 METS hr/wk; and strenuous, more than 60 METS hr/wk. Results of these comparisons are presented in Table IV.

Significant differences were observed between light-moderate and light-strenuous categories. Furthermore, there were more significant differences in the upper age groups 45-74 than in the 25-44 age categories. This suggests that physiological aging as reflected by STIs can be slowed in persons maintaining a more active lifestyle. In addition the same amount of leisure time physical activity results in greater differences among activity categories as age increased. This might be attributed to the fact that the same amount of activity is, in fact, a higher level for older subjects since maximal capacity decreases with age, or that greater fitness changes are possible in less fit persons. Once more the greatest differences were observed in postexercise measures. These included lowered HR, and increased Q-S_2 and LVET. Lowered HR was primarily a result of increased diastole and secondarily attributed to increased systole. A lengthened diastole permits greater ventricular filling, which, coupled with a longer time for emptying (increased Q-S_2 and LVET), results in increased stroke volume [17]. PEPs were also longer, in general, for the more active subjects, although the differences were significant only at one minute postexercise in the 35-44 and 45-54 age categories and at rest in the 45-54 age category. PEP has been associated with both the rate and force of ventricular contraction [1, 13].

A comparison of STIs uncorrected and corrected for HR revealed fewer significant differences with corrected values (4 compared to 34). Correcting for HR, therefore, is going to markedly alter one's interpretation of the significance of these measures. At this point, however, the authors are reluctant to nullify the physiological significance of the uncorrected measures.

Conclusions

From the results of this investigation it was concluded that (1) there was little relationship between age and STIs; (2) cardiac

Table IV. Comparisons Among Levels of Leisure Time Activity[a] According to Age Categories[b]

		25-34			35-44		Age Classifications	45-54			55-74	
STIs	L (n-54)	M (n=37)	S (n=15)	L (n=125)	M (n=77)	S (n=10)	L (n=88)	M (n=38)	S (n=4)	L (n=41)	M (n=14)	S (n=3)
Resting	*L*	*M*	*S*	*L*	*M*	*S*	*L*	*M*	*S*	*L*	*M*	*S*
HR	65 ± 9	61 ± 8	61 ± 10	65 ± 9	63 ± 10	67 ± 15	69 ± 11	61 ± 9	52 ± 2	67 ± 9	63 ± 10	52 ± 6
Q-S_2	393 ± 20	398 ± 27	407 ± 28	397 ± 24	401 ± 28	394 ± 17	393 ± 31	413 ± 23	443 ± 8	404 ± 30	406 ± 25	443 ± 20
LVET	298 ± 16	302 ± 19	310 ± 26	301 ± 21	308 ± 24	295 ± 18	297 ± 27	313 ± 15	330 ± 6	304 ± 26	306 ± 19	342 ± 20
PEP	93 ± 20	95 ± 18	98 ± 14	95 ± 18	95 ± 16	99 ± 6	97 ± 16	99 ± 18	114 ± 9	100 ± 15	99 ± 14	101 ± 6
One minute Postexercise	*L*	*M*	*S*	*L*	*M*	*S*	*L*	*M*	*S*	*L*	*M*	*S*
HR	83 ± 14	73 ± 11	74 ± 18	84 ± 15	77 ± 15	76 ± 19	89 ± 16	79 ± 14	63 ± 3	90 ± 18	85 ± 16	59 ± 6
Q-S_2	337 ± 27	353 ± 29	363 ± 35	337 ± 29	352 ± 33	352 ± 27	332 ± 35	349 ± 31	400 ± 25	335 ± 32	343 ± 36	395 ± 9
LVET	260 ± 22	277 ± 20	282 ± 30	264 ± 24	274 ± 27	272 ± 20	257 ± 29	272 ± 27	307 ± 9	259 ± 27	270 ± 29	317 ± 16
PEP	77 ± 18	75 ± 15	81 ± 16	73 ± 13	79 ± 14	80 ± 9	74 ± 13	77 ± 18	93 ± 18	77 ± 19	74 ± 11	77 ± 8

[a] L = light activity (<30 METS hr/wk)
M = moderate activity (30-60 METS hr/wk)
S = strenuous activity (>60 METS hr/wk)
[b] Underlined values are not significant (p > 0.05)

function as reflected by adaptation to the stress of exercise decreases with increased age, whereas little change is evident when comparing resting indices; (3) cardiac function is enhanced by increased leisure time physical activity. Differences between more and less active groups were more apparent in the older age categories; and (4) correcting for HR significantly affects the interpretation of STIs as to their ability to discern changes in myocardial function.

Acknowledgment

The authors would like to thank Rick Kukulka and Robert Mullen for their assistance with data tabulation and analysis.

References

1. Ahmed, S.S., Levinson, G.E., Schwartz, C.J. and Ettinger, P.O.: Systolic time intervals as measures of the contractile state of the left ventricular myocardium in man. Circulation 46:559, 1972.
2. American Heart Association: Exercise testing and training of apparently healthy individuals: A handbook for physicians. New York:American Heart Association, 1972.
3. Fardy, P.S.: Left ventricle time component changes in middle-aged men following a twelve week physical training intervention program. J. Sports Med. Phy. Fitness 13:219, 1974.
4. Fardy, P.S.: Effects of soccer training and detraining upon selected cardiac metabolic measures. Res. Q. 40:502, 1969.
5. Fardy, P.S., Maresh, C.M., Abbott, R. and Kristiansen, T.: An assessment of the influence of habitual physical activity, prior sport participation, smoking habits, and aging upon indices of cardiovascular fitness: Preliminary report of a cross-sectional and retrospective study. J. Sports Med. Phys. Fitness. (In press.)
6. Fardy, P.S., Maresh, C.M., Abbott, R. and Kristiansen, T.: Aging curves of left ventricular cardiac-cycle time components in former athletes: A cross sectional study. Paper presented A.A.H.P.E.R. Meeting, Anaheim, Calif., April 1974.
7. Frank, M.N, and Kinlaw, W.B.: Indirect measurement of isovolumetric contraction time and tension period in normal subjects. Am. J. Cardiol. 10:800, 1962.
8. Franks, B.D. and Cureton, T.K.: Effects of training on time components of the left ventricle. J. Sports Med. Phys. Fitness 9:80, 1969.
9. Franks, B.D. and Cureton, T.K.: Orthogonal factors of cardiac intervals and their response to stress. Res. Q. 39:3, 1968.
10. Franks, B.D., Wiley, J.F. and Cureton, T.K.: Orthogonal factors and norms for time components of the left ventricle. Med. Sci. Sports 1:171, 1969.
11. Harrison, T.R., Dixon, K., Russell, R.O. Jr. et al: The relation of age to the duration of contraction, ejection, and relaxation of the normal heart. Am. Heart J. 67:189, 1964.

12. Luonmanmaki, K. and Heikkilä, J.: Duration of the phases of left tricular mechanical systole in healthy men aged 45 to 64 years. Ann. Clin. Res. 1:156, 1969.
13. Martin, C.E., Shaver, J.A., Thompson, M.E. et al: Direct correlation of external systolic time intervals with internal indices of left ventricular function in man. Circulation 44:419, 1972.
14. Physical Fitness Research Digest. President's Council on Physical Fitness and Sports. Washington, D. C., Series 4, No. 2, April 1974.
15. Pouget, J.M., Harris, W.S., Mayron, B.R. and Naughton, J.P.: Abnormal responses of systolic time intervals to exercise in patients with angina pectoris. Circulation 43:289, 1971.
16. Rose, G.: Physical activity and coronary heart disease. In Symposium on the Meaning of Physical Fitness. Proc. Royal Soc. Med. 62:1183, 1969.
17. Weissler, A.M., Harris, W.S. and Schoenfeld, C.D.: Systolic time intervals in heart failure in man. Circulation 37:149, 1968.
18. Wilhelmsen, L. and Tibblin, G.: Physical inactivity and risk of myocardial infarction. The men born in 1913 study. In Larsen, O.A. and Malmborg, R.O. (eds.): Coronary Heart Disease and Physical Fitness. Proceedings of a Symposium, Munksgaard, Denmark, 1971.

Comparison of Maximal Bicycle and Treadmill Exercise ECG Tests in Middle-Aged Males

Gordon R. Cumming, John Fisher and Candace Stasynec

Introduction

Exercise tests are being used with increasing frequency in clinical cardiology with proponents for both bicycle [1, 16] and treadmill exercise [4, 5, 8, 11]. Comparisons of these forms of exercise are available for athletes and younger subjects [3, 10] but not for a large group of middle-aged subjects in whom clinical exercise tests are most frequently carried out. In a population under study, a maximal treadmill test [5] and a maximal bicycle test have been performed on 305 asymptomatic subjects aged 42 to 70 years.

Methods

Subjects performed the "Bruce" treadmill test [5] in 1974. They were encouraged to continue until markedly fatigued or short of breath. The same subjects had performed a bicycle ergometer test in 1973. At this time they had worked at 300 to 600 kpm/min for six minutes, immediately followed by 600 to 900 kpm/min for six minutes and then 300 kpm/min was added each minute until the subject could not maintain the cycling rate of 60 rpm. Considerable verbal encouragement was given to the subjects urging them to continue until severe leg fatigue required them to stop. An electric Elema ergometer was used and it was calibrated as previously described [6]. The maximal oxygen uptakes ($\dot{V}O_2$ max) from the treadmill test were predicted from published regression equations based on the endurance time [5]. The $\dot{V}O_2$ max for the bicycle test was predicted from the six-minute heart rates of both workloads according to Åstrand [2], and the mean of these was corrected using

Gordon R. Cumming, John Fisher and Candace Stasynec, Health Sciences Children's Centre of Winnipeg and Department of Pediatrics, University of Manitoba, Winnipeg, Manitoba, Canada.

actual maximal heart rates. The Åstrand nomogram was based on ergometer loads 9% higher than stated values because of the friction of the chain drive of the mechanical ergometer [6] and this discrepancy was taken into account in the calculations.

The aerobic requirement for the maximal workload reached on the treadmill was obtained from published values [5]. The oxygen requirement for steady state bicycle work is about 2.05 ml/kpm/min of work [2] (Cumming, unpublished data). Using this factor, the aerobic requirement for the final ergometer load that the subject was able to complete was determined to compare with the above value for treadmill exercise.

The ergometer workload required to produce a heart rate of 150 was determined by extrapolation from the two submaximal workloads and converted to $\dot{V}O_2$/kg (adding 3.5 ml/kg for resting $\dot{V}O_2$). Bruce et al [5] found a narrow range for $\dot{V}O_2$ during the treadmill test (17.4, 24.8, 34.3 and 43.8 ml/kg/min during the 3rd, 6th, 9th and 12th minutes of the test). Using these values and the heart rate recorded at the end of each stage, the estimated treadmill $\dot{V}O_2$ at a heart rate of 150 was determined by extrapolation.

The tests were carried out in an air-conditioned hospital laboratory maintained at 19 C by physical educators. A physician was available by intercom but was required for only one subject. During maximal treadmill exercise, a 45-year-old developed atrial fibrillation with a rapid ventricular rate that persisted for ten hours. Resuscitation equipment was available but was not required.

Bipolar chest lead CM5 of the ECG was recorded for heart rate and ST evidence of "ischemia." An abnormal ST change was arbitrarily defined as (a) 0.10 mv or greater ST depression with a horizontal or downsloping segment, (b) a slowly ascending ST segment with 0.2 mv J depression or greater and an ST slope of less than 1.0 mv/sec, with the ST segment failing to reach the isoelectric point before the onset of the T wave and (c) an additional 0.1 mv horizontal or downsloping ST depression in subjects with mild resting ST segment and/or T wave changes.

Eighteen subjects had their test terminated before severe fatigue had occurred because of three or more consecutive venticular ectopic beats, ST depressions of over 0.3 mv or neuromuscular complaints and lack of motivation. Subjects that did not complete both tests maximally were not included in the comparison for maximal work, but were included in the ECG comparison. Blood pressure was measured by sphygmomanometer and auscultation during exercise. The highest systolic pressure recorded was multiplied by maximal heart rate to provide a rough estimate of cardiac systolic work and myocardial oxygen requirement, and this value was termed the double product.

Actual exercise $\dot{V}O_2$ was measured on 18 of the subjects doing treadmill exercise using a Tissot spirometer, a Beckman F3 paramagnetic oxygen meter and a Beckman LB1 CO_2 analyzer. The analyzers were checked with three calibrating gases after each run. Measurements were made during the final minute of stage 3 of the Bruce test and during the last minute of maximal treadmill work. Direct measurement of $\dot{V}O_2$ max was made in all of the subjects from this population on the bicycle ergometer for each submaximal load and during the last minutes of maximal exercise during the first year of the study [7].

The subjects were initially recruited from municipal employees of varied occupations in 1969 [7]. Those with known heart disease, based on history, clinical examination, ECG changes other than minor resting ST and T wave changes, were excluded.

Results

The results of the two exercise tests are shown in Table I with the subjects separated into three age groups. Weights were the same for the two tests. There was no difference in mean maximal heart rates for the two tests. Maximal heart rates were in the acceptable normal range for age [2].

The resting heart rates two and five minutes after exercise were about 6 beats/minute higher following bicycle exercise in 40- and 59-year-olds. Subjects rested in the same chair with the feet elevated following each exercise so that postural differences were not responsible for this difference. In Table I the recovery rates are expressed as a percentage of the maximal heart rates.

The predicted maximal oxygen uptake values ($\dot{V}O_2$ max) for the treadmill exercise were 40% to 50% greater than for bicycle ergometer exercise. This difference was observed for each age group. The product of peak exercise systolic blood pressure times maximal heart rate was about 5% higher for bicycle work. At a heart rate of 150 beats/min, the estimated $\dot{V}O_2$ was about 9 ml/kg lower for bicycle compared to treadmill exercise.

The actual $\dot{V}O_2$ for stage 3 (third minute) of the Bruce test measured on 18 subjects was 33.7 ± 2.6 ml/kg/min, about the same as found by Bruce [5]. The actual $\dot{V}O_2$ for 900 kpm/min (fifth and sixth minutes) on the ergometer was 2.02 ± 0.14 L/min, confirming the calibration of the ergometer and validating the use of the

Table I. Comparison of Bicycle Ergometer and Treadmill Exercise Tests
Normal Males Aged 44 to 70 Years

Age group		40-49	50-59	60-69
Number of subjects		101	152	52
Mean age 1974		46.7 ± 2.5	53.6 ± 2.7	63.5 ± 3.0
Weight kg 1974		81.6 ± 11.1	85.0 ± 12.0	79.6 ± 9.0
Weight kg 1973		82.1 ± 11.8	84.5 ± 11.9	80.5 ± 9.2
Max HR	T	179 ± 11	169 ± 15	157 ± 15
	B	178 ± 14	168 ± 16	157 ± 16
2' recovery HR*	T	67 ± 6	65 ± 7	66 ± 7
	B	70 ± 7†	69 ± 8†	66 ± 8
5' recovery HR*	T	59 ± 5	58 ± 6	59 ± 5
	B	61 ± 7	62 ± 6	62 ± 5
Predicted $\dot{V}O_2$ max	T	36.7 ± 3.8	33.8 ± 4.6	30.9 ± 4.7
ml/kg/min	B	25.9 ± 4.5†	24.0 ± 5.1†	21.2 ± 4.4†
Systolic product	T	324 ± 4	318 ± 5	295 ± 5
mm Hg × beats/min	B	359 ± 4†	337 ± 5†	318 ± 5†
Aerobic requirement of	T	38.1 ± 4.2	35.3 ± 4.4	32.6 ± 4.4
max load ml/kg/min	B	37.0 ± 6.6	32.8 ± 6.8†	28.4 ± 6.8†
Aerobic requirement at	T	29.9 ± 4.2	30.5 ± 5.3	31.9 ± 6.4
HR 150 ml/kg/min	B	22.6 ± 3.8†	23.1 ± 4.6†	23.4 ± 4.7†

*Recovery heart rates are expressed as a percent of the maximal heart rates
†P < .05 treadmill vs bicycle, paired t test
T — treadmill
B — bicycle ergometer

predictive formula for estimating submaximal $\dot{V}O_2$ for bicycle exercise.

For treadmill exercise mean $\dot{V}O_2$ max directly measured was within 1.0 ml/kg of the predicted in the 18 subjects tested (r = 0.81).

A comparison of direct measurement of $\dot{V}O_2$ max and the Åstrand prediction of $\dot{V}O_2$ max with ergometer exercise is given in Table II. The prediction method underestimated $\dot{V}O_2$ max by as much as 0.42 L/min or 22% in this population.

The ECG results are given in Table III. A total of 27% of the subjects showed an abnormal exercise ECG as defined above in one or both tests. The ECG was abnormal for both treadmill and bicycle testing in 11% of the subjects. In 16% of the subjects the test was inconsistent; in 60% of these subjects only the treadmill exercise ECG was positive, and in 40% only the bicycle exercise ECG was positive.

Table II. Comparison Åstrand Prediction of $\dot{V}O_2$ Max
With Direct Measurements

Age group	40-45	46-50	51-55	56-60	61-65
Number of subjects	165	149	101	65	30
Mean actual $\dot{V}O_2$ max L/min	2.63	2.51	2.20	1.89	1.97
Mean Åstrand prediction L/min	2.16	2.09	1.94	1.83	1.74
Mean underprediction L/min	0.47	0.42	0.26	0.06	0.23
Percent underprediction	22	20	13	3	13

Table III. Frequency of Abnormal Exercise or Recovery ECG
Treadmill vs. Bicycle

Age	40-49	50-59	60-69	All	%
Number	107	157	59	323	100.0
Abnormal T and B	3	23	9	35	10.8
Abnormal T only	11	17	4	32	9.9
Abnormal B only	3	8	10	21	6.5
Abnormal total	17	48	23	88	27.3
Percent total abnormal	15.9	30.6	39.0	27.3	

T = treadmill
B = bicycle

Subjects answered the questions posed in Table IV ten minutes after completing the treadmill test. About three out of four subjects preferred the treadmill test over the bicycle. The bicycle tired their legs the most, the treadmill was the easiest to complete. There was little difference in the frequency of those responding to which test caused the most dyspnea. Fifty-eight percent of subjects indicated that the bicycle caused more marked general fatigue.

Table IV. Subjective Comparison Maximal Treadmill and
Bicycle Tests
300 Male Subjects Aged 44 to 70 Years

	Bicycle	Treadmill
What test did you like best?	27%	73%
What test stressed you the most?	58	42
What test made you the most out of breath?	49	51
What test made you most fatigued generally?	58	42
What test tired your legs out the most?	62	38
What test was easiest to complete?	34	66

Because this comparison of the two forms of exercise would have
been more suitably done in a random manner with tests a few weeks
apart, supporting data on the consistency of the bicycle test are given
in Table V. For two tests performed one to two years apart, the
mean results for maximal heart rate, recovery heart rate, workload at
a heart rate of 150 beats/min and maximal workload completed were
very similar.

A similar comparison for the Bruce treadmill test is given in
Table VI. The mean endurance times for the two tests one year apart
were not significantly different when subjected to the paired t test.
Despite slightly more work being done in 1975, the mean heart rates
at the end of exercise and two minutes into recovery were lower in
1975.

Discussion

Both treadmill and bicycle exercise produced nearly the same
degree of cardiovascular stress. The mean maximal heart rate was
almost identical for both tests. The double product of heart rate
times systolic blood pressure provides a rough estimate of myocardial
oxygen requirements and was slightly higher for bicycle exercise.

Table V. Comparison of Two Bicycle Tests
Obtained at Intervals of 1 to 2 Years

	Test 1	Test 2
Maximal heart rate	172 ± 14	171 ± 14
PWC 150 kpm/min	775 ± 242	757 ± 239
2' recovery heart rate	119 ± 17	117 ± 17
Max workload kpm/min	1315 ± 229	1312 ± 246

n = 415, age 42-67 years, mean age 53

Table VI. Bruce Treadmill Test Comparison 1974 to 1975
100 Men

Age group	40-49		50-59		60-71	
Number	29		45		26	
Year of test	1974	1975	1974	1975	1974	1975
Max HR	180 ± 7	178 ± 9	171 ± 13	169 ± 14*	159 ± 17	154 ± 17†
Endurance time minutes	10.7 ± 1.2	10.9 ± 1.0	9.5 ± 1.2	9.7 ± 1.2	8.8 ± 1.3	8.8 ± 1.5
2' recovery HR	120 ± 17	112 ± 17*	109 ± 14	104 ± 14†	103 ± 18	96 ± 16†

*p < .01
†p < .05

Subjective feelings of dyspnea and fatigue were said to be more severe for bicycle exercise in 55% of subjects and for treadmill exercise in 45%. The bicycle test was said to cause greater leg fatigue, and recovery heart rate was slightly higher following bicycle exercise. The projected aerobic requirement of the maximum workload was only about 7% less for the bicycle compared to treadmill exercise.

Bicycle exercise has some advantages over treadmill exercise and vice versa. Some of the points of comparison are listed in Table VII. If enough space is available, if mobility is not required, if sufficient staff to monitor and assist the patient are on hand, treadmill exercise is preferable because it is easier for the subject to reach near maximal workloads that fully stress the circulatory system. There is less localized muscular fatigue and it is not necessary to encourage the subject to continue as much as is necessary with bicycle work. The staff administering the tests preferred the treadmill. If space is

Table VII. Comparison of Bicycle and Treadmill Exercise

Bicycle	Treadmill
Minimal space requirement	3X space requirement
Low cost for mechanical	
Cost for electronic $2,000 to $3,000	Cost $2,500 to $6,000
No power, or ordinary requirements	Many require special power source
Electrical free of noise	Moderate to severe noise depending upon speed
Mild noise with mechanical	and subject
Leg fatigue predominant	Leg fatigue occurs, but dyspnea may be limiting
Subject needs continuous encouragement	symptom — less verbal encouragement required
Little muscle artifact during exercise	Can be considerable artifact during intense exercise
Better ECG monitoring	although electronic filtering possible
Less chance for lead wires to come off	Lead wires occasionally a problem
Blood pressure easier to record	BP recording can be difficult at higher loads
Lower $\dot{V}O_2$ max recorded	5% to 15% higher max $\dot{V}O_2$ usually recorded
Efficiency fairly constant	Efficiency can improve with practice
Negligible danger of falling	Must always be alert for falls
Most subjects not accustomed to bicycle work	Subjects not accustomed to treadmill walking either, nor hill walking or running
Low maintenance	More maintenance required
Little apprehension	Older persons may be extremely apprehensive at first
Lactate 2.5 × resting at 50% $\dot{V}O_2$ max	Lactate 2.5 × resting at 75% of $\dot{V}O_2$ max
Calibration problems	Need to check speed and incline

limited, if some mobility is required, if one technician only is available for testing, if special functions are to be measured with catheters, then the bicycle has definite advantages. Apprehensive patients (especially females) find the bicycle easier. The main consideration, as for any test procedure, is familiarity with the apparatus, proper maintenance and calibration. Artifact-free electrocardiograms were easier to obtain with bicycle exercise facilitating rhythm and ST segment monitoring during the exercise, but with attention to details satisfactory records are usually obtainable with treadmill exercise without resort to signal averaging.

The mean $\dot{V}O_2$ max of our subjects predicted from the treadmill test was remarkably similar to the values found by Bruce et al [5] in sedentary Seattle males using the same test.

A major difference existed between the predicted $\dot{V}O_2$ max for the treadmill and bicycle exercise, with the Bruce treadmill test providing values 41% to 46% higher than the Åstrand nomogram and the bicycle test.

The prediction of $\dot{V}O_2$ max from the work time of maximal tests has the advantage of simplicity. Direct measurement of oxygen uptake is tedious, expensive and requires considerable care to maintain accuracy. The standard error of predicting $\dot{V}O_2$ max from treadmill tests in sedentary men was ± 3.5 ml/kg/min in the studies of Bruce et al [5]. Using the same protocol, Froelicher et al [9] reported a standard error of ± 3.4 ml/kg/min. If the mean $\dot{V}O_2$ max was 30 ml/kg/min then the 95% confidence limits for a single prediction would be from 23.2 to 36.8 ml/kg/min. While there is a high correlation between $\dot{V}O_2$ max and work time in a population, the prediction in a given individual is not at all precise.

The Åstrand nomogram was set up on empiric grounds and was based on heart rate responses to set workloads in relatively fit subjects. One objective of the nomogram was to allow a prediction of $\dot{V}O_2$ max from submaximal work to avoid the discomfort and possible dangers of maximal exercise. The 95% confidence limits using the results on which the nomogram was based were 17% [2], about the same as cited for the treadmill above. Unfortunately, predictive tests that apply to one population may not apply to another, and there is no substitute for the direct measurement of $\dot{V}O_2$ max if this measurement is required for investigative purposes. The Bruce prediction method was based on subjects drawn from a population similar to ours, the Åstrand prediction method was based on a very different population.

Part of the 40% discrepancy between the Åstrand and treadmill predictions may be explained by the 5% to 15% higher values for

treadmill exercise found in young subjects for directly determined
$\dot{V}O_2$ max due to the larger muscle mass involved in the exercise and
the lesser degree of localized muscle fatigue [10]. This discrepancy
may be even greater in unfit middle-aged subjects. Some of the
discrepancy was seen to be due to a 20% underprediction of the
actual ergometer $\dot{V}O_2$ max with the Åstrand method in comparison
to direct measurements. The difference may be due to localized
muscle fatigue producing tachycardia greater than expected for a
given submaximal metabolic load in our subjects who were unaccus-
tomed to bicycle exercise. Von Döbeln et al [17] found that the
nomogram and correction factors for max heart rate underpredicted
$\dot{V}O_2$ max by 0.15 L/min in Swedish construction workers, while in
our population this underprediction was as high as 0.47 L/min.

The higher recovery heart rates for bicycle exercise may be
related to the higher lactate values observed after this type of
exercise [15], possibly due to more localized muscular stress.

The higher double product during bicycle exercise may be due to
the difficulty of obtaining a satisfactory blood pressure during the
higher loads of treadmill exercise, although the difference may be
real. Because of the large differences between brachial artery and
central aortic pressure during exercise [14], the observed small
differences in systolic product may not be important in terms of
myocardial oxygen requirements.

A basic difference between treadmill and bicycle exercise is that
within limits $\dot{V}O_2$ is independent of body weight for bicycle work
but is directly related to weight for treadmill work. There is a
tendency to use ergometer loads that are too low in heavy persons.
Table VIII compares the bicycle loads required to give the same $\dot{V}O_2$
per kilogram body weight as for the Bruce test in subjects of three
different weights. Note that a 90-kg man should be working at 1800
kpm/min to have the same metabolic stress produced by stage 4 of
the Bruce test.

Table VIII.

Bruce Treadmill Test		Bicycle Ergometer – Load for Equivalent $\dot{V}O_2$		
Speed mph	% Grade	50 kg kpm/min	70 kg kpm/min	90 kg kpm/min
1.7	10	400	560	720
2.5	12	510	710	920
3.4	14	770	1080	1390
4.2	16	1000	1410	1815

In 16% of the subjects the interpretation of the exercise ECG was inconsistent. Since the tests were not performed in random order, and a year separated the two tests, interpretation of this difference is difficult. More subjects had a positive treadmill test, but the difference was not statistically significant. The frequency of positive tests was slightly greater than that reported for some other series of "normal" males [12, 13], but little significance can be attached to this because of differences in ECG lead systems, criteria for abnormality and population selection.

Heart rate is said to be a reasonable guide for the metabolic stress for different exercise loads and is said to be the same for submaximal treadmill and bicycle exercise in fit young men [10]. Using predicted $\dot{V}O_2$ values, the metabolic demand at a heart rate of 150 beats/min appeared to be 23% higher for the treadmill than for the bicycle exercise in our subjects. However, the bicycle exercise loads were each of six-minute duration, the treadmill loads, three minutes. The mean increase in heart rate between three and six minutes of bicycle exercise was 5 beats/min. Using the three-minute instead of the six-minute heart rate values increased the bicycle work at a heart rate of 150 by 11%. Taking this difference into account, treadmill exercise allowed about 10% more metabolic work than bicycle exercise at a heart rate of 150 beats/min.

This comparison of bicycle and treadmill exercise is for well persons without cardiac symptoms. The patient with angina may behave in a completely different manner, being capable of doing much more work with one test than another. Thus, while these results indicate that maximal tests with the bicycle and treadmill are quite similar in terms of maximal heart rate and maximal metabolic load in asymptomatic subjects, the results obtained on patients may not be interchangeable from one test to another.

Since exercise-induced ST changes seem to be dependent upon heart rate, it may not be too important as to what type of repetitive exercise is used to induce the tachycardia. This study has shown clearly that indices of functional capacity (i.e., predicted $\dot{V}O_2$ max) cannot be compared for treadmill and bicycle exercise.

References

1. Astrand, I.: Exercise electrocardiograms recorded twice in an 8 year interval in a group of 204 women and men 48-63 years old. Acta Med. Scand. 178:27, 1965.
2. Astrand, I.: Aerobic work capacity in men and women with special reference to age. Acta Physiol. Scand. 49, Suppl. 169, 1960.

3. Åstrand, P.O. and Saltin, B.: Maximal oxygen uptake and heart rate in various types of muscular activity. J. Appl. Physiol. 16:977, 1961.

4. Balke, B. and Ware, R.W.: An experimental study of physical fitness of Airforce personnel. U.S. Armed Forces Med. J. 10:675, 1959.

5. Bruce, R.A., Kusumi, F. and Hosmer, D.: Maximal oxygen intake and nomographic assessment of functional aerobic impairment in cardiovascular disease. Am. Heart J. 85:546-562, 1973.

6. Cumming, G.R. and Alexander, W.D.: Calibration of bicycle ergometers. Can. J. Physiol. Pharmacol. 46:917-919, 1968.

7. Cumming, G.R., Borysyk, L. and Dufresne, C.: The maximal exercise ECG in asymptomatic men. Can. Med. Assoc. J. 106:649-653, 1972.

8. Ellestad, M.H., Allen, W., Wan, M. and Kemp, G.: Maximal treadmill fitness testing for cardiovascular evaluation. Circulation 39:517-522, 1969.

9. Froelicher, V.F., Brammell, H., Davis, G. et al: A comparison of the reproducibility and physiologic response to three maximal exercise protocols. Chest 65:512-517, 1974.

10. Hermansen, L. and Saltin, B.: Oxygen uptake during maximal treadmill and bicycle exercise. J. Appl. Physiol. 26:31, 1969.

11. Kattus, A.A., Jorgensen, C., Worden, R. and Alvaro, A.: ST segment depression with near maximal exercise in detection of preclinical coronary heart disease. Circulation 44:585-595, 1971.

12. Lester, F.M., Sheffield, L.J. and Reeves, T.J.: Electrocardiographic changes in clinically normal older men following near maximal and maximal exercise. Circulation 36:5-14, 1967.

13. Punsar, S., Pyorala, K. and Siltanen, P.: Classification of electrocardiographic S-T segment changes in epidemiological studies of coronary heart disease. Ann. Med. Inter. Fenn. 57:53, 1968.

14. Rowell, L.B., Brengelmann, G.L., Blackmon, J.R. et al: Disparities between aortic and peripheral pulse pressures induced by upright exercise and vasomotor changes in man. Circulation 37:954, 1968.

15. Shephard, R.J., Allen, C., Benede, A.J.S. et al: Standardization of submaximal exercise tests. Bull. WHO 38:765-775, 1968. Standardization of maximal exercise tests. Bull. WHO 38:757-764, 1968.

16. Strandell, T.: Electrocardiographic findings at rest, during and after exercise in health old men compared with young men. Acta Med. Scand. 174:479-499, 1963.

17. Von Döbeln, W.V., Åstrand, I. and Bergstrom, A.: An analysis of age and other factors related to maximal oxygen uptake. J. Appl. Physiol. 22:934, 1967.

L'électrocardiogramme à l'effort programmé sur tapis roulant comme critère indispensable à l'évaluation cardiocirculatoire des dyslipidémiques

R. Carrier et R. Potvin

Introduction

Le regroupement étiologique des atteintes cardiocirculatoires au sein d'une clinique des maladies lipidiques a permis à notre milieu hospitalier de préciser ses éventails diagnostique et thérapeutique et de les adapter aux plus récents concepts de la morbidité de l'artériosclérose [1, 4].

La clinique des maladies lipidiques de l'hôpital Saint-François-d'Assise qui fonctionne depuis plus de deux ans, ne reçoit que des malades dirigés par les médecins de la région. Les principales raisons de la consultation sont, bien sûr, l'hypercholestérolémie ou l'hypertriglycéridémie ou les deux à la fois, soit l'artériosclérose et ses manifestations les plus courantes: claudication intermittente, accident cérébrovasculaire, accident coronarien, soit l'obésité et le diabète, ou encore toute autre pathologie de type métabolique généralement référée à un spécialiste et surtout susceptible de progresser vers une dyslipidémie à son tour à l'origine d'atteinte vasculaire.

La diversité ou plutôt les variations considérables de l'échantillonnage n'ont en commun que les probabilités statistiques reliées à la léthalité et davantage à la morbidité rattachée aux dyslipidémies classés par Fredrickson [3, 6] cette classification étant encore de nos jours un guide thérapeutique de choix.

Si le microtraumatisme peut faire partie des facteurs étiologiques de l'artériosclérose [5], il appert que les artères touchées par le phénomène sont par ordre d'importance: les coronaires, les iliaques ou sacro-iliaques ou fémoro-iliaques et les carotides; les "by-pass"

R. Carrier et R. Potvin, Services de biochimie et de cardiologie, Hôpital Saint-François-d'Assise, Québec, Canada.

vasculaires prennent une part toujours plus considérable des activités chirurgicales des milieux hospitaliers généraux.

Après avoir décrit le groupe de malades référés par leurs caractéristiques usuelles: âge, sexe, etc., nous décrirons sommairement des résultats obtenus de l'électrocardiographie au repos et à l'effort en nous réservant dans une étape subséquente les études de corrélation entre les paramètres radiologiques, biochimiques, et même les éléments électrocardiographiques entre eux sur un nombre de cas plus considérable.

Matériel et méthodes

Au cours des 15 premiers mois d'opération, la clinique a acceuilli 335 sujets référés pour diverses pathologies dont la majorité était dyslipidémique. Aucun critère de sélection ne fut utilisé à part la raison de consultation.

Chaque patient référé fut examiné cliniquement et soumis à une exploration biologique et radiologique pertinente avant d'être évalué, si c'était nécessaire, par l'électrocardiographie au repos et subséquemment à l'effort; cette dernière épreuve a été faite sur tapis roulant selon la programmation inscrite au tableau I.

L'évaluation clinique comprend l'examen physique complet, l'accent étant mis particulièrement sur les manifestations cutanées des phénomènes artériosclérotiques: xanthomes, xanthélasmas, tubérosités, etc., sur les pulsations artérielles carotidiennes, fémorales et la présence de souffle trahissant des rétrécissements.

L'évaluation biologique comprend les paramètres usuels statiques d'abord et dynamiques si ce complément s'avère judicieux. Les principaux éléments sont le bilan lipidique, la formule sanguine complète, la protéinémie, l'électrophorèse et l'immunoélectrophorèse si nécessaire, le bilan thyroïdien: T_3 et T_4; la glycémie, l'azotémie et l'uricémie; la sédimentation globulaire; une mosaïque enzymatique

Tableau I. Epreuve électrocardiographique à l'effort programmé sur tapis roulant*

Stade	Vitesse (m.p.h.)	Pente du tapis (%)	Temps (minutes)
I	1.7	10	3
II	2.5	12	3
III	3.4	14	3
IV	4.2	16	3
V	5.0	18	3

*Bruce et Kasser: Circulation 39:750-774, 1969.

comprenant l'ATGO, l'ATGP, les LDH totales, la phosphatasémie alcaline et la gammaglutamyltranspeptidase, la radiographie pulmonaire et cardiaque, la mesure radiologique des tendons d'Achille [2] font également partie de cette évaluation. Si des paramètres dynamiques doivent s'ajouter, l'hyperglycémie provoquée, la fluoroscopie cardiaque et l'échocardiographie en plus de l'électrocardiographie à l'effort sur tapis roulant sont susceptibles de compléter les premières observations.

Résultats et discussion

L'âge des patients du groupe varie de 11 ans à 74 ans, la moyenne étant de 45,97 ans (s = 12,45). Le groupe comprend 198 hommes (59.1%) et 137 femmes (40.9%). Selon les groupes d'âge, les dyslipidémiques se sont distribués d'une façon relativement constante entre 30 ans et 60 ans comme le démontre le tableau II. Cette distribution n'est cependant pas constante pour les diverses catégories de dyslipidémie; en effet, le tableau III révèle que plus de 50% appartenaient au groupe IV de Fredrickson [3] pendant qu'un pourcentage important (15.8%) appartenait à la classe IIB.

La morbidité reliée à ce groupe de malade demeure importante. En effet, le tableau IV montre que plus du tiers souffrait d'hypertension artérielle sur la base d'une tension systolique de 140 mm de Hg et plus et/ou d'une diastolique de 100 mm de Hg et plus; ces mesures ayant été faites en position assise et au repos après dix minutes ou plus. Le surpoids demeure également appréciable car le quart des patients ont un excédent de 21% et plus selon l'indice de Broca [7].

Tableau II. Distribution des dyslipidémiques en fonction de l'âge

Age (années)	Nombre	Pourcentage
Moins de 30	36	10.8
De 31 à 35	36	10.8
De 36 à 40	43	12.8
De 41 à 45	42	12.5
De 46 à 50	50	14.9
De 51 à 55	48	14.3
De 56 à 60	34	10.2
61 et plus	46	13.7
Total	335	100.0

Age moyen : 45.97 (s = 12.45)

Tableau III. Caractéristiques du groupe étudié
sur le plan dyslipidémique

Classification	Nombre	Pourcentage
II A	30	9.0
II B	53	15.8
III	6	1.8
IV	176	52.5
Normaux	30	9.0
Autres	40	11.9
Total	335	100.0

Tableau IV. Quelques traits pathologiques relevés
au sein du groupe des patients référés à la
consultation des maladies lipidiques

Caractéristiques	Nombre	Pourcentage
Hypertension artérielle	118	35.2
Surpoids:		
Moins de 20%	260	77.6
de 21% à 30%	35	10.4
de 31% à 40%	8	2.4
41% et plus	32	9.6
Total	335	100.0

Le tableau V présente le pourcentage des cas qui ont subi l'électrocardiographie statique et dynamique. En effet, nous notons que 178 patients soit 53.1% du groupe ont subi l'E.C.G. au repos et que 143 soit 42.7% ont été acheminés vers l'épreuve d'effort sur tapis roulant. Il va de soi que le cardiologue veille au respect des contre-indications au test d'effort en réexaminant lui-même le malade à cette fin.

Au cours de L'E.C.G. en position couché et au repos, nous avons pu relever 15.7% de cas pathologiques (tableau VI) pendant que

Tableau V. Distribution de l'électrocardiographie
au repos et à l'effort en fonction du nombre total

E.C.G.	Nombre	Pourcentage
Repos	178	53.1
Effort	143	42.7

Nombre total : 335

**Tableau VI. Résultats de l'évaluation
électrocardiographique au repos**

Classe	Nombre	Pourcentage
Normaux	150	84.3
Pathologiques	28	15.7
Total	178	100.0

l'E.C.G. à l'effort sur tapis roulant permettait d'en observer 32 soit
22.4% (tableau VII). Le tableau VIII cependant permet de constater
que 33 cas, soit 9.9% de l'ensemble ou 23.1% de ceux qui ont subi
l'E.C.G. à l'effort, ont vu leur statut cardiocirculatoire mieux
reconnu en couplant l'épreuve dynamique à l'épreuve statique: les
trois quarts dans le sens d'une détérioration et le quart dans la
direction contraire; il va de soi que la thérapeutique fut plus
adéquate ainsi.

Nous devons ajouter que chez plus du tiers des patients ayant
subi une épreuve d'effort monitorisée à l'E.C.G., le cardiologue a
signalé une faible tolérance à l'effort. Nous devons ajouter ici que
toute anomalie cardiocirculatoire décelée tant par l'E.C.G. au repos

**Tableau VII. Résultats de l'évaluation électro-
cardiographique sur tapis roulant**

Classe	Nombre	Pourcentage
Normaux	111	77.6
Pathologiques	32	22.4
Total	143	100.0

**Tableau VIII. Résultats obtenus chez quelques
patients ayant subi une évaluation électrocardiographique dynamique complémentaire**

Electrocardiographie	Nombre	Pourcentage
Normal au repos et anormal à l'effort	26	78.8
Anormal au repos et normal à l'effort	7	21.2
Total	33	100.0

qu'à l'effort recevait l'appui des paramètres radiologiques avec lesquelles la corrélation était parfaite.

D'autres études de corrélation dont celles portant sur différents paramètres composants de l'électrocardiographie: fréquence cardiaque cible et atteinte, travail accompli, tension artérielle systolique et diastolique mesurées, etc., sont présentement en cours sur une population plus considérable, ce qui nous permettrait de soutenir davantage la prescription de l'E.C.G. à l'effort programmé sur le tapis roulant, avec plus de conviction et surtout d'évidence statistique.

Résumé et conclusion

Nous avons sommairement décrit un groupe de dyslipidémiques référés à une clinique spécialisée. Par les techniques électrocardiographiques au repos et à l'effort, nous avons pu relever un pourcentage appréciable de cas, soit plus de 20% (23.1%) qui ont bénéficié d'une évaluation électrocardiographique dynamique puisque leur traitement a été plus approprié, leur statut pathologique ayant été mieux explicité.

Références

1. Beaumont, J.L.: Les facteurs de risque et la pathogénie de l'athérosclérose. Triangle 14 (1):9-16, 1975.
2. Desrochers, M.: Utilité de la mensuration radiologique des tendons d'Achille chez des dyslipidémiques. Communication personnele 1975.
3. Fredrickson, D.S. et Levy, R.I.: Familial Hyperlipoproteinemia. *Dans* The Metabolic Basis of Inherited Disease, ed. 3. 1972, pp. 545-614.
4. Kaunel, W.B. et Gordon, T.: The Framingham study. An epidemiological investigation of cardiovascular disease, Sections 1-27, Washington, U.S.: Government Printing Office, 1971.
5. McCullagh, K.G.: Revised concepts of atherogenesis, a review. Cleve. Clin. Q. 43 (4):247-266, 1976.
6. Motulsky, A.G.: The genetic hyperlipidemias. N. Engl. J. Med. 294 (15):823-827, 1976.
7. Schimert, G.C.: Conséquences cardiovasculaires de l'obésité. Triangle 13 (2):31-40, 1974.

Cardiac Rate Investigation in Sportsmen

D. Vasiliauskas

An investigation was undertaken of heart rate response and ECG in 12 of the U.S.S.R. top-rate rally racers during a 500-km night race. The ECG and rhythmogram analyses were performed and the data obtained were compared with that of a group of 40 professional drivers (20 healthy subjects and 20 with myocardial infarction history) engaged in their daily work — driving urban communication means. The racers were all under 35, with 5- to 10-year racing experience.

The drivers were considered healthy if this was the inference obtained in terms of ischemic heart disease on the basis of a WHO epidemiological investigation. The other subgroup encompassed the drivers who had had a myocardial infarction in 1973 and had resumed their previous work.

ECG V_5-lead recordings of 8- to 12-hour duration were taken on a portable magnetograph, developed on the basis of a "Sputnik-401" cassette recorder and an electrocardiorecorder (Avionics-Satra, USA) prior to and during driving. Special adhesive ring electrodes were used for signal acquisition. The ECG recordings were played back on a display and then recorded on paper. The rhythmograms were fed into an automatic measuring and recording device; the R-R interval value series (500) coming from working day beginning, middle, and end epochs were punched on tape and later computer-processed in statistical terms.

Also, all the subjects were subject to physical exertion on a veloergometer (Monark, Sweden). In parallel, I, III, aVF, V_2, V_4, V_6 leads of ECG were recorded on an Elcar-6. A starting load was 25 w for five minutes and was then increased to 50 w, 75 w, 100 w. The subjects who managed with a load of 100 w or more in five minutes were considered load-resistant. Heart rate was measured from an ECG or rhythmogram. An analysis of sinus rhythm kinetics in terms of rate and character was performed, along with that of ECG

D. Vasiliauskas, Institute for Cardiovascular Research, Kaunas, U.S.S.R.

111

waveform kinetics and rhythm disturbances. Two kinds of an S-T downward displacement, ischemic and "junction"-type, were distinguished.

Racers and healthy drivers did not significantly differ in their load resistance. In the majority of cases it was high in both groups (100% for racers; 85% for healthy drivers). The MI group failed in performance as compared with the two above: only 20% were highly resistant, while 65% displayed medium- and 15%, low-effort resistivity. There was not a complete correspondence of a response to test effort to events that were found to occur on driving a car. Therefore, six drivers with MI history who were highly resistant on load test exhibited S-T displacement exceeding 1.5 mm and inversion of T wave when working. Hence it can be inferred that under real conditions it is psychological responses which exert a key influence upon the cardiovascular system. This phenomenon is quite common in terms of rhythm responses for healthy drivers (ectopic beats, in 45%; sinus tachycardia, in 20% of cases) and racers (42% and 67% with heart rate incidentally reaching 140/min, respectively) who were free of rhythm disturbances on veloergometric test.

Rhythm kinetics was analyzed for the three groups during a work day. At the beginning and during the following two hours (five hours for drivers with MI history) healthy subjects, both drivers and racers, displayed a rhythm acceleration. The healthy subjects reached their acceleration peak (up to 90/min on the average) more rapidly as compared with patients whose heart rate at the peak acceleration reached 95/min by the fifth hour. By that time the healthy subjects would recover to a steady level, 80/min. By the end of a day there was a certain slowing of heart rate, which was more pronounced in healthy subjects. Individual differences were quite ample.

In rhythmogram analysis, the sinus rhythm variance, periodic character and kinetics of the rhythm make-up were taken into consideration, in addition to rate, as assessed visually from rhythmogram recordings and from univariate R-R distributions, correlation functions and spectral density.

The sinus rhythm in patients differed from that in healthy subjects by displaying smaller variance, slower decay of a correlation function and, often, the absence of respiratory arrhythmia. All these findings are indicative of the enfeeblement of parasympathetic influences in sinus rhythm control. The parasympathetic rhythm control was predominant in healthy drivers and sportsmen. Also, the sinus rhythm response to driving, in terms of the above characteristics, was more pronounced in this group. Rhythm rate acceleration was paralleled by appearance of clear-cut slow waves (which is evidently an indication of emotional strain with sportsmen) and became manifest during the race. It was not until the end of competition that the normal heart rate would recover and T-wave would increase, those being the signs of reinstatement of para-sympathetic control. By the end of the race ectopic beats were characteristic of five subjects, with a preceding tachycardia of up to 140 beats per minute in one case.

To summarize, it may be stated that a detailed analysis of sinus rhythm character contributes a considerable amount of information concerning the functional state of the heart and its autonomic control. The responses to occupational loads and to test loads being mutually comparable, concern must be nevertheless given to the important role that is played by a psychological response of drivers (patients or healthy subjects) to driving in producing clear-cut cardiac rate and ECG responses. This factor is of great importance in sportsmen selection for competition, as well as in tackling problems related to enabling drivers with MI to resume their previous work.

Hypertrophie du coeur chez les coureurs de fond et leurs examens vectocardiographiques

Fikret Durusoy et Aydin Karamehmetoglu

Introduction

Les coureurs de fond appartiennent à la catégorie d'athlètes qui ont à suivre un entraînement physique des plus astreignants. C'est pourquoi, l'hypertrophie cardiaque constatée chez ces sportifs est un sujet qui a préoccupé bien des cardiologues. Cette hypertrophie a été observée pour la première fois par Williams et Arnold [10] qui l'ont découverte par percussion et en ont communiqué les résultats. Herxheimer [4] a déterminé radiologiquement l'hypertrophie cardiaque chez les coureurs de fond ayant participé aux Jeux Olympiques d'Amsterdam. Par ailleurs, Reindell s'est penché lui aussi sur la question et a entrepris des recherches très détaillées où il analysait par la méthode radiologique [7] le rapport entre le volume du coeur et le poids du corps chez les sportifs d'endurance. Il a ainsi démontré que l'index du rapport volume cardiaque/poids du corps qui était de 11.3 ml/kg chez des sujets normaux devenait 13.5 ml/kg chez les coureurs de fond. Beckner et Winsor [2], après des recherches électrocardiographiques chez les coureurs de fond, lors desquelles ils ont utilisé comme base l'index Sokolow-Friendlander, ont confirmé à leur tour l'existence de l'hypertrophie. Récemment, on a utilisé le vectocardiogramme dans la détermination de l'hypertrophie cardiaque [1] et on en a conclu que, d'une manière générale, chez les sportifs d'endurance, ces données restaient dans les limites normales tout en manifestant une certaine variation. C'est dans ce sens que nous avons voulu faire une étude comparative entre les données vectocardiographiques d'une part, le volume cardiaque déterminé radiologiquement et les tracés électrocardiographiques d'autre part chez les meilleurs coureurs de fond de notre pays.

Fikret Durusoy et Aydin Karamehmetoglu, Faculté de médecine de l'université Hacettepe, Ankara, Turquie.

115

Matériel et méthodes

Nos recherches ont porté sur six coureurs de fond choisis parmi ceux qui ont accompli les meilleures performances au cours des deux dernières années. Après un examen physique classique, leur capacité vitale a été mesurée avec le Collins Vitalometer, puis les dérivations standard bipolaires et unipolaires des extrémités et les dérivations V_{1-6} précordiales ont été enrégistrées à l'aide de Viso-Cardiette Sanborn. Pour l'évaluation de l'électrocardiogramme, la somme des amplitudes R de V_1 et S de V_5 a été utilisée pour l'hypertrophie ventriculaire gauche comme le préconisait Sokolow. Le volume cardiaque de ces sportifs a été calculé d'après la méthode Rohrer-Kahlstorf modifiée par Musshoff et Reindell [6] en évaluant l'ombre du coeur des téléradiographies prises avant-arrière et latérales, droite-gauche. Les vectocardiogrammes ont été pris au repos sur le plan horizontal et frontal selon le système de Grishman Cube à l'aide d'une caméra polaroïde. Ont été aussi étudiées les valeurs du vecteur total QRS, de l'amplitude QRS, celles du sens du vecteur mi-surface [3] et du vecteur T.

Résultats et discussion

Les valeurs des paramètres de la constitution physique des athlètes choisis au repos: âge, taille, poids, surface du corps, capacité vitale et capacité vitale prévue, calculée d'après la formule de Baldwin et Cournand, de même que la pression artérielle systolique et diastolique sont donnés au Tableau I.

Comme on peut le voir, l'âge moyen de nos athlètes est relativement peu élevé (22.3 ans), ils ont un poids moyen de 57.1 kg, leur taille oscille autour de 1.71 m, la surface du corps est en moyenne de 1.651, ce qui montre des jeunes de constitution moyenne. Leur capacité vitale présente des valeurs moyennes et aussi

Tableau I.

	Age	Poids	Taille	Surf. corps	CV	CVpr.	Press. artér. syst.	diast.	Pouls au repos
1.	21	56	1.67	1.62	4100	4250	110	75	58
2.	26	62	1.76	1.75	5200	4350	115	75	48
3.	22	53	1.73	1.63	4850	4350	110	70	66
4.	25	56	1.70	1.608	4100	4250	130	80	60
5.	20	60	1.75	1.704	4400	4450	120	80	51
6.	20	56	1.65	1.60	4200	4175	130	80	60
	22.3	57.1	1.71	1.651	4475	4304	119	78	56.6

légèrement au-dessus de la moyenne. Il n'y a rien à signaler en ce qui concerne leur pression artérielle. Comme chez tous les sportifs d'endurance, nos sujets présentent aussi au repos une bradicardie caractéristique.

Les tracés électrocardiographiques de nos coureurs ne présentent pas de troubles particuliers, sauf en ce qui concerne la heuteur des amplitudes QRS et T des dérivations précordiales. Toutefois, les sujets 1 et 4 présentent $\dots$ la dérivation V_1 un bloc incomplet droit qu'on rencontre souvent ﬁez des sportifs jeunes [8] et qui correspond à une surcharge du côté droit. L'axe électrique QRS calculé à l'aide des dérivations bipolaires des extrémités [5] et les résultats de $R_{V1} + S_{V5}$ et de $S_{V1} + R_{V5}$ utilisés pour la détermination de l'hypertrophie ventriculaire d'après Sokolow-Friedlander ont été indiqués au Tableau II.

Comme on peut le constater, l'axe électrique cardiaque des coureurs est, en général, semi-vertical. Les amplitudes RS de même qu'une hypertrophie ventriculaire gauche peuvent être observées chez les sujets 4,5 et 6 dont les valeurs sont supérieurs à 35 mm, pris comme limite maximale. Smith et coll. ont observé ce phénomène chez 16 marathoniens sur 21 [9]. Une hypertrophie ventriculaire droite ne se trouve d'une manière approximative que chez le coureur 3. Beckner et coll. ont constaté cette hypertrophie dans un tiers des cas [2], Smith seulement dans un dixième des cas [9].

Les valeurs du volume cardiaque déterminé par la méthode radiologique se trouvent dans le Tableau III, où le volume cardiaque est calculé par kg de poids du corps. On peut voir que le rapport du volume du coeur au poids du corps est de 14.17, ce qui prouve une très forte hypertrophie cardiaque. Chez Reindell [7] cet index est de 11.3 pour des sujets normaux et de 13.5 pour les coureurs de fond. Chez nos athlètes, ces valeurs sont encore plus élevées.

Le Tableau IV donne les résultats des examens vectocardiographiques. On peut voir d'après les valeurs que chez les coureurs le

Tableau II.

	$R_{V1} + S_{V5}$	$S_{V1} + R_{V5}$	Axe QRS
1.	4	26	60°
2.	8	35	95°
3.	10	34	45°
4.	7	41	28°
5.	2	47	62°
6.	7	41	35°
	6.3	37.3	54°

Tableau III.

	Volume cardiaque	Vol. card./poids du corps
1.	776	13.90
2.	893	14.40
3.	678	12.78
4.	781	13.94
5.	1019	16.98
6.	730	13.03
	812.8	14.17

Tableau IV.

	QRS Fr.	Hor.	Amplit. Fr.	Hor.	Mi-surface Fr.	Hor.	Sens Fr.	Hor.	T Fr.	Hor.
1.	22°	−20°	0.7	0.7	12°	−40°	s.c.	s.c.	5°	−20°
2.	50°	0°	0.9	0.55	50°	0°	s.a.	s.c.	40°	− 5°
3.	40°	0°	0.5	0.38	40°	15°	en 8	s.c.	42°	10°
4.	18°	−10°	0.6	0.6	0°	−10°	s.c.	s.c.	18°	−15°
5.	3°	−10°	0.7	0.6	20°	−15°	s.c.	s.c.	45°	15°
6.	25°	− 5°	0.9	0.8	−20°	− 5°	s.c.	s.c.	25°	−10°
	26°	− 7°	0.7	0.6	17°	−10°			29°	− 3°

Fr: Frontal   Hor: Horizontal
s.c.: sens contraire aux aiguilles d'une montre
s.a.: sans des aiguilles d'une montre

sens de la boucle du vecteur QRS et son amplitude ne correspondent pas aux critères définissant l'hypertrophie cardiaque [3]. D'après la littérature que nous avons pu consulter à ce propos, Arstila et Koivikko [1] sont les auteurs qui ont le plus étudié les variations vectocardiographiques du coeur des sportifs d'endurance. Du point de vue vectocardiographique, ces auteurs ont constaté la proportion de 1/10 d'hypertrophies cardiaques gauches et les tracés électrocardiographiques confirment ces données chez les mêmes athlètes dans un quart des cas. Toutefois, il paraît évident que des sportifs plus âgés ayant fourni un entraînement pendant de longues années présentent une hypertrophie plus marquée que celle d'athlètes plus jeunes. L'hypertrophie ventriculaire gauche est nettement plus fréquente chez des marathoniens un peu plus âgés. C'est pourquoi, il nous semble possible d'expliquer l'absence de critères dus à l'hypertrophie dans les vectocardiogrammes de nos athlètes de par leur jeune âge. De longues années d'entraînement la feront apparaître.

Sur le plan radiologique, l'hypertrophie visible dans l'ombre du coeur et la bradicardie due à l'entraînement chez ces sportifs confirment la dilatation fonctionnelle décrite par Reindell, mais rien ne permet de vraiment affirmer, à la lumière de ces observations, qu'il s'agit d'une hypertrophie musculaire. Avant de pouvoir développer cette assertion, il faut attendre les résultats des recherches longitudinales qui seront effectuées chez ces mêmes athlètes.

Références

1. Arstila, M. et Koivikko, A.: J. Sports Med. 6:166, 1966.
2. Beckner, G.L. et T. Winsor: Circulation 9:835, 1954.
3. Bristow, J.D.: Am. Heart J. 61:242, 1961.
4. Herxheimer, H.: Klin. Wschr. 8:402, 1931.
5. Holzmann, M.: Klin. Elektrokardiographie, 1961.
6. Musshoff, K., H. Reindell: Dtsch. med. Wschr. 81:1001, 1956.
7. Reindell, H. et coll.: Herz-Kreislaufkrankeiten und Sport, 1960.
8. Roskamm, H. et coll.: Sportarzt 17:251, 1966.
9. Smith, W.G. et coll.: Br. Heart J. 26:469, 1964.
10. Williams, H. et Arnold, H.D.: Phil. Med. J. 3:1233, 1899.

Hemodynamic Changes in 50- to 70-Year-Old Men Due to Endurance Training

R. Rost, W. Dreisbach and W. Hollmann

Introduction

Physical activity is increasingly recommended for prevention and rehabilitation of coronary heart disease, but a therapeutic effect is not generally accepted. A very often mentioned argument to demonstrate the benefit of training is the reduction of myocardial work at a given workload. Myocardial work is determined by arterial pressure, cardiac output and blood acceleration. According to a great many reports in the literature all of these parameters can be lowered by training, but these results are challenged by others.

Cross-sectional studies between endurance athletes and sedentary people usually did not show such a decrease of pressure or volume work, but rather a reduction of heart rate, an increase of stroke volume and circulation time. The last finding could be considered to be a hint for a decrease of acceleration work. However, these results cannot be extrapolated to the effect of training with minor intensity as it can be performed by subjects prone to coronary disease. Training like this will not yield a dimensional adaptation as an enlargement of the heart; the effects will be more functional. The problem of a reduction of cardiac work in this state of adaptation may be another one and the findings in literature are very contradictory.

A decrease of arterial pressure as a consequence of the reduced sympathic tone has been described from authors like Bouchard, Clausen and Mellerowicz [2-5, 15], while others like Ekblom, Frick and Saltin [6, 7, 10, 11, 17] could not find it. As to the results concerning the influence of training on the volume work, there seems to be a great confusion in literature. Earlier authors generally stressed

R. Rost, W. Dreisbach and W. Hollmann, Institute for Sports Medicine and Circulation Research, German Sports University, Cologne, Federal Republic of Germany.

121

the improvement of capillarization by training and therefore assumed a higher perfusion of the trained muscle. Today a contradicting tendency can be observed, but not unanimously. Varnauskas [19] was the first, using modern methods, to describe a decrease of cardiac output during exercise after training, but he still thought this to be a result of a more pronounced collateral vasoconstriction in the nonworking tissues. According to the results of Rowell [16], however, the contrary was true and indeed as to the reduced sympathic tone a less effective vasoconstriction seems to be more probable.

Consequently, other investigators like Clausen [3-5], who could find a diminution of cardiac output as well, suggested that this was the result of a decreased muscle blood flow after training. This reduction, which could be demonstrated by plethysmographic methods as well as by the Xenon technique, was considered to be made possible by a better oxygen utilization in the skeletal muscle. According to this suggestion training will improve the arteriovenous difference by the well-known fact of the elevated enzymatic capacity and a more hypothetic improvement of the intramuscular blood distribution. The results will be a decreased muscle perfusion and therefore a reduced cardiac output with a lower requirement of the myocardium.

In fact such a reduction of cardiac output could be found by a few investigators, for example Andrew, Ekblom, Hanson and Tabakin [1, 6, 13, 18], but it should not be forgotten that in nearly the same numbers of publications such a decrease could not be realized, in the papers of Freeman, Frick, Hartley and Saltin [9-11, 14, 17] and even another one of Clausen [3-5].

Methods

Further investigation seemed necessary. We did perform a training program for three months five times a week with 20 healthy, sedentary 50- to 70-year-old men. This age group was elected because they have a high coronary risk. The training consisted of jogging, swimming, gymnastics and basketball. In the first group of ten persons we did measure the following parameters before and after the training at rest and during exercise: cardiac output by dye dilution technique, arterial pressure by direct measurement, circulation time and arterial oxygen pressure. Exercise was performed on the bicycle in a supine position.

The second group consisted of the same number of members. Here we explored the conditions of perfusion and utilization by

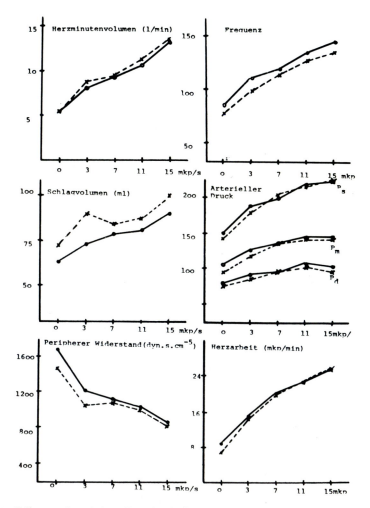

FIG. 1. Effects of training. Results before training: straight line, after training dashed line. Figures on the left side represent cardiac output, stroke volume and peripheral resistance, on the right side heart rate, arterial pressure and cardiac work, beginning with the upper one.

venous occlusion plethysmographic method and by analysis of the femoral venous blood with respect to the oxygen and metabolic parameter. In addition, in all members we measured the performance capacity by the maximal oxygen uptake, the cardiac volume, the lactic acid concentration and partly the myocardial wall thickness by ultrasonic methods.

Results

After training there was a significant improvement of performance capacity and of maximal oxygen uptake, a significant decrease of lactic acid concentration and of heart rate at a given workload. There was only a little and insignificant decrease of mean arterial pressure and no reduction of cardiac output. The lowered heart rate therefore was equalled by an increased stroke volume (Fig. 1).

We also found a decrease of postexercise hyperemia in the working muscle, but the analysis of femoral venous blood could not demonstrate an elevated utilization during exercise. Metabolic parameters demonstrate a shift from the oxygenation of carbohydrates to fat, and it should be stressed that this demands a higher amount of oxygen.

Our results are in contradiction to some of the literature, but the plethysmographic findings of a reduced perfusion of the muscle after exercise cannot be taken as proof for a reduced muscle blood flow during exercise, as Elsner [8] has stated. The application of the Xenon technique, which in contrast to our findings demonstrates a reduced muscle blood flow during exercise, must be considered critically if we analyze the results available in literature.

References

1. Andrew, G., Guzman, C. and Becklake, M.: J. Appl. Physiol. 21:603, 1966.
2. Bouchard, C., Hollmann, W., Venrath, H. et al: Sportarzt und Sportmedizin 7:348, 1966.
3. Clausen, J.P., Klausen, K., Rasmussen, B. and Trap-Jensen, J.: Acta Physiol. Scand. 82:35, 1971.
4. Clausen, J.P., Larsen, O. and Trap-Jensen, J.: Circulation 40:143, 1969.
5. Clausen, J.P. and Trap-Jensen, J.: Circulation 42:611, 1970.
6. Ekblom, B.: Acta Physiol. Scand. Suppl. 38:328, 1969.
7. Ekblom, B., Astrand, P.O., Saltin, B. et al: J. Appl. Physiol. 24:518, 1968.
8. Elsner, R. and Carlson, L.: J. Appl. Physiol. 17:436, 1962.
9. Freedman, M.E., Snider, J.G., Brosthoff, P. et al: J. Appl. Physiol. 8:37, 1955.
10. Frick, M. and Katila, M.: Circulation 37:192, 1968.
11. Frick, M., Kontinen, A. and Sarajas, H.: Am. J. Cardiol. 12:142, 1963.
12. Grimby, G., Häggendal, E. and Saltin, B.: J. Appl. Physiol. 22:305, 1967.
13. Hanson, J., Tabakin, B.S., Levy, G. and Nedde, W.: Circulation 38:783, 1968.
14. Hartley, L. and Saltin, B.: Scand. J. Clin. Lab. Invest. 22:217, 1968.
15. Mellerowicz, H.: Rehabilitative Kardiologie 16, 1974.
16. Rowell, L., Blackmon, J. and Bruce, R.: J. Clin. Invest. 43:1677, 1964.
17. Saltin, B., Blomquist, G., Mitchell, J. et al: Circulation 38 (suppl. 7), 1968.
18. Tabakin, B.: Br. Heart J. 27:205, 1965.
19. Varnauskas, E., Bergmann, H., Houk, P. and Björnstrop, P.: Lancet 2:8, 1966.

On the Specific Effects of Various Physical Activities on the Cardiovascular and Metabolic Functions in Older People

S. E. Strauzenberg

Introduction

It is a well-known fact, corroborated recently again by Robinson et al [1], that regular physical training not only detains the age-dependent degradation of performance and function but also may act against significant additional damage caused by physical inactivity and psychic stress.

However, the greatest part of relevant results in this field stems from investigations using bicycle ergometer training or running for exercise workload. These training methods are linked with considerable expense especially within a big city and may only be applied under favorable conditions.

According to the social program of the GDR which, by constitution, warrants equal rights of health protection for all citizens, we feel it is our obligation to make the beneficial effects of physical training accessible not only to an elite group but to as many people as possible. In addition, it is generally known and underscored once again by Teräslinna [2] that physical conditioning is bound to be abandoned by older people very soon if such an endeavor is attached to preconditions that render training more difficult. Our basic aim, however, is to insure that an efficient training program grows into a lasting habit.

For this reason it was our intention to investigate whether and under what conditions a calisthenics program, that can readily be performed at home, or walking at a quick pace can bring about similar favorable effects as obtained by running or bicycle ergometer training.

S. E. Strauzenberg, Zentralinstitut des Sportmedizinischen Dienstes, Kreischa, German Democratic Republic.

Material and Methods

In 44 healthy middle-aged men (mean age 53.5 years), with impaired performance capacity due to sedentary life, the effect of a calisthenics program (I) lasting ten minutes and performed six times a week over a period of four weeks was investigated. Before and on the last day of the training period the heart rate at rest and at the end of a bicycle ergometer test (100 W 10 min) was monitored electrocardiographically. Blood pressure was measured by the Riva Rocchi method. Maximum oxygen uptake, serum cholesterol, neutral fat and uric acid levels were determined. The same examinations were made before and after a four-week training program consisting of walking at a pace of 1.4 meters/sec (about 5 km/hr) (II) and another program consisting of walking at a pace of 1.8 meters/sec (about 6.5 km/hr) (III) performed six times per week for a duration of 20 minutes. The whole group was divided into three subgroups, each starting with another training program. Between each series of exercises, training was interrupted for four weeks.

In 26 male patients, mean age 54.2 years, who had suffered from myocardial infarction, the actual effects of various calisthenic exercises and walking at the abovementioned speeds on heart rate and blood pressure were studied.

Results

Effects on Heart Rate (Fig. 1)

The calisthenics program (I) and walking at a pace of 1.4 meters/sec (II) did affect the heart rate at rest only insignificantly. Walking at 1.8 meters/sec (III), however, caused a significant reduction of heart rate at rest. The heart rate at the end of the test load and in the third minute of recovery was significantly reduced in both cases. The reduction was most pronounced after program III.

Blood Pressure (Fig. 2)

Within the whole group, the blood pressure at rest remained practically unchanged. The systolic blood pressure at the end of exercise and at three minutes of recovery shows a significant reduction by each training program. Diastolic blood pressure was reduced significantly only by program III (Fig. 2).

In 16 patients showing initially hypertonic blood pressure we found a significant reduction in systolic blood pressure, even at rest, that was most pronounced after program III (Fig. 3).

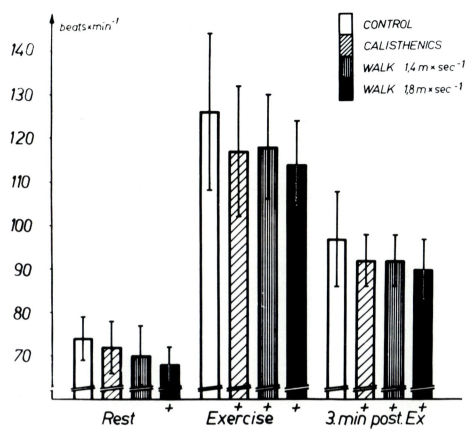

FIG. 1. Pulse rate at rest, at the end of the test load (exercise) and three minutes post exercise (+ = significant at the p = 0.05 level).

Maximum Oxygen Uptake

Calisthenics and walking at 1.4 meters/sec resulted only in an insignificant increase in maximum O_2 uptake whereas walking at a speed of 1.8 meters/sec led to a significant rise from 40.8 to 46.9 ml/kp/min.

Change in Serum Cholesterol, Neutral Fat and Uric Acid Levels

Calisthenics caused no significant changes. Walking at both speeds resulted in an insignificant decrease of blood cholesterol and uric acid concentration (Fig. 4). Walking at a pace of 1.8 meters/sec, however, resulted in a significant reduction of the cholesterol level

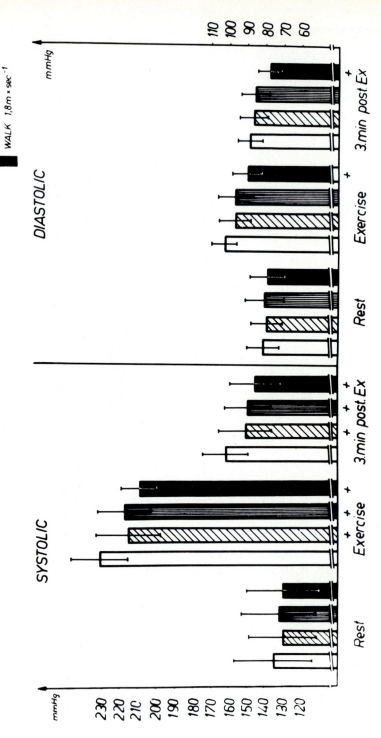

FIG. 2. Systolic and diastolic blood pressure (+ = statistically significant).

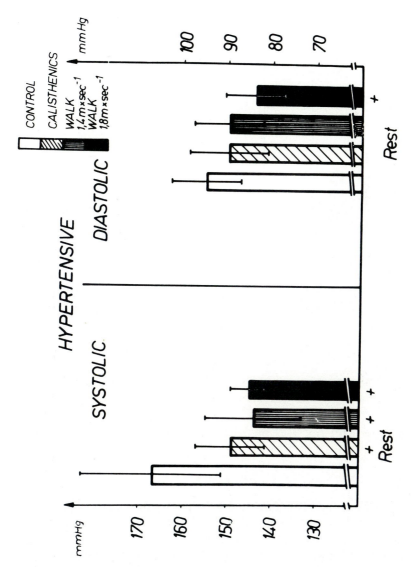

FIG. 3. Blood pressure at rest in initially hypertonic patients (+ = statistically significant).

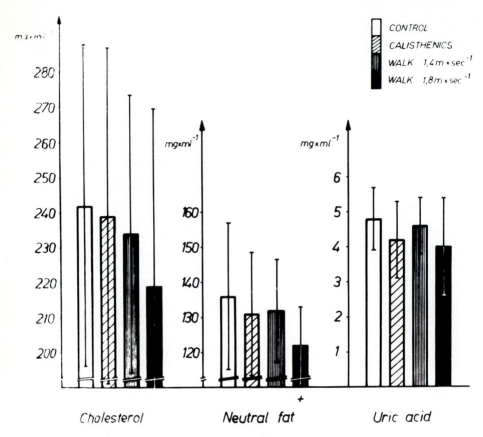

FIG. 4. Influence of the different training programs on serum levels of cholesterol, neutral fat and uric acid.

from 344 to 256 mg/100 ml with all patients that initially showed hypernormal levels.

Discussion

Our studies show that in people with impaired physical capacity a calisthenics program of ten-minute duration performed every day may cause similar changes in circulation as found with running or ergometer training at medium intensity. But it should be pointed out that the effects of such exercises substantially depend upon the quantity of the participating muscle mass. Our investigations of the actual effect of physical exercises reveal that the effects are the more pronounced the greater the muscle mass involved (Fig. 5). On the

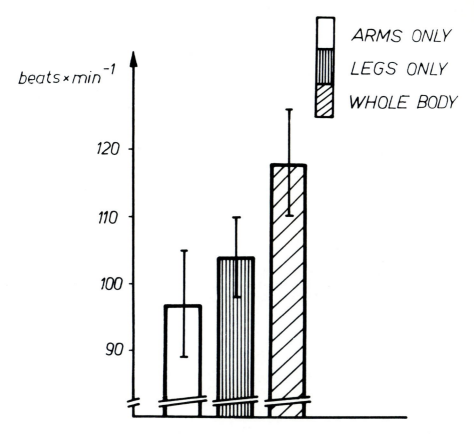

FIG. 5. Pulse rate after three minutes of exercise including arms only, legs only and the whole body (run on the spot). Intensity was limited to 30 actions resp. double steps per minute.

other hand, it is striking that the calisthenics program as well as the walking program (II) had no significant bearing on metabolic parameters.

Regarding the heart rate, the intensity of the calisthenics program turned out to be of the same order as walking at a pace of 1.4 meters/sec. Walking at the higher speed of 1.8 meters/sec, however, caused significant changes also with metabolic parameters. Therefore, we think that the difference of the results between program I and II versus program III is caused by the different intensities. Based on these results calisthenics at home and quick walking can be recommended as efficient exercise programs for older people with reduced performance if other possibilities are not readily available. The easy feasibility even in big cities is an important prerequisite for the aspired regularity of physical exercises.

To insure the efficiency of physical training, however, the exercise load must be defined quantitatively with respect to duration and intensity. It is necessary that the greater part of the whole muscle mass be involved and that the intensity requires about 60% of maximum oxygen capacity. As to duration, ten minutes seems to be the lower limit for effectiveness. A duration as short as ten minutes is effective only if the exercises are performed every day. The effectivity of daily training can further be enhanced by extending its duration.

References

1. Robinson, S., Dill, D.B., Tzankoff, S.P. et al: Longitudinal studies of aging in 37 men. J. Appl. Physiol. 38(2):263-267, 1975.
2. Teräslinna, P., Partanen, T., Oja, P. and Koskela, A.: Some social characteristics and living habits associated with willingness to participate in a physical activity intervention study. J. Sports Med. Phys. Fitness 10(3):138-144, 1970.

Physical Activity and Cardiac Rehabilitation

O. D. Karatun, W. H. Osness, P. K. Wilson,
J. W. Edgett and R. M. Green

Introduction

Cardiac rehabilitation, including graded exercise testing (GXT), medically supervised physical activity, patient education and reduction of coronary risk factors, is becoming a part of the medical practice in the management of coronary heart disease (CHD). The investigations in this area [3, 4, 8, 12] reveal significant changes in exercise tolerance and physical working capacity in coronary patients. Nevertheless, Saltin's studies [13] indicate that this positive physiologic adaptation to exercise is lost in a short time if the exercise program is not continued. Therefore, the long-term prophylactic effects of a cardiac rehabilitation program should not only reflect the improvements in exercise parameters, but also related physical, habitual and behavioral factors.

The purpose of this study was to investigate these total changes in cardiac patients. The parameters investigated were relative weight, resting heart rate, systolic and diastolic blood pressure, rate pressure product in rest (modified tension time index), longevity on medication, subsequent heart problems during the treatment period, occupational and leisure time physical activity, relaxation ability, depression, diet and nutrition (Table III).

Methodology

The design of the investigation is based on comparative analysis between the rehabilitated (R) and nonrehabilitated (NR) cardiac patients. The patients in the LaCrosse, Wisconsin, Cardiac Rehabilitation program represented the R sample. The matched NR sample

O. D. Karatun, W. H. Osness, P. K. Wilson, J. W. Edgett and R. M. Green, University of Kansas, Lawrence, Kansas, and University of Wisconsin, LaCrosse, Wisc., U.S.A.

133

subjects were selected from the Lawrence, Kansas, Memorial Hospital.

The total number of subjects studied was 209. The final analysis included 140 matched subjects. The patients, who voluntarily accepted to be subjects for the investigation, signed the consent form and accepted the release of the confidential medical information to the investigator.

Both samples had the same number of postmyocardial infarction (MI), postcoronary revascularization (CR), non-MI coronary artery disease (CAD) and prone (P) to CHD subjects. Infarct locations and infarct sizes were used for matching MI cases. Degree and locations of the occlusions, number of grafts and their locations were used for matching post CR cases. ECG, peak serum enzyme levels, coronary arteriography and operation reports were used for these purposes. The physician's diagnosis was utilized for CAD and P cases. Additional criteria for general sample matching were age, sex, height, weight at the onset of the cardiac condition, treatment period, hospital stay and family history of the subjects. These matching characteristics have provided a complete uniformity for comparison of two samples (Tables I and II).

The treatment period was 6 to 36 months in both populations.

Rehabilitation through exercise consisted of the three phases as it is commonly practiced [10, 11]. Phase I was the "in hospital rehabilitation" and included 14 steps for post MI cases and 11 steps for post CR cases. Early ambulation activities started with passive range of motion (ROM) exercises to extremities in bed, then progressed to semipassive full active ROM exercises at the bedside and was followed by a progressive walking program. At the end of this phase, the patients were subjected to a low intensity functional graded exercise test (FGXT) for the assessment of the exercise level to be initiated in the Phase II program. In Phase II, patients followed a self-walking program. This activity started as a one street block distance (approximately 350 meters), which increased progressively every two weeks. Eventually, the patients were expected to cover 5 to 6 km in 72 minutes at the end of the eighth week. During Phase II, the exercise heart rate of the patients was kept under 115 beats per minute. After the completion of this phase, the patients received another FGXT, which measured the functional level of the patients and enabled the program director to determine an exercise prescription for the next phase. Phase III was the aggressive exercise stage and included (a) 2½ months elementary backstroke swimming after a 15-day initial walking in the shallow end of the pool; (b) 3 months

Table I. Characteristics of Samples at the Onset of CHD
(Sample Matching)

Criteria	Rehabilitated Mean, S.D.	Nonrehabilitated Mean, S.D.	Statistical Difference	
Sex (%)	91.4 ± 8.6 (F)	92.9 ± 7.14 (F)		
Age (yr)	54.15± 8.95	54.60± 7.86	F = 0.09	NS
Height (cm)	174.68± 7.26	176.08± 7.79	F = 1.21	NS
Weight (kg)	85.78±13.64	84.28±18.01	F = 1.62	NS
Resting heart rate (beats/min)	81.14±10.74	81.87± 9.14	F = 0.007	NS
Family history (+)$_1$	2.60± 1.28	2.80± 1.29	F = 0.84	NS
Diet (+)$_1$	4.18± 1.14	4.37± 1.02	F = 0.90	NS
Nutrition (+)$_1$	1.70± 1.04	1.70± 0.93	F = 0.00	NS
Hospital stay (days) (MI and Post OP cases)	14.81± 5.87	18.15± 7.76	F = 3.77	NS
Treatment period (mos.)	13.68± 9.68	15.07± 9.13	F = 2.44	NS
Pathology (cases)				
Post MI (+)$_2$	21	21		NS
CAD	14	14		NS
Postcoronary revascularization	11	11		NS
Prone CHD	24	24		NS
Total cases	70	70	N = 140	

(+)$_1$ Coded Score (5 = increased risk, 1 = decreased risk in CHD)
(+)$_2$ See Table II for MI and coronary revascularization case matching.
NS = Nonsignificant difference
*Significant difference

beginners walking-jogging and running; (c) 6 months advanced jogging-running.

The patients who were in the program more than 12 months and did not have any complications were chiefly in the advanced group. Changes in exercise intensity and new exercise prescription are always based on periodic GXTs. Patients with CAD or P to CHD started directly in the Phase III program.

The patients in the NR sample did not engage in an organized, medically supervised exercise program either during their hospital stay or their convalescent period. They were mostly physically inactive. The exceptional ones, who attempted to be active, did not receive a GXT; therefore, they did not receive an exercise prescription based on their functional level.

In the data analysis the "T — Test" was used to test the differences at pre- and posttreatment levels. Univaried analysis of

Table II. Pathologic Matching
(Coronary Revascularization and Myocardial Infarction Cases)

Matching Criteria	Rehabilitated Sample	Nonrehabilitated Sample
No. of MI Cases	21	21
Infarct Locations:		
Anterior MI	10	10
Inferior MI	10	10
Posterior MI	1	1
Infarct Size (predicted by SGOT level)		
Mean Peak SGOT level	91.89 Units	91.05 Units
SGOT Distribution:		
SGOT 70 Units	11 case	13 case
SGOT 70 - 140 Units	5 case	4 case
SGOT 140 Units	5 case	4 case
Coronary Revascularization Cases	11 case	11 case
Total R.C.A. lesions	11	9
Total L.A.D. lesions	9	10
Total L.CX lesions	5	3
No. of total grafts	25	22

variance ("ANOVA") was used on nonrepeated measure variables and analysis of covariance ("ANCOVA") was used on repeated measure variables. Numeric values were used for the comparison in parametric variables. Nonparametric variables were measured with a 1 to 5 coded score scale. The upper level of the scale represented the increased risk of CHD and/or worsened condition, the lower level, the reduced risk of CHD and/or positive improvement in condition.

Results

Pre- and posttreatment differences of the samples are given in Table III. The data indicated that rehabilitation made significant changes in relative weight, resting heart rate, systolic and diastolic blood pressure, leisure time physical activity, dietary and nutritional parameters. Occupational physical activity did not show any change, because most of the R sample subjects were able to return to their jobs and working conditions.

The NR sample showed significant improvement only in the relative weight and systolic blood pressure. Other parameters did not show any significant changes.

In cigarette smoking there was a significant change in both the R and NR samples. Nevertheless, this change was at a higher level in the R sample.

Table III. Rehabilitation and Nonrehabilitation Pre- and Posttreatment and Total Group Comparisons

Variable N = 140	Test	"R" Means, S.D. Pre	"R" Means, S.D. Post	Pre-Post Difference	"NR" Means, S.D. Pre	"NR" Means, S.D. Post	Pre-Post Difference	"R" – "NR" Difference
Relative weight	ANCOVA	121.62 ±17.98	114.47 ±15.80	t = 7.60* P 0.01	115.47 ±15.77	112.18 ±15.18	t = 3.70* P 0.01	4.08 * 0.05
Resting heart rate	ANCOVA	81.74 ±10.79	74.42 ±18.90	t = 3.02* P 0.01	81.87 ±9.14	80.07 ±7.35	t = 1.18 NS	29.18 * 0.01
Systolic blood pressure	ANCOVA	151.55 ±19.39	132.55 ±16.47	t = 7.48* P 0.01	142.68 ±22.42	133.05 ±16.13	t = 3.80* P 0.01	0.69 NS
Diastolic blood pressure	ANCOVA	93.95 ±11.58	85.45 ±14.73	t = 4.60* P 0.01	87.68 ±12.80	85.45 ±10.38	t = 1.62 NS	0.36 NS
Longevity on medication $(+)_1$	ANOVA	—	3.01 ±1.28		—	3.74 ±1.59		6.34 * 0.05
Subsequent heart problems $(+)_1$	ANOVA	—	1.60 ±1.39		—	2.55 ±1.62		15.68 * 0.01
Relaxation ability $(+)_1$	ANOVA	—	2.71 ±1.09		—	3.58 ±1.14		21.16 * 0.01
Occupational physical activity	ANCOVA	3.42 ±1.39	3.61 ±1.23	t = 1.90 NS	2.80 ±1.32	3.41 ±1.34	t = 1.29 NS	0.79 NS
Leisure time physical activity	ANCOVA	3.55 ±1.09	1.44 ±0.65	t = 16.23* P 0.01	3.18 ±1.33	2.97 ±1.46	t = 0.52 NS	106.47 * 0.01
Diet	ANCOVA	4.18 ±1.14	2.75 ±1.26	t = 7.94* P 0.01	4.37 ±1.02	3.52 ±1.17	t = 1.70 NS	12.72 * 0.01
Nutrition	ANCOVA	1.70 ±1.04	1.31 ±0.87	t = 3.54 P 0.01	1.70 ±0.93	1.70 ±0.90	t = 0.00 NS	7.28 * 0.01
Rate pressure product	ANCOVA	124.67 ±23.57	96.01 ±18.23	t = 3.24* P 0.01	116.75 ±23.79	107.88 ±19.06	t = 2.79* P 0.01	13.95 * 0.01

*For explanation of symbols, see Table I.

R-NR comparison included also nonrepeated measure variables (Table III) such as longevity on medication, subsequent heart problems during the treatment period, relaxation ability and depression according to the Zung scale.

Discussion

Some psychosomatic changes are the expected outcome of the cardiac episode in most patients. The role of the cardiac rehabilitation program is to hopefully orient these changes in the direction of reducing the risk factors in CHD, teaching patients how to cope with the problem and live within the limits of a new functional level. In this study they were investigated and evaluated from the following perspectives.

Habitual Changes

One of the most important significant changes in both of the R and NR populations was on the cigarette smoking habit. Before the treatment, the number of smokers was more than double in both of the populations when compared with the number of smokers after the treatment. However, the change in percentage from smokers to nonsmokers was higher in the R population.

As seen in Table III, data also indicated that the food consumption was extremely high in both populations before the cardiac problem. Since this has been found to be a key parameter for the obesity and high cholesterol level [9], their eating habits portrayed a typical picture of a high-risk man for CHD: overeater, overweight and probably increased cholesterol level. Results indicated significant positive changes in this parameter for the R population. The objective of the nutritional parameter was to investigate if the patient consumed a nutritionally balanced meal at the pre-measure level and avoided the high cholesterol containing food during the treatment. Examination of pretreatment data indicated that both populations consumed a very well-balanced meal before the onset of the cardiac problem. This measure is also parallel to the diet measure. During the treatment period, avoiding the cholesterol rich food intake was managed significantly better by the R population.

The next important habitual parameter studied was the physical activity level of both populations before the onset of the cardiac problem and the change in this activity level with treatment. Data indicated that prior to the cardiac problem, the subjects of both the R and NR populations were on the "physically inactive" side of the scale. Their low level of occupational physical activity was almost the only physical activity that the individuals engaged in, because their leisure time activity was also very low.

Results indicate that leisure time physical activity level was significantly increased in the R population. On the other hand, occupational physical activity level was not significantly different between the two populations.

Behavioral Changes

Several investigations [5, 7, 15] indicated behavioral patterns and tension as very important risk factors. Tension can be accepted as an outcome of the emotional disturbances and loss of relaxation ability. The patients in the R program had significantly better relaxation ability [14] scores than the NR patients. This result shows that probably the most important influence of the rehabilitation program was a reduction of tension and an increase in the relaxation state in cardiac patients with exercise.

The degree of depression was measured according to the Zung self depression scale [16] and indicated a significantly higher level in the NR population. There was also a significant negative correlation $(r = 0.67)$ between the relaxation ability and the depression scores.

Physical Changes

At the onset of the cardiac problem, the characteristics of the samples (Table I) showed no significant difference between the R and NR populations in reference to physical parameters. They were generally overweight, endomorphic and had a high relative weight index. Both populations showed weight reduction during the treatment period. The weight reduction in the R population was in conformity with the other related parameters, such as increased physical activity level and better controlled diet. On the other hand, without this correspondence between the contributing other parameters and with the higher level of depression, the weight reduction in the NR population is not known whether it was truly an expected outcome of the treatment or a weight loss related to pathology.

Physiological Changes

Except in a few individual practices, the NR population was not subjected to any organized physical activity, even as a form of exercise testing. Therefore, the exercise parameters were not the objectives of this investigation and it was assumed that changes in the resting heart rate, systolic/diastolic blood pressure and rate pressure product indicated the basic cardiovascular responses to the treatment conditions. While the treatment made no change on the resting heart rate of the NR population, it showed a significant decrease in the R population. According to several investigations [1, 2, 6] this can be accepted as an indication of cardiovascular fitness and an increase in cardiac reserves. In this investigation rate pressure product (SBP $\times$ HR $\times$ 10^{-2}) reflects the myocardial oxygen demand in the resting metabolic level of the cardiac man. This demand was significantly lower in the R population after the treatment. Both the R and NR treatments were successful to about the same extent on the management of the hypertension (Table III).

Changes in Pathology

It was assumed that an increased or decreased level of subsequent heart problems and medication level were directly related to the patients' pathologic condition. NR population had significantly more subsequent heart problems and used more medication during the treatment period. These two parameters probably also had a great influence on the behavioral parameters of the NR patients.

Conclusion

Rehabilitation through exercise has made significant changes in the physical, habitual, behavioral and resting cardiovascular parameters of the cardiac patients studied in this investigation.

The NR cardiac patient confronts an increased number of subsequent heart problems and utilizes more medication than a patient who participates in a structured cardiac rehabilitation program.

References

1. Astrand, P.O.: Method of measurement of physical fitness in population studies. *In* Larsen, A. and Malmborg, R.O. (eds.): CHD and Physical Fitness. Baltimore, London, Tokyo:University Park Press, 1971, pp. 82-97.
2. Bevegard, S., Holmgren, A. and Johnson, B.: The effect of body position on the circulation at rest and during exercise, with special reference to the influence on the stroke volume. Acta Physiol. Scand. 49:279-298, 1960.
3. Boyer, J.L. and Kasch, F.D.: Changes in maximum work capacity resulting from 6 months training in patients with ischemic heart disease. Med. Sci. Sports 1:156-159, 1969.
4. Brock, L.: Early reconditionings for post-MI patients: Spalding Rehabilitation Center. *In* Naughton, J.P., Hellerstein, H.K. and Mohler, I.C. (eds.): Exercise Testing and Exercise Training in Coronary Heart Disease. New York:Academic Press, 1973, pp. 315-335.

5. Bruhn, J.G., Chandler, B. and Wolf, S.: Psychological study of survivors and non-survivors of M.I. J. Psychosom. Med. 31:8-19, 1969.
6. Cooper, K.H.: The New Aerobics. New York:M. Evans and Company Inc., 1970, pp. 92-118.
7. Friedman, M. and Rosenman, R.H.: Type "A" behavior pattern, its association with CHD. Ann. Clin. Res. 3:300-312, 1971.
8. Kellerman, J.J., Modan, B., Levy, M. et al: Return to work after MI, comparative study of rehabilitated and non-rehabilitated patients. Geriatrics 23:151-156, 1968.
9. Masironi, R.: Dietary Factors in CHD. Bull. WHO 42:103-114, 1970.
10. National Heart and Lung Inst.: Needs and opportunities for rehabilitating the coronary heart disease patient. DHEW publication No.: (NIH) 75-750, Bethesda, Md., 1974.
11. Pyfer, H., Doane, B., Mead, W. and Frederick, R.: Group exercise rehabilitation for cardiopulmonary patients: A five year study. Med. Sci. Sports 5:71, 1973.
12. Rechnitzer, P.A., Pickard, H.A., Paivio, A.U. et al: Long term follow up study of survival and recurrence rates following myocardial infarction in exercising and control subjects. Circulation 45:853-857, 1972.
13. Saltin, B., Blomquist, G., Mitchell, J.H. et al: Response to exercise after bed rest and after training. Circulation 48:VII/1-55, 1968.
14. Vitale, F.: Individualized Fitness Programs. New Jersey:Prentice-Hall Inc., 1973, p. 247.
15. Weis, E., Dlin, B., Rollin, H.R. et al: Emotional factors in coronary occlusion. Arch. Intern. Med. 99:628-640, 1957.
16. Zung, W.W.: A self rating depression scale. Arch. Gen. Psychiatry 16:543-547, 1967.

Fluid and Mineral Needs of Post-Coronary Distance Runners

T. Kavanagh and R. J. Shephard

Extent of Fluid Loss

Post-coronary patients can lose substantial quantities of fluid if they run over marathon distances. Table I recalls our experience with the first group of post-coronary patients who competed at Boston in 1973 [4]. There were eight volunteers from our rehabilitation program. All had sustained proven myocardial infarctions one to four years previously, and before their heart attacks they had been leading a very sedentary existence. They ran much more slowly than the average young marathoner, taking as long as five hours to cover the 42 km. Nevertheless, the day was humid. Temperatures rose to the upper seventies, 25 to 26 C, and our runners suffered an average weight loss of 4 kg despite a fluid intake averaging some 800 ml. Their total sweat production was thus about 4.6 liters.

Such heavy losses pose several nutritional problems:

1. How much of the weight loss is true dehydration?
2. From which body compartment does the fluid come?
3. How far can the loss be prevented?
4. What recommendations should be made for replenishment of fluid, mineral and vitamin stores?

The likely origins of a 4-kg weight loss are set out in Table II. First, there is metabolism. The caloric cost of the race for a runner of average body weight is about 3700 kcal, irrespective of his speed of running. Our group derived about 200 kcal from the ingestion of sweetened drinks, but the remaining 3500 kcal came from body stores. Putting the average energy yield of these stores at 6.5 kcal/gm, a total of 0.54 kg of food reserves would have been broken down to 0.32 kg of water plus carbon dioxide, for a net weight loss of 0.22 kg.

The direct water yield of metabolism would then be 320 ml, but this could be supplemented by the potential reserve of up to 1600 ml

T. Kavanagh and R. J. Shephard, Toronto Rehabilitation Centre and Department of Preventive Medicine and Biostatistics, University of Toronto, Toronto, Ontario, Canada.

Table 1. Fluid Balance Data for Participants in 1973 Boston Marathon [4]

Patient	Fluid Intake	Weight (kg) Initial	Final	(Δ%)	Na⁺ (mEq/l) Initial	Final	K⁺ (mEq/l) Initial	Final	Cl⁻ (mEq/l) Initial	Final	HCO₃⁻ (mEq/l) Initial	Final
L†	180 ml Lucozade prior to race. Four or five small drinks (20-25 ml.) each and 6 quarter oranges en route	85.7	82.1	(-4.2)	146	145	4.5	4.7	100	112	25	12
Ro	90 ml Lucozade prior to race, sips of water and pieces of orange en route	60.8	56.2	(-7.6)	143	155	4.0	6.9*	99	100	28	14
Rl	180 ml Lucozade prior to race, "about 2.7 liters of water en route"	91.2	88.0	(-3.5)	145	151	3.7	5.4	102	96	23	16
S	None before 130 ml during event	76.7	72.6	(-5.3)	143	149	4.2	4.1	98	106	26	23
C	45 ml Lucozade prior, 80 ml water, 6-7 quarter oranges en route	64.9	61.7	(-4.9)	149	148	6.2*	4.4	99	102	20	22
B	180 ml Lucozade prior, "as much as I could drink during the event "	64.2	59.4	(-7.0)	143	154	4.4	4.9	96	107	26	21
N	Nil prior to race, about 900 ml in second half of race	81.2	77.1	(-5.0)	141	147	4.7	4.5	99	104	26	21
V	Nil prior to race, taking fluid "continually" during race	70.3	65.8	(-6.4)	141	153	4.2	3.7	97	107	27	24
Average, all patients		74.4	70.4	(-5.5)	143.8	150.2	4.2	4.5	98.8	104.3	25.1	19.1
Laboratory normal range					135-142		3.6-5.0		98-105			

† completed only half of the race.
* sample showed some hemolysis.

**Table II. Likely Basis of a 4-kg Weight Loss During
Participation in a Marathon Race [5]**

Catabolism	$\dot{V}O_2$ 2.5 liter/min	= 12.5 kcal/min
		= 3700 kcal for race
	Ingestion	= 200 kcal
	Net loss	= 3500 kcal
	If 6.5 kcal/gm 0.5 kg food	
	converted to 0.3 kg water	
Weight loss	4 kg	
	Catabolism 0.2 kg	
	Water loss 3.8 kg	
	But 0.3 kg from catabolism	
	1.6 kg from glycogen	
Dehydration about 1.9 kg		

tied to glycogen molecules. Assuming that glycogen stores were virtually exhausted over five hours of running, a total of 1920 ml of water would have been liberated.

Tissue water loss would thus have been the difference between 4 kg and the sum of metabolic weight loss plus metabolic water liberation [5]. The answer to this calculation, 1.86 liters, is a substantial dehydration, although the fluid depletion is less serious and more readily replaced than has been assumed by those who have neglected liberated water.

Site of Fluid Loss

Almost any method of calculating the site of fluid loss is open to objection on the part of the subject or the investigator. Perhaps for this reason, exercise and heat stress have been reported as causing both similar and dissimilar patterns of dehydration.

One of our early approaches to this problem was to relate changes in plasma sodium ion concentrations to the overall degree of dehydration (Table III). Plasma sodium rose more than predicted from the fluid loss; in some instances ingestion of sodium ions could have been a contributing factor, but in other experiments where water was provided, a selective depletion of plasma volume seemed likely.

A second possible noninvasive approach is to look at hemoglobin and hematocrit levels (Table IV). The first pair of formulas are suggested by Costill [1]. They correct for changes of red cell size provided that there is no hemoglobin loss. The third has been used by Beaumont, who has claimed in some of his reports that there is no change of red cell size [8]. Another possibility is to study changes in

T. KAVANAGH AND R. J. SHEPHARD

Table III. Estimates of Fluid Gain or Loss
Over Selected Marathon Events With Corresponding Changes
in Plasma Sodium Ion Concentrations

Year	Fluid Gain or Loss (liter)	Plasma Sodium Ions (mmol/liter)		
		Initial	Final	Δ
Boston 1973 [4, 5]	−1.86	143.8	150.3	+6.5
Hawaii 1973 [3]	+0.87	144.3	144.6	+0.3
Toronto 1974 [2]				
water	+0.19	144.5	146.0	+1.5
Erg	−0.11	145.3	148.3	+3.0
special	−0.16	147.0	149.0	+2.0
Boston 1975 [7]	−0.73	144.3	148.0	+3.7

All patients undergoing rehabilitation following myocardial infarction; at Boston, fluid was mainly Lucozade and in Hawaii Erg was drunk exclusively.

Table IV. Formulas Used in Calculating Changes
of Plasma Volume During Exercise

(1) $PV_1 = 100 - HCt_1$

$PV_2 = 100 \, (Hb_1 / Hb_2) - 100 \, (Hb_1 / Hb_2) \, HCt_2$

$\Delta PV = 100 \, (PV_1 - PV_2) / PV_2$

(2) $\Delta MCV = 100 \, [(MCHC_1) - (MCHC_2)] / MCHC_1$

(3) $\Delta PV = \dfrac{100}{(100 - HCt_1)} \times \dfrac{100 \, (HCt_1 - HCt_2)}{HCt_2}$

(Hematocrits corrected by 0.96 × 0.91 for trapping, etc.)

plasma protein concentrations. By choosing a high molecular weight globulin, exercise-induced exchanges with the tissue fluid should be minimized. In the 1973 Hawaii marathon, we found no changes of mean corpuscular volume (Table V). Thus both the hemoglobin and the simple hematocrit formulas led to similar conclusions. Our three runners enjoyed a cool day, and we persuaded them to drink large quantities of Erg, a sodium- and potassium-containing fluid, to the point that they were urinating en route. The average hyperhydration was 870 ml. According to the hematology data, all of this excess fluid was initially in the plasma, with 22% to 23% expansion of plasma volume at the end of the race, and a 4.5% to 4.7% expansion

Table V. Estimates of Dehydration for December 1973 Hawaii Marathon

Weight loss	1.3 kg	
Sweat production	2890 ml	
Hyperhydration	870 ml	
(If 57 kg lean tissue, and body water = 73% LBM, 2.1% dehydration)		
Plasma volume	(Hb)	
Immediate	+23.0% (622 ml)	
3 hours	+ 4.7% (127 ml)	
	(HCt)	
Immediate	+22.0% (595 ml)	
3 hours	+ 4.5% (122 ml)	
No change of mean corpuscular volume		

three hours later. Saltin (personal communication to R.J.S.) has had a similar experience in athletes whose fluid balance has been well sustained. There are obvious advantages to an expansion of plasma volume during sustained work, although the regulating mechanism (shifts of protein, altered antidiuretic hormone secretion) remains to be explored.

In the 1975 Boston Marathon (Table VI), fluid intake was less favorable, with an estimated dehydration of 730 ml. The high molecular weight protein, IgM, indicated a dehydration of this order. On the other hand, the blood studies again suggested a small increase of plasma volume. Whereas the hematological data supported the traditional view of tissue fluid depletion, both the sodium ion

Table VI. Estimates of Dehydration for 1975 Boston Marathon

Weight loss	2.75 kg	
Sweat production	3520 ml	
Dehydration	730 ml	
(If 57 kg lean tissue, and body water is 73% LBM, ~ 1.8%)		
IgM concentration		+1.8%
Plasma volume (Hb)		+4.6%
Plasma volume (HCt + MCV)		+1.8%
Plasma volume (HCt)		+5.9%

concentrations and the IgM readings apparently indicated that the plasma was at least equally depleted. The sodium readings may have been augmented by drinks taken en route, and there is no guarantee that the use of IgM as a marker obviates the problem of protein shifts during exercise [7]. Possible errors in the hematological approach include the release of sequestrated cells and hemolysis. Our data [7] showed a decrease of serum haptoglobin levels in some subjects, suggesting there was indeed some hemolysis over the course of the race.

The possibility of avoiding all dehydration (Table VII) depends upon the rules of the contest, the environmental conditions and the pace of running. Among our 26 participants, the worst situation was in the 1973 Boston race where sweat production averaged 4570 ml [4, 5]. At Boston, we have found difficulty in administering more than 1 liter of fluid, but with less crowded events we have given 1.8 to 2.0 liters, that is, 500 to 600 ml/hr per subject [3]. Given a water liberation of 1920 ml, the average middle-aged runner should then suffer dehydration of no more than 600 to 700 ml, even on a warm and humid day.

The changes in mineral composition of the plasma seem to proceed almost independently of the fluid provided. In Boston, our group drank what was available at watering stations, often Lucozade. Plasma sodium rose substantially [4, 5, 7], mainly because of the secretion of sweat with a lower sodium ion concentration than the plasma. In Hawaii [3], Erg was used. This provided low concentrations of both sodium and potassium ions. In the scientific marathon in Toronto [2], Erg was compared with water and with a fluid containing 50 mmol/liter of sodium ions. With all three solutions, there was a rise in plasma sodium and potassium. Further, the runners taking water achieved the largest fluid intake. We would thus conclude that there is no good basis for providing mineral ions over the marathon distance.

During the recovery period, one might anticipate a need to replace both fluid and mineral ions. After the 1975 Boston race [7], the first urine samples had a very high potassium content (Table VIII). This cannot reflect secretion of a concentrated urine, since sodium readings were in the low normal range. The vigorous early renal excretion of potassium suggests an attempt at homeostasis as a reaction to muscle leakage and the drinking of potassium-containing fluids while running. Normal blood potassium levels were restored within three hours in the Hawaii marathon [3]. The drop in chloride excretion presumably reflects the excretion of alternate anions such

Table VII. Changes in Plasma Sodium and Potassium Ion Concentrations Over Marathon Distances in Relation to the Fluids Provided en Route [2]

Group	Weight Loss kg	Net Fluid Intake liter	Sweat Loss kg	Sodium Ion Initial mEq/liter	Δ mEq/liter	Potassium Ion Initial mEq/liter	Δ mEq/liter
8 Participants 1973 Boston	4.0 (3.2–4.8)	0.79 (0.08–2.70)	4.57 (3.06–5.68)	143.8 (141–149)	+6.5 (–1 to +12)	4.28 (3.7–4.7)	+0.27 (–0.5 to +1.7)
3 Participants, 1973 Hawaii	1.27 (1.1–1.6)	1.84	2.89 (2.72–3.22)	144.3 (143–145)	+0.3 (–3 to +12)	4.17 (3.9–4.4)	+0.50 (+0.2 to +1.0)
Scientific Marathon 1974							
"Erg" (3 participants)	–2.3 (–2.1 to –2.7)	1.72 (1.39–2.28)	3.53 (2.88–3.95)	147.0 (145–149)	+2.0 (0 to +3)	4.40 (4.2–5.0)	+0.40 (0.1–0.7)
Special solutions (4 participants)	–2.25 (–1.8 to –2.5)	1.25 (0.82–1.73)	3.01 (2.71–3.40)	145.3 (143–149)	+3.0 (1–5)	5.00 (4.4–5.8)	+0.30 (0–0.6)
Water (2 participants)	–1.95 (–1.8 to –2.1)	2.19 (2.07–2.29)	3.43 (3.37–3.49)	144.5 (144–145)	+1.5 (0–3)	4.70 (4.6–4.7)	+0.60 (0.4–0.8)

Table VIII. Urine Compositions Immediately After
the 1975 Boston Marathon [7]

Urine (1975)	Post-Race mEq/liter	Normal mEq/liter
K$^+$	120 + 39	25–125
Na$^+$	75 + 27	50–150
Cl$^-$	73 + 50	150–250
Protein	33 + 33	Nil

Blood (1973)	Pre-Race mEq/liter	Immediate mEq/liter	3hr Post-Race mEq/liter
K$^+$	4.17	4.67	4.20
PO$_4$$^{---}$	4.33	4.53	4.73

as phosphate, liberated by the breakdown of ATP. In Hawaii, blood phosphate levels were still increasing three hours after the contest [3].

Substantial quantities of iron and magnesium were lost in the sweat [7]. Sweat was collected by small pads of iron-free gauze attached to the medial aspect of the arm. This technique largely avoids maceration and iron enrichment of sweat from superficial layers of the epidermis and at the same time avoids evaporation of locally secreted sweat en route. Sweat concentrations were, respectively, 0.46 mg/liter for iron and 7.6 mg/liter for magnesium. The iron figures are of the order encountered in sauna experiments, but the magnesium levels are about four times higher (Stromme — personal communication to R.J.S.). This may reflect regional differences in sweat composition. However, if sustained over the entire body, the loss would amount to 1.8 mg of iron and 30 mg of magnesium. The magnesium represents some 10% of normal dietary intake. The iron is about a sixth of that found in the average diet, although we have found intakes as high as 33 mg/day in one of our distance runners [6].

Unfortunately, if one eats 12 mg of iron, only about 1 mg of dietary iron is absorbed, particularly if a substantial fraction of calorie needs are met from fat. Repeated marathon races could thus lead to a progressive iron depletion.

In our post-coronary group, four of eight subjects had an initial serum iron below the anticipated normal range of 100 to 150 μg/100 ml. Table IX shows data for Hawaii, where we observed a further

Table IX. Serum Iron Levels for Participants in the Hawaii Marathon [3]

	Serum Iron ($\mu g \cdot 100\ ml^{-1}$)		Total Iron-Binding Compounds ($\mu g \cdot 100\ ml^{-1}$)		Percentage Saturation	
	Initial	Final	Initial	Final	Initial	Final
	112	60	400	384	26	17
	74	50	436	400	17	13
	80	77	416	448	19	17
Mean	89	62	417	411	21	16

Kavanagh & Shephard [2]

decrease over the course of the event [3]. After the race, two of the three subjects had a latent deficit, with a saturation of less than 20%, and the third with a saturation of less than 15% was showing what many would regard as a frank iron depletion.

We would conclude that if conditions allow a middle-aged runner access to fluids, serious dehydration is not necessary in a marathon race. However, large volumes of sweat are secreted, and some depletion of iron reserves can occur if such exercise is repeated frequently.

References

1. Costill, D.L. and Fink, W.J.: Plasma volume changes following exercise and thermal dehydration. J. Appl. Physiol. 37:521-525, 1974.
2. Kavanagh, T. and Shephard, R.J.: On the choice of fluid for the hydration of middle-aged marathon runners. In preparation.
3. Kavanagh, T. and Shephard, R.J.: Maintenance of hydration in "post-coronary" marathon runners. Br. J. Sports Med. 9:130-135, 1975.
4. Kavanagh, T. and Shephard, R.J.: Marathon running after myocardial infarction. JAMA 229:1602-1605, 1974.
5. Shephard, R.J. and Kavanagh, T.: Biochemical changes with marathon running. Observations on post-coronary patients. In Howald, H. and Poortmans, J. (eds.): Metabolic Adaptation to Prolonged Physical Exercise. Basel:Kirkhauser Verlag, 1975.
6. Shephard, R.J., Kavanagh, T., Conway, S. et al: Nutritional demands of sub-maximum work: Marathon and TransCanadian event. In Pawluk, J. (ed.): Proceedings of International Conference on Athletic Nutrition. Warsaw: Polish Sports Federation, October 1975.
7. Shephard, R.J., Kavanagh, T. and Moore, R.: Fluid and mineral balance of post-coronary distance runners. Studies on the 1975 Boston marathon. In Venerando, A. (ed.): Proceedings of International Conference on Nutrition, Dietetics, and Sport. Milan:Minerva Med, 1976.
8. Van Beaumont, W.: Red cell volume changes with changes in plasma osmolarity during maximal exercises. J. Appl. Physiol. 35:47-50, 1973.

Caractéristiques des sujets porteurs d'une hypertension artérielle

Nancy-Michelle Robitaille, Andrée Christian,
Gilles R. Dagenais, Paul J. Lupien et Jean Rochon

Introduction

Depuis 1962, plusieurs études épidémiologiques démontrent qu'environ 50% des sujets ayant une tension artérielle égale ou supérieure à 160/95 mm Hg (hypertension artérielle: HTA) ignorent qu'ils ont une telle anomalie [2, 4, 6-8]. De plus, ces études révèlant que la moitié des sujets hypertendus qui connaissent leur état ne sont pas traités, la moitié des hypertendus traités ont une médication insuffisante; donc seul un huitième des hypertendus est sous contrôle thérapeutique adéquat [5].

On a prétendu que le coût des visites médicales, les faibles effectifs médicaux et l'éloignement par rapport aux milieux universitaires spécialisés peuvent être des facteurs responsables de cette situation [3]. Dans la région immédiate de Québec, la population bénéficie de la gratuité des services médicaux, du plus haut rapport médecin/patient au Québec et de la proximité des hôpitaux universitaires. La disponibilité et la gratuité des services médicaux ne semblent pas avoir d'impact sur le dépistage de l'hypertension puisqu'on observe que 48% des hpertendus ne sont pas diagnostiqués.

Le présent rapport fait état de certains facteurs pouvant contribuer à la détection de l'hypertension dans la région de Québec. Nous avons comparé deux sous-groupes d'hypertendus: des sujets hypertendus détectés lors d'un dépistage (group A — inconnu) et des sujets sachant qu'ils ont une hypertension (groupe B — connu). Les facteurs considérés ne constituent qu'une partie de notre analyse et sont l'âge, le degré de scolarité, la valeur des chiffres tensionnels, la symptomatologie et les complications de l'hypertension.

Nancy-Michelle Robitaille, Andrée Christian, Gilles R. Dagenais, Paul J. Lupien et Jean Rochon, Institut de cardiologie de Québec, Département de médecine sociale et préventive, Université Laval et Centre de recherche des maladies lipidiques, CHUL, Québec, Canada.

Sujets et Méthode

Dans le cadre du Projet Joseph C. Edwards, nous avons procédé à l'échantillonnage, au hasard, de la population mâle, canadienne française, âgée de 35 à 64 ans, habitant 7 villes de la banlieue de Québec.

L'échantillon original (tableau I) comprend 9007 noms d'hommes, obtenus au hasard à partir des listes électorales. Les enquêteuses ont réussi à contacter 7108 sujets et 4667 ont accepté de participer au projet. Ceci représente une participation de 66%. Cent quatre-vingt-dix-neuf concitoyens se sont portés volontaires. Comme ils étaient comparables à l'échantillon original pour l'âge et la présence de facteurs de risque, ils sont inclus dans la population totale des participants. Donc, 4866 hommes se sont présentés aux cliniques de dépistage.

Des infirmières procédaient à un bref questionnaire sur la consommation de cigarettes, deux mesures de tension artérielle au repos, à 5 minutes d'intervalle et un prélèvement sanguin pour mesure du cholestérol. Les infirmières avaient reçu une formation spéciale en techniques d'interview et mesure de la tension artérielle. La fidélité de leur lecture de tension a été vérifiée par comparaison avec celle de médecins et des mesures intra-artérielles en salle de cathétérisme.

Chez 2090 sujets, les seuls facteurs de risque identifiés sont l'âge et le sexe. Ils constituent le group à bas risque ou contrôle. Par ailleurs, 2776 sujets étaient, en plus, porteurs d'un ou de plusieurs facteurs de risque dits modifiables. Ils forment la population à haut

Tableau I. Population dépistée
(hommes, 35 à 64 ans, Québec)

Echantillon au hasard (listes électorales)		9007	
Perdus (erreur de listing, absents, etc.)	1899		
Identifiés		7108	100%
Refus	2441	. . . .	34%
Participants	4667	4667	66%
Volontaires		199	
Population dépistée		4866	
Groupe contrôle (à bas risque)	2090		
Groupe à haut risque (un ou plusieurs facteurs)		2776	
— cigarettes > 20/jour	1905	(39.2%)	
— cholestérol ≥ 240 mg/100 ml	490	(10.1%)	
— tension artérielle ≥ 160/95 mm Hg	1040	(21.4%)	

risque: 1905 hommes fument plus de 20 cigarettes par jour, 490 ont
un cholestérol égal ou supérieur à 240 mg/100 ml et chez 1040
sujets, la moyenne de deux tensions artérielles est égale ou supérieure
à 160/95.

Des 1040 sujets hypertendus en dépistage, 790 ont accepté de se
rendre à l'étape suivant (tableau II). On procédait à un examen
d'urines, glycémie, azotémie, bilan lipidique à jeun et un électrocardiogramme. Des médecins-résidents effectuaient une histoire clinique et un examen physique consignés sur un questionnaire stand-
ardisé, analysé par ordinateur.

Au cours de cet examen, on effectuait deux mesures de tension
artérielle au repos et à 5 minutes d'intervalle. Nous avons établi
arbitrairement que la moyenne de ces deux lectures doit être égale ou
supérieure à 160/95 pour qu'un individu soit classifié hypertendu.
Chez 301 sujets, les chiffres de tension sont inférieurs. Les 489 sujets
confirmés hypertendus ont été divisés en 2 groupes selon que leur
hypertension est découverte lors du dépistage ou qu'ils sont des
hypertendus connus.

Donc, on diagnostique une hypertension, pour la première fois,
chez les 235 sujets du group A. Les 254 individus du groupe B se
savent hypertendus, mais leur hypertension n'est pas contrôlée
médicalement. Nous avons comparé les caractéristiques cliniques de
ces 2 groupes.

Résultats

Caractères généraux (tableau III)

Les groupes A et B sont formés d'hommes du même âge ayant le
même degré de scolarité. Peu de sujets ont été hospitalisés au cours
de l'année précédant le dépistage. Les taux de prévalence du

**Tableau II. Hypertension artérielle (TA ⩾ 160/95 mm Hg)
(1040 hommes, 35 à 64 ans, Québec)**

TA ⩾ 160/95 mm Hg, lectures des infirmières	1040
Refusant l'examen médical 250	
Examen médical	790
– TA < 160/95 mm Hg: lectures des médecins . 301	
– hypertendus connus, traités,	
contrôlés 77	
– sans traitement 224	
– TA ⩾ 160/95 mm Hg	489 . . . . . 100%
– Groupe A: inconnu, non traité	235 . . . . . 48%
– Groupe B: connu, non contrôlé	254 . . . . . 52%

Tableau III. Prévalence des caractéristiques cliniques
(489 hommes, 35 à 64 ans, TA ≥ 160/95 mm Hg, Québec)

	Groupe A (235 sujets)	Groupe B (254 sujets)	p chi-square
Age			
− 35 à 44 ans	70	60	N.S.
− 45 à 54 ans	89	97	N.S.
− 55 à 64 ans	76	97	N.S.
âge moyen (ans)	50.36 ± 7.92	50.62 ± 8.18	N.S.
Degré de scolarité	9.23 ± 5.0	9.46 ± 4.74	N.S.
Hospitalisation antérieure	12	20	N.S.
Facteurs de risque associés			
− cigarettes ≥ 20/jour	74	82	N.S.
− cholestérol ≥ 240 mg/100 ml	74	78	N.S.
Anomalies au bilan lipidique	147	157	N.S.
− cholestérol ≥ 240/100 ml, ou			
− triglycérides ≥ 160 mg/100 ml			
Obésité	62	67	N.S.
Vision trouble	21	40	N.S.
Tinnitus	18	40	*
Cephalées	32	64	*
Syncope	2	16	**
Vertige	26	52	*
Un ou plusieurs symptomes	66	124	**
Angine	14	28	N.S.
Infarctus	9	11	N.S.
Accident cérébro-vasculaire	5	11	N.S.
Claudication intermittente	5	12	N.S.
Electrocardiogramme anormal	88	129	*
− HVG	20	43	*

N.S. non significatif   *p < .01   **p < .001

tabagisme (> 20 cigarettes par jour) et d'hypercholestérolémie (> 240 mg/100 ml) sont légèrement supérieurs à 30%, dans les groupes A et B. Dans les 2 groupes, 62% des sujets ont une anomalie au bilan lipidique, c'est-à-dire soit un cholestérol ≥ 240 mg/100 ml, soit des triglycérides ≥ 160 mg/100 ml, soit les deux. L'indice pondéral est calculé à partir des tables de la Compagnie d'Assurance Métropolitaine. Le poids idéal est le point milieu, pour ossature moyenne selon la taille. Nous avons défini arbitrairement l'obésité comme un poids observé excédant de 30% ou plus le poids idéal. L'obésité ainsi définie se retrouve chez 26% des sujets des deux groupes.

Tension artérielle

La figure 1 illustre les polygones de fréquence des tensions artérielles diastoliques (à gauche) et systolique (à droite). Le groupe A est en ligne pleine et le groupe B en ligne pointillée. Ces polygones sont superposables et les moyennes sont comparables:
diastolique moyenne:
    A: 99.9 mm Hg ± SEM: 7.73
    B: 101.8 mm Hg ± SEM: 10.72
systolique moyenne:
    A: 159.2 mm Hg ± 16.11
    B: 170.1 mm Hg ± 21.5

Symptômes généraux (tableau III)

La vision trouble, le tinnitus, les céphalées, la syncope et les vertiges sont des symptômes généraux qu'on a longtemps associés à l'hypertension. Dernièrement, leur haute prévalence dans des populations dites saines, a jeté le discrédit sur leur rôle d'indicateur d'hypertension [1]. Cependant, dans notre étude, les sujets connus du groupe B présentent plus fréquemment ces symptômes et la différence est statistiquement significative pour chaque symptôme pris isolément à l'exception de la vision trouble.

Complications de l'hypertension (tableau III)

Une hypertension qui évolue assez longtemps s'accompagne souvent de complications cardiaques, cérébrales, vasculaires ou

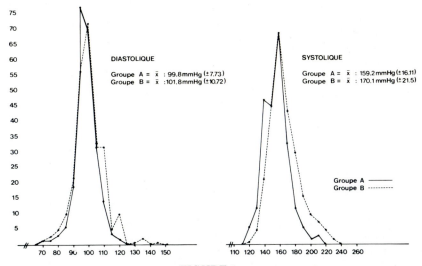

FIGURE 1.

rénales. Ces complications se manifestent par une angine de poitrine, un infarctus, une insuffisance cardiaque, un accident cérébro-vasculaire ou une claudication intermittente. Nous avons retrouvé un nombre comparable de ces complications chez les 2 groupes d'hypertendus. Quant à l'atteinte rénale, nous avons identifié un sujet du groupe B présentant une azotémie élevée.

L'examen médical comprenait une funduscopie. Cet examen est sujet à de grandes variations d'interprétation entre observateur et, par conséquent, ne peut faire l'objet de comparaison entre les 2 groupes.

Enfin, tous les sujets ont eu un électrocardiogramme au repos et tous les tracés ont été interprétés par le même observateur. Les anomalies électrocardiographiques sont plus fréquentes dans le groupe B. La différence est non significative pour l'arythmie (4 dans le groupe A, 11 dans le groupe B), les troubles de conduction (14 et 13 respectivement), l'hypertrophie ventriculaire droite (respectivement 8 et 7), les anomalies de la repolarisation (31 et 37 cas) et les infarctus anciens (7 et 14 cas). Par ailleurs, l'hypertrophie ventriculaire gauche définie par critère de voltage avec ou sans anomalie du segment ST est significativement plus fréquente dans le groupe B (43 cas) que dans le groupe A (20 cas).

Discussion et conclusion

La différence dans la détection de l'hypertension ne s'explique donc pas par des facteurs tels que l'âge, le degré de scolarité, les hospitalisations antérieures, la présence de facteurs de risque associés, l'obésité, les valeurs de tension artérielle ou les complications de l'hypertension. Cependant, chez les hypertendus connus, on retrouve une prévalence significativement plus élevée d'anomalies électro-cardiographiques et de symptômes généraux.

Il est possible que ces symptômes aient amené les sujets à consulter et ainsi favorisé la détection de l'hypertension. Mais, il est aussi possible que les hypertendus connus du groupe B soient plus symptomatiques parce qu'ils se savent hypertendus et portent plus d'attention à tous ces symptômes que leur médecin recherche à chaque visite. L'étude actuelle ne nous permet pas de dire définitivement si les individus du groupe B sont connus parce que sympto-matiques ou symptomatiques parce que connus.

D'autres données, incluant les examens médicaux pré-assurance sont actuellement soumis pour analyse. Enfin, une fois de plus, cette étude met en évidence que 48% des hypertendus ne sont pas détectés et que 60% d'entre eux ont en plus un autre facteur de risque de la maladie coronarienne.

Références

1. Bulitt, C.J., Dollery, C.T. and Carne, S.: Br. Heart J. 38:121, 1976.
2. Report of Inter-Society Commission for Heart Disease Resources: Guidelines for the detection, diagnosis, and management of hypertensive populations. Circulation 44:A263, 1971. (Revised August 1972.)
3. Sheps, S.G. and Kirkpatrick, R.A.: Hypertension. Mayo Clin. Proc. 50:709, 1975.
4. Silverberg, D.S., Smith, S.O., Juchli, B. and Van Dorsser, E.: Use of shopping centers in screening for hypertension. CMA Journal, 111:769, 1974.
5. Stamler, J., Stamler, R. Schoenberger, J.A. and Shekelle, R.B.: The problem and the challenge. *In* The Hypertension Handbook. Merck, Sharp and Dohme, 1974, p. 21.
6. U.S. Department of Health, Education and Welfare United States, 1960-62. National Center for Health Statistics Series 11, number 13, 1969.
7. Wilber, J.A.: Detection and control of hypertensive disease in Georgia, U.S.A. *In* Stamler, J., Stamler, R. and Pullman, T.N. (eds.): The Epidemiology of Hypertension. New York:Grune and Stratton, 1967, p. 439.
8. Wilber, J.A. and Barrow, J.G.: Reducing elevated blood pressure — experience found in a community. Minnesota Med. 52:1303, 1969.

Hemodynamic Response to Graded Exercise of Hypertensive Patients Following Chronic Beta Adrenergic Blockade

Tony Reybrouck, Antoon Amery, Leon Billiet
and Robert Fagard

Introduction

Previous studies in man have shown that maximal aerobic capacity is maintained [5, 6] or decreased [7, 14] following beta adrenergic blockade (BB). Since these studies were acute experiments, using BB agents lacking cardioselectivity, the purpose of the present experiments was to investigate the influence of chronic BB on the maximal exercise capacity, using BB agents with preferential action on cardiac beta receptors.

Subjects and Methods

A group of 31 subjects (14 males and 17 females) with high blood pressure was selected. The mean values for age were 36.3 ± 3.30 years for male and 46 ± 2.94 for female subjects. All subjects were admitted to the hospital and had not taken anti-hypertensive drugs for at least three weeks. Right heart and brachial artery catheterization was performed. Brachial and pulmonary artery pressures ($\bar{P}_p$) were measured by electronic pressure-transducers. Cardiac output ($\dot{Q}$) was determined by the direct Fick method for O_2. In arterial and mixed venous blood oxygen content was calculated from the product of oxygen saturation (reflection oxymetry), hemoglobin concentration (cyanmethemoglobin method) and the combining factor 1.34. Oxygen uptake and CO_2 output were measured by the open-circuit method with electronic gas analyzers. Measurements of hemodynamic and respiratory variables were made

Tony Reybrouck, Antoon Amery, Leon Billiet and Robert Fagard, Hypertension and Cardiovascular Rehabilitation Unit, University of Leuven, Leuven, Belgium

at rest in the supine (RR) and sitting position (RS) on the bicycle ergometer (Elema Schönander). The subjects performed an uninterrupted graded exercise test starting at 20 w; the workload was increased every four minutes by 30 w until exhaustion [5]. Cardiac output ($\dot{Q}$) and derived variables were converted to index values by expressing it per square meter of body surface. BB was performed with a newly available compound, Atenolol* [5], which was shown to be cardioselective and devoid of membrane stabilizing, sympathomimetic or quinidine-like properties in animal experiments [3]. Subject received subsequently placebo tablets and active treatment. The active drug was increased in a stepwise fashion at weekly intervals from 75 to 150, 300 and 600 mg daily.

Results

At Rest and During Submaximal Exercise

During BB a strong negative chronotropic effect decreased the heart rate (HR) at rest and during submaximal exercise by 30% on average (Fig. 1A). This negative chronotropic effect was partly compensated by an increase in stroke index (SI) varying from 15% at rest to 24% to 29% during submaximal exercise (Fig. 1B). Despite this compensatory increase in SI, BB induced a significant reduction in cardiac index (CI) varying from 24% at rest to 12% and 16% during submaximal exercise (Fig. 1C). To compensate for this decline in CI, the (a-v)O_2 difference was further increased by 10% on average (Fig. 1D). Finally, these rearrangements resulted in a small ($\pm$ 15%) but significant decrease in $\dot{V}O_2$ at rest from 152 $\pm$ 41.7 before versus 128 $\pm$ 46.8 ml/min/m^2 during BB. During mild exercise $\dot{V}O_2$ was slightly (6%) decreased during BB, but at heavier workloads the mechanical efficiency remained unchanged before and during BB.

At rest and during exercise beta blockade significantly reduced the pressures in the brachial artery, varying respectively from 12% to 22% for the systolic, 17% for the diastolic and 16% for the mean pressure (Fig. 1E). The calculated total peripheral resistance index (TPRI) was not changed on average by beta blockade.

The $\bar{P}_p$ tended to increase during beta adrenergic blockade (Fig. 1F); this was compensated at rest by an increase in pulmonary capillary wedge pressure ($\bar{P}_c$) from 6.2 $\pm$ 0.76 to 8.2 $\pm$ 1.30 (0.05 < p < 0.10), while the pulmonary vascular resistance index

---

*4-(2-hydroxy-3-isopropylamino-proxy) phenyl acetemide (ICI 66,082 or Tenormin®), generously supplied by ICI Pharmaceuticals Division, England.

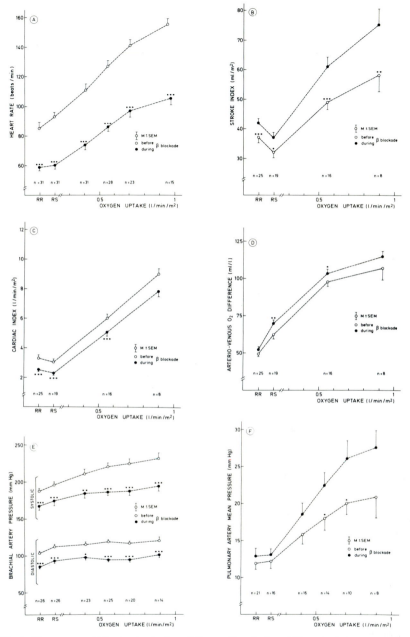

FIG. 1. Heart rate (A), stroke index (B), cardiac index (C), arteriovenous oxygen difference (D), brachial artery pressure (E) and pulmonary artery pressure (F) at rest and during graded exercise before and during beta adrenergic blockade. As the number of paired comparisons declined with increasing intensity of exercise, the points representing submaximal exercise data are connected by hatched lines. (* = p < 0.05; ** = p < 0.01; *** = p < 0.001.)

remained unchanged (3.10 ± 0.73 units before and 3.61 ± 0.71 during BB, $p > 0.25$). No significant changes were observed for right atrial mean pressure and right ventricular end diastolic pressures at rest recumbent, before and during BB.

At Maximal Exercise

For an analysis of the effect of beta adrenergic blockade at maximal exercise, hemodynamic parameters were compared before and during beta blockade at the highest load which could be maintained during four minutes (Table I). No significant changes were found for maximal working capacity and $\dot{V}O_2$ at maximal exercise. The maximal exercise HR was inhibited by 34% on average; this was compensated by a 31% increase in SI and resulted finally in a 14% decrease in maximal CI which was further compensated by an 8% increase in (a-v)O_2. For brachial artery pressure and TPRI at maximal exercise the same changes were observed as during submaximal work. No changes were found for maximal arterial lactate concentration, nor for the respiratory gas exchange ratio (RQ).

Table I. Hemodynamic Variables at Maximal Exercise (mean ± S.E.M.)

	Before Beta Blockade	*During Beta Blockade*	*No.*	*p Value*
External workload (watt)	107 ± 8.70	106 ± 8.20	29	>0.25
Oxygen uptake (ml/min/m²)	941 ± 54.3	893 ± 52.8	30	0.05-0.10
Heart rate (beats/min)	167 ± 4.10	110 ± 3.20	29	<0.001
Stroke index (ml/systole/m²)	52.3 ± 3.88	68.7 ± 6.52	11	<0.005
Cardiac index (l/min/m²)	8.7 ± 0.77	7.50 ± 0.74	11	0.01-0.02
Arteriovenous O_2 difference (ml/l)	114 ± 4.70	123 ± 4.20	11	0.05-0.10
Brachial artery mean pressure (mm Hg)	172 ± 4.76	147 ± 4.87	26	<0.001
Total peripheral resistance index (units/m²)	20.25 ± 1.57	20.27 ± 1.99	11	>0.25
Pulmonary artery mean pressure (mm Hg)	23.1 ± 2.10	27.7 ± 2.46	11	0.10-0.20
Respiratory gas exchange ratio	1.04 ± 0.02	1.03 ± 0.02	29	0.05-0.10
Arterial lactate (mg%) highest value	71.7 ± 4.36	71.9 ± 4.15	17	>0.25

Discussion

Although an increased sympathetic adrenergic activity is found during exercise [11] cardiac BB did not prevent the increase in HR, stroke volume (SV) and Q during graded exercise. However, controversy exists whether maximal aerobic capacity is maintained [5, 6] or decreased [7, 14] during acute BB. Following chronic BB no change occurred in $\dot{V}O_2$ at maximal exercise in our experiments.

It has to be stressed, however, that no plateau in $\dot{V}O_2$ was reached in the present exercise testing procedure using an uninterrupted graded exercise test. Values for maximal HR, RQ and arterial lactate were similar to the normal criteria for attainment of $\dot{V}O_2$ max as described by Issekutz et al [10]; but the maximal (a-v)O_2 of 114 ml/l in the present series was somewhat lower than values of 135 ml/l reported by McDonough et al [13] for normal untrained subjects at maximal exercise, where several of them reached a plateau in $\dot{V}O_2$. It appears that our subjects exercised at close to their maximal effort.

With regard to the degree of BB, difference exists in the findings in acute and chronic experiments. When the degree of BB was estimated by the percentage inhibition of maximal HR, it averaged 34% in the present series against 13.3% to 23% in different acute experiments [5-7, 14] where $\dot{V}O_2$ max was maintained [5, 6] or decreased [7, 14]. Therefore, the unchanged maximal exercise capacity as found in the present experiments cannot result from a lesser degree of BB compared to the other studies [5-7, 14].

Differences in the effect of BB on $\dot{V}O_2$ max result from different patterns of SV response to the decrease in HR during acute and chronic experiments. At rest and exercise, following the inhibition of HR with acute cardioselective or nonselective BB agents, the SV may remain unchanged [2, 5-7, 15] or even decrease [2, 16]. With chronic cardioselective or nonselective BB agents on the other hand, SV increases significantly [12]. In our series SV increases significantly following chronic BB which is consistent with the observations of Lund-Johansen [12]. The enhancement of the SV following BB appears to be a hemodynamic adaption to chronic BB.

From these data the mechanism of adjustment of the SV during BB can be assessed. Since SV is dependent upon (a) preload, (b) impedance and (c) contractility of the myocardium [4], the contribution of each of these factors can be discussed. When changes in impedance are estimated from changes in blood pressure, a pronounced reduction in impedance occurred in our series following

BB, which could favor the enhancement in SV. In addition, the rise in pulmonary artery and pulmonary capillary wedge pressure could lead to an increased preload with increased SV. Other investigators have noted an increased end-diastolic volume of the left ventricle during BB [9, 17]. As the positive inotropic stimulation to the heart was antagonized during BB, this factor did not contribute to the enhancement in SV during BB. In acute studies, in contrast, no change occurred in SV although BB produced a significant negative chronotropic effect [1, 2, 5, 7, 8, 15] and an increase in preload [2, 7, 15]. However, blood pressure decreased only to a minor extent in acute experiments [1, 2, 5, 7, 8, 15] compared to the clear hypotensive action shown during chronic BB. Therefore, both the decrease in impedance and the increase in preload played a major role in the enhancement of SV following chronic BB. Nevertheless the strong compensatory action of the SV during BB was not enough to restore the Q to its initial value; therefore, the peripheral oxygen extraction compensated further to maintain oxygen delivery to the tissues during exercise.

In conclusion following chronic BB, adequate hemodynamic readjustments occurred which maintained maximal physical working capacity. A critical factor was the enhancement in SV to the decrease in HR, which appeared to be a hemodynamic adaption to chronic BB.

Summary

In 31 patients with high blood pressure, the hemodynamic response to exercise was studied during a control period and repeated after one month of beta adrenergic blockade (BB). Similar readjustments were observed at rest and during submaximum and maximum exercise. No significant change occurred in maximal physical working capacity during BB. Maximal exercise heart rate was reduced by 34%, and this was compensated for by a 31% enhancement in stroke index. Consequently, cardiac index decreased by only 14%. In the Fick equation the decrease in cardiac index was further compensated by an increase of the total (a-v)O_2 difference of 8%, thereby maintaining O_2 delivery to the tissues. At maximal exercise brachial artery mean pressure dropped 14.5%, while pulmonary artery mean pressure increased by 20%. It is concluded that the compensatory action of the stroke volume, resulting from the interaction of an increased preload and decreased impedance, played a major role in the hemodynamic readjustments following chronic BB to maintain maximal working capacity.

Acknowledgments

This study was supported by a grant of the Belgian Research Council. We gratefully acknowledge the helpful advice and comments of J. Conway, M.D., Ph.D. and Prof. J. A. Faulkner, Ph.D. (Dept. of Physiology, University of Michigan).

References

1. Aström, H.: Hemodynamic effects of beta-adrenergic blockade. Br. Heart J. 30:44-49, 1968.
2. Aström, H. and Vallin, H.: Effects of a new beta-adrenergic blocking agent ICI 66,082, on exercise hemodynamics and airway resistance in angina pectoris. Br. Heart J. 36:1194-1200, 1974.
3. Barrett, A.M., Carter, J., Fitzgerald, J.D. et al: A new type of cardioselective adrenotropic blocking drug. Br. J. Pharmacol. Chemotherap. 48:340, 1973.
4. Braunwald, E.: On the difference between the heart's output and its contractile state. Circulation 27:416-432, 1971 (editorial).
5. Conway, J., Wheeler, R. and Sannerstedt, R.: Sympathetic nervous activity during exercise in relation to age. Cardiovasc. Res. 5:577-581, 1971.
6. Ekblom, B., Goldbarg, A.N., Kiblom, A. and Astrand, P.O.: Effects of atropine and propranolol on the oxygen transport system during exercise in man. Scand. J. Clin. Lab. Invest. 30:35-42, 1972.
7. Epstein, S.E., Robinson, B.F., Kahler, R.L. and Braunwald, E.: Effects of beta adrenergic blockade on the cardiac response to maximal and submaximal exercise in man. J. Clin. Invest. 44:1745-1753, 1965.
8. Hansson, L., Zweifler, A.J., Julius, S. and Hunyor, S.N.: Hemodynamic effects of acute and prolonged β-adrenergic blockade in essential hypertension. Acta Med. Scand. 196:27-34, 1974.
9. Horwitz, L.D., Atkins, J.M. and Leshin, S.J.: Effects of beta adrenergic blockade on left ventricular function in exercise. Am. J. Physiol. 227:839-842, 1974.
10. Issekutz, B., Birkhead, N.C. and Rodahl, K.: Use of respiratory quotients in assessment of aerobic work capacity. J. Appl. Physiol. 17:47-50, 1962.
11. Kötchen, T.A., Hartley, L.H., Rice, T.W. et al: Renin, norepinephrine and epinephrine responses to graded exercise. J. Appl. Physiol. 31:178-184, 1971.
12. Lund-Johansen, P.: Hemodynamic long-term effects of a new beta-blocker (ICI 66,082) in essential hypertension. Br. Clin. Pharmacol. (In press.)
13. McDonough, J.R., Danielson, R.A., Wills, R.E. and Vine, D.L.: Maximal cardiac output during exercise in patients with coronary artery disease. Am. J. Cardiol. 33:23-29, 1974.
14. Pirnay, F., Delvaux, J.M., Deroanne, R. et al: Effect of beta adrenergic blockade in the circulatory response during muscular work. Int. Z. Angew. Physiol. 29:88-93, 1970.
15. Stenberg, J., Wasir, H., Amery, A. et al: Comparative hemodynamic studies in man of adrenergic $_I$ receptor blocking agents without (H93/26 = metoprolol) or with (H 87/07) intrinsic sympathomimetic activity. Acta Pharmacol. Toxicol. 36 (suppl. 5):76-84, 1975.

16. Ulrych, M., Frolich, E.D., Dustan, H.P. and Page, I.H.: Immediate hemodynamic effects of beta-adrenergic blockade with propranolol in normotensive and hypertensive man. Circulation 37:412-416, 1968.
17. Vatner, S.F., Franklin, D., Higgings, C.B. et al: Left ventricular response to severe exertion in untethered dogs. J. Clin. Invest. 51:3052-3060, 1972.

Effects of Heavy Resistance Weight Training on Arterial Blood Pressure and Other Selected Measures in Normotensive and Borderline Hypertensive College Men

T. R. Baechle

Introduction

The primary purpose of this study was to determine the effects of a ten-week heavy resistance weight training program on the systolic (SP) and diastolic (DP) blood pressures of normotensive and borderline hypertensive college-age men. The study further attempted to identify whether the heavy resistance weight training program would affect the blood pressure of normotensives differently than borderline hypertensives. In addition to these primary concerns was a secondary concern which related to the effect of the training program on other selected measures, these being pulse pressure (PP), mean blood pressure (MP) and heart rate (HR).

Subjects

During the first week of the spring semester 1976, two groups of students currently enrolled at the University of South Dakota, Vermillion campus, were involved in this study. One of the groups was designated experimental and was drawn from a potential population of 62 students who were members of the 1975 University of South Dakota football team. The other was designated the control group and was drawn from a potential population of 42 male students who had enrolled in any one of four sections of PE 200, "Beginning Golf" classes offered at the University of South Dakota during the spring semester. The selection of experimental subjects

T. R. Baechle, University of South Dakota, Vermillion, S.D., U.S.A.
This research was conducted under the direction of Dr. Fred Petersen in partial fulfillment of the Doctor of Education Degree.

was delimited to those persons who had not followed a regular program of exercise during the two-month period following the 1975 football season. The selection was also limited to those who had not participated in any form of weight training during or after the football season which preceded this study.

The control group included subjects who had not been following a regular program of exercise preceding this investigation and had not been weight training during the study or for a five-month period prior to the study. All control and experimental subjects were Caucasian and were not younger than 18 nor older than 26 years of age.

Procedures

After subjects were seated, the left arm was measured to determine the suitability of using the 12 to 14 cm Tycos Pre Calibrated Blood Pressure Cuff before measurements began. After being snugly positioned, the cuff was inflated while the brachial artery was palpated. Inflation continued until the disappearance of the pulse occurred. This occurrence marked the SP (by palpation) and was recorded. The cuff was inflated an additional 10 mm Hg and the auscultatory method of measurement was employed with the stethoscope placed directly over the brachial artery at the antecubital depression. The cuff was deflated at a rate of approximately 2 to 3 mm Hg per second and the SP was recorded as the first appearance of faint, clear tapping sounds, while the DP was recorded as the disappearance of sound.

After the cuff was removed, the HR was determined by palpation of the radial artery at the wrist for a 30-second period. All measurements were taken at the University of South Dakota Medical School under ideal conditions by a qualified and well-experienced exercise physiologist who was also a registered nurse. Furthermore, all readings were taken after subjects had been seated for 15 minutes and were repeated again 15 minutes later during both the pre- and posttest sessions. Eating, smoking and/or muscular movement were not permitted during measurement sessions and subjects were requested to refrain from these activities (except walking) for a two-hour period prior to being tested.

The initial statistical procedures employed in this study involved averaging SP, DP and HR during the pretest. The number recorded as the SP for each subject was the average of two auscultatory and two palpatory readings. The DP recorded for each subject was the average of two auscultatory readings.

In this study the use of 141 as the SP and 85 mm Hg as the DP served as discriminative points. Subjects with average blood pressures of 100/60 to 140/84 mm Hg were considered as normotensive while those with blood pressures of 141/84 to 159/94 mm Hg were considered borderline hypertensive.

Emanating out of this classification procedure came four groups which at the time of posttesting totaled 28 subjects in the normotensive and 14 in the borderline hypertensive experimental groups (EN and EB, respectively), 14 in the normotensive and 7 in the borderline hypertensive control groups (CN and CB, respectively). The HR recorded were the result of two readings taken 15 minutes apart which were averaged. PP were determined by subtracting the average SP from the average DP (pulse pressure = systolic – diastolic). The MP was recorded as the sum of the average SP plus two (average) DP, divided by the number three (mean blood pressure = systolic + 2 diastolic/3).

Nature of the Treatment

The experimental groups (EN and EB) engaged in a ten-week, three-day-a-week program of heavy resistance weight training which included nine different exercises: supine bench press, supine lying lateral raise, parallel squat, quarter squat, two-arm bicep curl, two-arm tricep curl, bent over rowing, standing military press and two raise. As the men gained in strength, as reflected by their ability to perform more than five repetitions in an exercise, an additional five pounds was assigned. All exercises were performed for two or three sets and were completed usually within a 1½ hour time period.

During the same ten-week period the control group began participating in the nonvigorous activities normally included in a beginning golf class. Beginning golf classes were selected because the amount of physical activity involved in them was negligible in comparison to the jogging, fencing, gymnastics, wrestling and aquatic classes which were offered at the University at the time of the study. It was important that a minimal amount of vigorous physical activity be a characteristic of exercise class selected because studies have shown that those activities of a more vigorous nature tend to alter posttraining blood pressure levels. Other than that already stated, no special treatment was given to either experimental or control normotensive or borderline hypertensive groups.

After ten weeks all members of both experimental and control groups involved in the study had SP, DP, PP, MP and HR determined again in the previously described manner to ascertain if any changes had occurred since the initial measurement session.

Summary of Findings

Changes in Normotensives After Weight Training (Table I)

All measures under investigation showed a decline in the EN after weight training; however, the within group analysis using the pair-wise t-test disclosed that only the HR was significantly lowered (p <.01). The between group analysis (EN and CN) involving the Student t-test found none of the measures to be significantly lowered, including HR.

The report by Steinhaus is germane to these findings. In discussing the findings of various blood pressure studies, Steinhaus suggested that investigations not yielding significant reductions involved comparatively mild training over short periods of time, whereas significant reductions were observed in more strenuous programs [5].

It is unlikely that the weight training program included in the study was not strenuous, but it is possible that the length of training was too short. Although not really a bona fide part of this study, observations nonetheless were made simultaneously of a two-day-a-week weight training class of normotensives. These men were following a program of exercises similar to that in this study except

Table I.

| | Experimental Normotensives | | | | | |
| | Pretest | | Posttest | | Mean | |
Description	$\overline{X}$	SD	$\overline{X}$	SD	Differences	t-Value
Systolic (mm Hg)	123.39	7.16	121.50	5.48	1.88	1.51
Diastolic (mm Hg)	77.75	3.37	76.39	4.72	1.36	1.58
Pulse pressure (mm Hg)	45.68	7.19	44.68	5.09	1.00	.77
Mean blood pressure (mm Hg)	92.57	3.67	90.25	5.01	2.32	1.83
Heart rate (bpm)	71.68	7.05	68.32	6.27	3.35	2.84*

Note: A t-value of 2.160 was required for significance at the .05 level of confidence.
*Significant at the .01 level of confidence. N = 28

the amount of weight handled during exercises was comparatively light. A comparison of pre- and posttest results revealed that no noticeable increase or decrease in blood pressures had occurred after ten weeks in the weight training class. So while the EN group may not have had statistically significant reductions in SP and DP, there were reductions. And these reductions seemed to have occurred in response to a more strenuous program which would tend to support Steinhaus' thinking relative to intensity and duration of exercise and blood pressure reductions.

Changes in Borderline Hypertensives After Training (Table II)

The pair-wise t-test analysis of pre- and posttest changes in EB revealed significant reductions in SP (p <.01), DP (p <.05), MP (p <.01) and HR (p <.01). The Student t-test between EB and CB, however, revealed otherwise. These blood pressure results are somewhat similar to those found in the study by Boyer and Kasch [1]. Their investigation involved 23 essential hypertensives and the same number of normotensives. After a six-month walking, jogging and calisthenic program, they reported significantly lower SP and DP in the hypertensive group. They also reported significant reductions in DP, but not in SP within the normotensive group.

Studies by Damato, discussed by Johnson and Grover [4], and Hanson and Nedde [3] involving basically endurance exercises have also reported reductions of blood pressure in hypertensive subjects.

Table II.

Description	Pretest $\bar{X}$	SD	Posttest $\bar{X}$	SD	Mean Differences	t-Value
Systolic (mm Hg)	142.07	8.27	133.50	10.79	8.57	3.61†
Diastolic (mm Hg)	85.21	4.98	81.50	4.26	3.71	2.62*
Pulse pressure (mm Hg)	56.86	11.99	53.21	9.07	3.64	1.21
Mean blood pressure (mm Hg)	104.36	2.70	98.36	4.94	6.00	4.50†
Heart rate (bpm)	75.71	12.46	69.79	13.19	5.93	4.91†

Note: A t-value of 2.160 was required for significance at the .05 level.
*Significant at the .05 level of confidence.
†Significant at the .01 level of confidence. N = 14

In the latter study the investigators reported that after a six-month program of isotonic and isometric strengthening exercises and other forms of conditioning, blood pressures in labile and prehypertensives were reduced from 150/86 to 134/75 mm Hg.

Differences Found Between EN and EB After Weight Training Compared to CN and CB Differences (Table III)

The pre- and posttest differences found for all measures between EN and EB were compared by a two-way analysis of covariance to those found between CN and CB. This analysis revealed that the differences found between EN and EB groups as a result of weight training were not significant. It should be mentioned that even though the differences found between the experimental normotensive and borderline hypertensive groups were not significant, they did exist, and that the EB group had greater reductions in all measures under investigation when compared to the EN group. The findings of this study somewhat parallel the nature but not extent of those by Choquette and Ferguson [2]. While reporting that SP and DP were lowered significantly after endurance training in both normotensives and borderlines, they also reported that the greatest decreases were found in the latter group.

It should be noted that Choquette and Ferguson did not involve a control group, whereas this study did. The difference in experimental designs is important to mention because inclusion of the control in this study brought about some unanticipated results. The

Table III.

	Mean Differences EN − EBL	Differences	Mean Differences CN − CBL	Differences	Mean Square	F-Value
Systolic (mm Hg)	1.88 − 8.57	6.69	2.36 − 6.29	3.93	.074	.002
Diastolic (mm Hg)	1.36 − 3.71	2.35	2.71 − 3.71	1.00	36.990	1.889
Pulse pressure (mm Hg)	1.00 − 3.64	2.64	+1.50 − +.06	+1.44	171.351	3.991
Mean blood pressure (mm Hg)	2.32 − 6.00	3.68	1.79 − 4.71	2.92	.275	.011
Heart rate	3.35 − 5.93	2.58	5.36 − 2.14	3.22	.140	.005

Note: An F-value of 4.00 was required to reach the .05 level of confidence.

+ indicates an increase from pre- to posttest; all other scores reflect a decrease.

comparisons between the experimental and control groups, somewhat surprisingly, disclosed decreases in the control group's SP and DP as well as MP and HR. These observed reductions served to reduce the size of the net mean differences between groups and, consequently, may have been responsible for finding that the decreases noted in the experimental groups were not significant.

The greater familiarity of the subjects with the nature of the procedures during posttesting, when compared to pretesting, may have contributed to decreases noted in the control groups. Sometimes anxiety accompanies blood pressure measurements and therefore its absence, via familiarity, would tend to have a lowering effect on blood pressure.

It is also possible that the control group's involvement in the beginning golf class may have also been a contributing factor in SP, DP, MP and HR reductions which occurred, but it seems unlikely. What does appear to be an important factor is that of the wide blood pressure fluctuations which occur naturally in response to various stimuli. Observations of the results of this study, where rigorous controls were instituted during measurement sessions and yet great variations in blood pressure existed, make it abundantly clear that findings of blood pressure studies not involving control groups and especially those with a small number of subjects should be weighed with these limitations in mind.

References

1. Boyer, J.L. and Kasch, F.: Exercise therapy in hypertensive men. JAMA 211 (4):1671, 1970.
2. Choquette, G. and Ferguson, R.: Blood pressure reduction in borderline hypertensives following physical training. Can. Med. Assoc. J. 108:701, 1973.
3. Hanson, J.S. and Nedde, W.H.: Preliminary observations on physical training for hypertensive males. Circ. Res. 27 (suppl. I):1-52, 1970.
4. Johnson, W.P. and Grover, J.A.: Hemodynamic and metabolic effect of physical training in four patients with essential hypertension. Can. Med. Assoc. J. 96:847, 1967.
5. Steinhaus, A.H.: Chronic effects of exercise. Physiol. Rev. 13:117, 1933.

A Histochemical Study of the Effect of Mobilization and Immobilization on the Metabolism of Healing Muscle Injury

Markku Järvinen and Tapani Sorvari

Introduction

In sport medical practice today early mobilization as a treatment of muscle injuries has superseded the earlier use of immobilization because of the lower frequency of reruptures. In order to study the effects of these two treatments on the healing of muscle injury we have developed an experimental model in the rat where a standard contusion injury can be induced in the gastrocnemius muscle [7].

According to our histological, microangiographical and tensiometrical studies, repair of injured muscles occurred more rapidly when treated by mobilization [3-5]. The purpose of this histochemical work was to study the background of the differences in repair of muscle injuries in rats treated either by immobilization or by early mobilization.

Material and Methods

Sixty male Wistar rats, about 16 weeks old, whose body weight varied from 250 gm to 300 gm were fed laboratory chow and water ad libitum. Before traumatization all animals were taught to run a treadmill. Then the standard partial contusion injury was induced in the left gastrocnemius muscle of each animal [7]. The day of traumatization is called Day 0, and the following days Day 1, 2, etc.

The animals were then divided into two groups, 30 rats each, and treated as follows (Fig. 1):

1. Mobilized rats were kept running on a treadmill with an inclination of 15° at a speed of 40 cm/sec about one hour/day. This mobilization schedule has been used in all our earlier studies.

Markuu Järvinen, Sports Medical Research Unit, Department of Physiology, University of Turku and Tapani Sorvari, Department of Pathology, University of Kuopio, Turko, Finland.

177

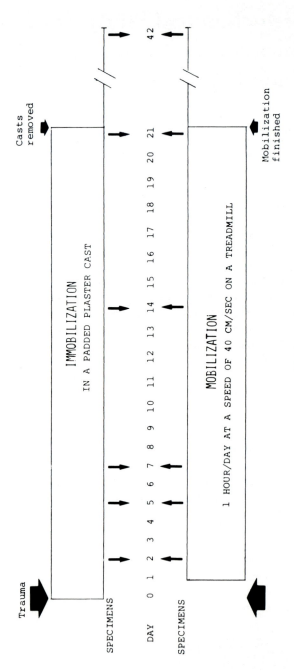

FIGURE. 1.

2. Immobilized rats were kept in their cages with the trauma-tized leg immobilized with a padded plaster cast as used also earlier [8].

After various time intervals the animals were anesthetized with pentobarbital (Nembutal®, Abbot, England) and the muscle injury area was removed and kept a few hours in ice-cold balanced chlorhexidine solution (Histocon®, supplied by Bethlehem Trading, Göteborg, Sweden) [2]. Then the tissue specimens were frozen in propane at −195 C and cut with a cryostat at −20 C. The enzymes stained histochemically with their interpretation are presented in Table I.

Results

Most of the results are summarized in Table II. It seems that the enzyme activities are closely related to the different tissue elements,

Table I. Enzymes Studied Histochemically and Their Interpretation

Marker Enzyme	Interpretation
Phosphorylase	Glycogen breakdown
Glucose-6-phosphate dehydrogenase	Pentose phosphate shunt
Lactate dehydrogenase	Anaerobic glycolysis
Succinate dehydrogenase	Citric acid cycle
Glutamate dehydrogenase	Amino acid metabolism
$NADH_2$-diaphorase	Electron transport
$NADPH_2$-diaphorase	Electron transport
Adenosine triphosphatase (ATPase)	ATP breakdown
Acid phosphatase	Catabolism
Aminopeptidase	Catabolism

Table II. Comparison of Enzyme Activities of Degenerated Muscle Fibers, Myotubes and Degenerated Muscle Fibers With Activities of Normal Uninjured Muscle Fibers

	PHOS	G-6-PDH	LDH	SDH	$NADH_2$-diaph. $NADPH_2$-diaph.	APase	AcPase
Degenerated muscle Days 2 to 5	0	↓↓↓	↓↓	↓↓	↓↓	0	0
Myotubes Days 5 to 10	0	↑↑↑	↑↑↑	↑↑	↑↑	↑↑	↑↑↑
Regenerated muscle Days 10 to 14	↓	↑	↑↑	↑	↑(↑)	0	↑↑

0 no activity; ↑ ↓ activity increased or decreased, respectively, as compared to uninjured normal muscle.

e.g., degenerated myofibers, myotubes and regenerated myofibers and the enzyme pattern in each of those tissue elements was similar in both groups. In degenerated muscle fibers, which were more abundant in immobilized injuries, the lack or decrease of enzyme activities was clearly demonstrable. In the regenerated muscle fibers, especially in the myotubes, the activity of many enzymes was increased when compared to normal muscle near the injured area. In particular, lactic acid dehydrogenase and glucose 6-phosphate dehydrogenase stained intensively, indicating metabolism *via* glycolysis and the pentose phosphate shunt, respectively. Later during maturation the enzyme activities in regenerated muscle fibers approached those found in normal muscle.

In inflammatory cells the catabolic enzymes, aminopeptidase and acid phosphate, as well as lactic acid dehydrogenase stained intensively.

A high aminopeptidase activity was found in the fibroblasts in the injured area. Even at the end of our observation period (Day 42) this catabolic activity was evident in the fibroblasts of the scar.

Discussion

Our results are in agreement with the opinion that the metabolic activity of muscle tissue is closely dependent upon adequate blood supply [12]. During the first days after the trauma we observed a decrease or lack of all enzyme activities connected with energy metabolism in the injured muscle tissue. Possibly this is due to the lack of blood flow observed in microangiographical studies [4]. The regeneration of muscle at the myotube phase is considered to occur in close connection with capillaries [1, 4, 12]. According to the present studies the glycolysis and pentose phosphate shunt are the two most active pathways in myotubes needed for anaerobic energy production and nucleic acid synthesis, respectively. Apparently, the scarcity of mitochondria in myotubes, reported by Reznik [10], is the reason for the limited energy production *via* the citric acid cycle.

Another main feature in the healing of injured muscle is the formation of connective tissue scar. Although the production of connective tissue is more pronounced under mobilization treatment, there were no differences in the amount of scar tissue between the groups six weeks after the trauma [3, 8]. In this histochemical study the strong activity of catabolic enzymes, acid phosphatase and especially aminopeptidase in fibroblasts of the scar was clearly evident during the entire observation period. Since the function of aminopeptidase seems to be similar to that of collagenase in healing tissue [9, 11], the greater production of connective tissue scar observed in the early phase of repair in mobilized muscle may be followed by increased lysis of young collagen by catabolic enzymes in the late phase of healing.

These histochemical results agree well with our earlier histological, microangiographical and tensiometrical observations [6, 8] showing that treatment by early mobilization provides better healing of injured muscle than immobilization.

References

1. Carlson, B.M.: Histological observations on the regeneration of mammalian and amphibian muscle. *In* Mauro, A., Shafig, S.A. and Milhorat, A.T. (eds.): Regeneration of Striated Muscle and Myogenesis. Amsterdam:Excerpta Medica, 1970.
2. Heyden, G.: Ett nytt vävnadstransportmedel i histopatologisk rutin. Tandläkartidningen 64:248-254, 1972.
3. Järvinen, M.: Healing of a crush injury in rat striated muscle. II. A histological study of the effect of early mobilization and immobilization on the repair processes. Acta Path. Microbiol. Scand. 83:269-282, 1975.
4. Järvinen, M.: Healing of a crush injury in rat striated muscle. III. A micro-angiographical study of the effect of early mobilization and immobilization on capillary growth. Acta Path. Microbiol. Scand. 84:85-94, 1976.
5. Järvinen, M.: Healing of a crush injury in rat striated muscle. IV. Effect of early mobilization and immobilization on the tensile properties of gastrocnemius muscle. Acta Chir. Scand. 142:47-56, 1976.
6. Järvinen, M.: Healing of a crush injury in rat striated muscle. Doctoral thesis. Turku, Finland, 1976.
7. Järvinen, M. and Sorvari, T.: Healing of a crush injury in rat striated muscle. I. Description and testing of a new method of inducing a standard injury to the calf muscles. Acta Path. Microbiol. Scand. 83:259-265, 1975.
8. Kvist, H., Järvinen, M. and Sorvari, T.: Effect of mobilization and immobilization on the healing of contusion injury in muscle. Scand. J. Rehab. Med. 6:134-140, 1974.
9. Raekallio, J.: Biochemical and histochemical observations on isocitrate dehydrogenase activity in early wound healing. Experimentia 26:1301, 1970.
10. Reznik, M.: Current concepts of skeletal muscle regeneration. *In* Pearson, C.M. and Mostofi, F. K. (eds.): The Striated Muscle. Baltimore:The Williams and Wilkins Company, 1973, Chap. 10.
11. Schmidt, A.J.: Cellular Biology of Vertebrate Regeneration and Repair. Chicago, Ill.:The University of Chicago Press, 1968, pp. 209-213.
12. Snow, M.H.: Metabolic activity during the degeneration and early regenerative stages of minced skeletal muscle. Anat. Rec. 176:185-204, 1973.

Changes in Synovial Fluid Deprived Articular Cartilage of the Patella: An Experimental Study

Richard V. Worrell and Arthur Cosmas

Introduction

Chondromalacia of the patella is a condition which is characterized by softening and fibrillation of the articular cartilage of the patella. Its immediate cause is unknown. Several etiologic theories have been proposed [2, 4-8]. It has been suggested that mechanical forces may give rise to fatigue failure of the cartilage [3]. Aging has been cited as an important factor [1]. However, its occurrence in young people suggests that factors other than those related to mechanical forces and aging may initiate this condition. The authors are currently studying histochemical and morphological changes produced by many factors in the articular cartilage of the canine patella. One facet of this study relates to changes produced by alteration of the synovial fluid lubrication of the patella. The findings obtained to date are presented in this paper.

Materials and Methods

Four adult, mongrel dogs were used in this study. All surgery was performed on the right patella of each dog. The left patella was used as a control. The same surgical procedure was performed on each dog. The surgery consisted of the interposition of suprapatellar fibrocartilaginous discs and synovium between the articular cartilage of the patella and the articular cartilage of the patellar bed of the femur. The patella was thereby isolated from the normal movement of synovial fluid caused by flexion and extension of the knee. Some synovial fluid was present in the pouch formed by the interposed

Richard V. Worrell, Chief of Orthopaedic Surgery, Veterans Administration Hospital, Newington, Connecticut; University of Connecticut School of Medicine, Farmington, Conn. and Arthur Cosmas, Veterans Administration Hospital, Newington, Connecticut; School of Allied Health, University of Connecticut, Storrs, Conn., U.S.A.

suprapatellar fibrocartilaginous discs and synovium. Each animal was sacrificed in a time interval ranging from six weeks to six months.

Results

Both patellae of each dog were excised at the time of sacrifice. Samples of cartilage of each patella were obtained for transmission electron microscopy and histochemical studies. Slides for light microscopy were made using safranin-O fast green and iron hematoxylin, alcian blue and PAS, and routine hematoxylin and eosin stains. Areas of softening and fibrillation were noted in each right patella. Light microscopic examination of the cartilage of each right patella revealed fibrillation and depletion of proteoglycans. The loss of proteoglycans was determined by the absence of safranin-O staining (red) or alcian blue in the superficial and intermediate zones of the cartilage. Transmission electron microscopy of samples of cartilage of each right patella revealed disruption of the cartilaginous matrix and midzonal chondrocytes containing rather prominent endoplasmic reticulum. The cartilage of each left patella was normal when examined by light and transmission electron microscopy.

Discussion

The changes noted in the articular cartilage of each right canine patella were similar to changes noted in chondromalacia of the patella in man. Accordingly, one can speculate that alteration in the synovial lubrication of the patella in this study adversely affected the nutritional status of the chondrocytes thereby giving rise to a decrease in the production of proteoglycans which in turn led to softening and subsequent fibrillation of the cartilage and "leakage" of proteoglycans. The findings of this study suggest that factors which adversely affect the nutrition of the chondrocyte may play a role in the initiation of softening and fibrillation of the articular cartilage of the patella in man.

Summary

In this study experimental chondromalacia of the canine patella was produced by altering the normal synovial lubrication of the articular cartilage of the patella. These findings suggest that factors which adversely affect the nutrition of the chondrocyte may initiate the changes which are characteristic of chondromalacia of the patella in man.

References

1. Bennett, G.A., Waine, H. and Bauer, W.: Changes in the Knee Joint at Various Ages. New York:The Commonwealth Fund, 1942.
2. Darracott, J. and Vernon-Roberts, B.: The bony changes in chondromalacia patellae. Rheumatol. Phys. Med. 11:175, 1971.
3. Freeman, M.A.R. and Meachim, G.: Ageing, degeneration and remodelling of articular cartilage. *In* Freeman, M.A.R. (ed.): Adult Articular Cartilage. New York:Grune & Stratton, 1973, p. 287.
4. Haliburton, R.A. and Sullivan, C.R.: The patella in degenerative joint disease. A clinicopathologic study. A.M.A. Arch. Surg. 77:677, 1958.
5. Outerbridge, R.E.: Further studies on the etiology of chondromalacia patellae. J. Bone Joint Surg. 46-B:179, 1964.
6. Outerbridge, R.E.: The etiology of chondromalacia patellae. J. Bone Joint Surg. 43-B:752, 1961.
7. Outerbridge, R.E. and Dunlop, J.A.Y.: The problem of chondromalacia patellae. Clin. Orthop. 110:177, 1975.
8. Wiles, P., Andrews, P.S. and Devas, M.B.: Chondromalacia of the patella. J. Bone Joint Surg. 38-B:95, 1956.

Lumbar Lesion in Athletes: The Correlation Between the Lumbar Motion in Athletes and Its Biochemical Meaning Concerning the Etiology of Spondylolysis

Nobuyasu Ichikawa, Kenji Hirohashi, Masaaki Koshimune
and Akira Koshikawa

Introduction

Since 1970 we have been studying the lumbar disorders of active athletes. We have obtained interesting facts from a radiological and orthopedic viewpoint, based on various kinds of sports, duration. etc. Figure 1 shows typical radiological findings in a 29-year-old male rugby athlete who has played for ten years. The X-ray of the lumbar spine shows vertebral deformity. Figure 2 shows spondylolysis has occurred in four vertebra in a 22-year-old male volleyball player of nine years. Spondylolysis was found in quite a high incidence in athletes in our study compared with that in the general population.

In the lower lumbar spine, large load bearing and mobility are required because of its anatomical position and functional needs. Especially in the case of athletes, excessive load and movement are often required in the lower lumbar spine for many years, while the athletes continue rigorous training. The suggestion here then is that lumbar disorders and morphological changes occur with greater frequency in athletes than in the average person. Even when an organic change of spine is radiographically proven, it does not necessarily accompany lumbago. Only when it accompanies additional factors do the subjective and clinical symptoms of waist and back ache appear. The onset of lumbago is further modified by the improving and aggravating factors (Fig. 3). Therefore, we studied the

Nobuyasu Ichikawa, Kenji Hirohashi, Masaaki Koshimune and Akira Koshikawa, Department of Orthopedic Surgery, Osaka City University Medical School, Asahi-machi, Abeno-ku, Japan.

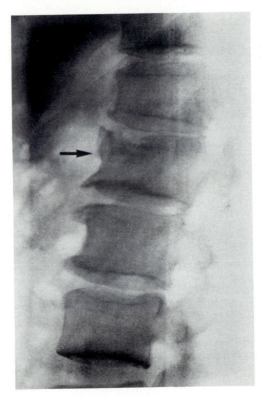

FIG. 1. T.H., 29-year-old male rugby player.

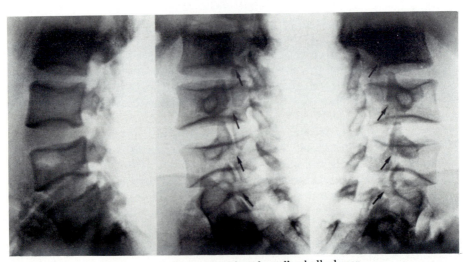

FIG. 2. H.A., 22-year-old male volleyball player.

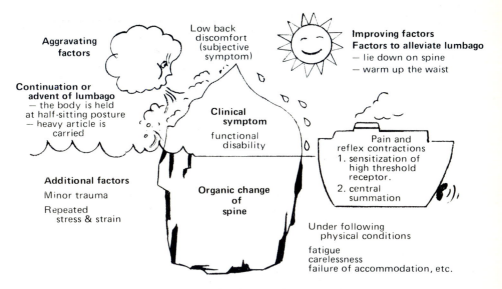

Aggravating
factors

Low back
discomfort
(subjective
symptom)

Improving factors
Factors to alleviate lumbago
— lie down on spine
— warm up the waist

Continuation or
advent of lumbago
— the body is held
at half-sitting posture
— heavy article is
carried

Clinical
symptom

functional
disability

Pain and
reflex contractions
1. sensitization of
high threshold
receptor.
2. central
summation

Additional factors

Minor trauma

Repeated
stress & strain

Organic change
of
spine

Under following
physical conditions

fatigue
carelessness
failure of accommodation, etc.

FIG. 3. Relation between lumbago and organic change of spine.

relation between physioanatomical changes of the lumbar spine and low back pain. We then made a spinal model to simulate the lumbar vertebra of an average person. We will report its biomechanical study later in this paper.

Materials and Methods

In order to learn the causes of lumbar physioanatomical changes and low back pain we gathered data such as history, symptoms, and so on, including the studied clinical and radiological findings of the regular orthopedic examination. The subjects of this study were 367 active athletes of the first order ranked in eight kinds of sports including rugby, boxing and weightlifting. They were males from 13 to 49 years of age with an average age of 21.9. As a control we selected 74 people who were active in sports only two to three times a week. They were males from 18 to 35 years of age with an average age of 24.8 (Tables I and II).

Results

We did a comparative study between athletes and ordinary athletic people on the radiological changes in the anterior and posterior component of the lumbar spine divided by the posterior

Table I. Study of Athletes

	No. of Examinees	Follow up (2-4 yrs.)	Total No. of Examiness
Rugby	68	19	90
Judo	99	33	149
Kendo	38	21	60
Boxing	50	14	64
Am.Football	23	0	23
Weight-lifting	52	0	52
Gymnastics	18	0	18
Crewing	18	6	24
Total	367	93	480
Comparison Sporting Public	74	0	74

Pd. of Time : 1970~1975

Subject   : Athletes including Japanese

Athletes   champions, Olympic trainess, etc.
(adults, college, high school, and junior high students)
Practice more than 2-4 hours daily 6 days a week.

Comparison : judo or kendo, etc. 2-3 times a week

Sporting Public

Table II. Age and Amount of Practice of Athletes

	Age			Amount of Practice		
	Min.	Max.	Avr.	Mon/yr.	Day/W.	hr./day
Rugby	18	41	24.6	10	6	2
Judo	13	49	23.0	12	6	3
Kendo	20	36	23.6	12	6	4
Boxing	15	22	19.3	10	6	2
Am.Football	18	22	20.2	7	6	2
Weight-lifting	18	31	21.3	10	6	3
Gymnastics	13	32	18.2	12	6	4
Crewing	22	32	24.9	10	3	2
Sporting Public	18	35	24.8	8~10	2~3	1~2

longitudinal ligament. The results are shown in Figure 4. The incidence of pathological radiological changes in the anterior component of the spine of the athlete was found to be close to twice that of athletic people. However, it was interesting to note that the incidence of osteophyte formation of athletic people was twice that of the athletes. If we exclude osteophyte formation, the incidence of radiological changes in athletes is found to be almost three times that in ordinary athletic people (72% vs. 24%). In the posterior component there was a prominent difference in the incidence of spondylolysis between the athletes and athletic people. We found spondylolysis in 99 athletes which is 27% of the total, while in athletic people, it was found in only 8, or about 11% of the total. That is, spondylolysis occurred in the athletes about 2.5 times as often as in the athletic people.

Next, we studied the relation between chronic low back pain and spondylolysis. As shown in Tables III and IV, 221 athletes (60.2%) complained of low back pain, while 26 ordinary athletic people complained of low back pain. As for spondylolysis, it was found in 68 athletes which is 18.5% of the total and in 3 athletic people (4.1%). Thirty (8.4%) of the athletes and 5 (6.8%) of the athletic people who had spondylolysis did not complain of low back pain. The result of our study is that spondylolysis was found to be at a

Radiological Change of Lumbar spine of Athletes

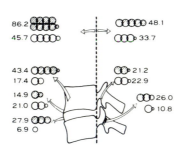

⊘ Athletes   ○ Sporting Public

%	anterior portion of the Vertebrae						posterior portion of the Vertebrae		
	vertebral body			osteophyte formation	Intervertebral Disc		Bony sclerosis (Facet / Pedicle)	Spondylolysis	Scoliosis
	concave spine	lumber index	deformity		narrowing	instability			
Athletes	13.3	13.0	17.1	14.9	16.8	11.1	21.2	26.9	14.9
Sporting Public	12.1	4.0	1.3	21.6	5.4	1.3	22.9	10.8	9.4

FIGURE 4.

Table III. Lumbago and Spondylolysis of Athletes

lumbago						Spondylolysis	
lysis (+)	lysis (−)	No. of Persons	%	List of Sports	No. of Examinees	No. of Persons	%
9	16	25	55.6	Rugby	68	17	25.0
21	54	75	75.8	Judo	99	27	27.0
2	8	10	25.6	Kendo	39	8	20.5
7	13	20	40.0	Boxing	50	11	22.0
1	13	14	60.9	Am. Football	23	4	17.4
20	24	44	84.6	Weight-lifting	52	21	40.4
4	12	16	88.9	Gymnastics	18	5	27.8
4	13	17	94.0	Crewing	18	6	33.3
68	153	221	60.2	Total	367	99	27.0
3	23	26	35.1	Sporting Public	74	8	10.8

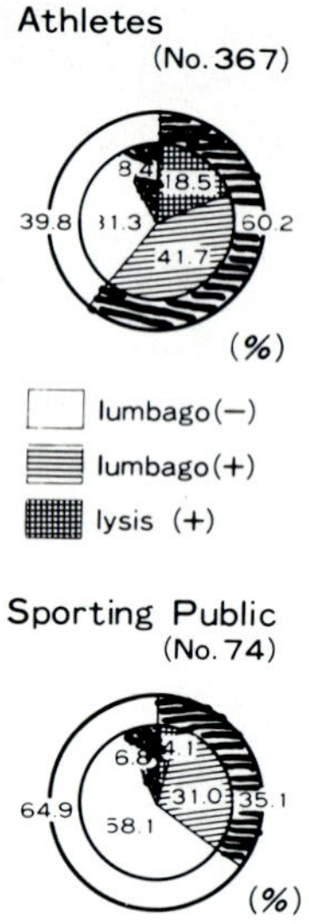

Table IV. Spondylolysis of Athletes

List of Sports	No. of Examinees	Spondylolysis		No. of lamina with spondylolysis			Total	Location				Clest type	Pseudo-arthrotic type
		No. of Persons	%	Both Sides	One Side	2 places		$L_{2,3}$	L_4	L_5	L_6		
Rugby	68	17	25.0	30	1	4	35	2(L_3)	2	25	6	7	28
Judo	99	27	27.0	42	5	4	51		4	47		21	30
Kendo	39	8	20.5	8	3	4	15	2(L_2)		13		1	14
Boxing	50	11	22.0	14	4	0	18			18		3	15
Am.Football	23	4	17.4	4	2	0	6			5	1	3	3
Weight-lifting	52	21	40.4	32	4	4	40		4	36		20	20
Gymnastics	18	5	27.8	6	2	0	8			6	2	2	6
Crewing	18	6	33.3	12	1	0	13	1(L_3)		12		1	12
Total	367	99	27.0	148	22	16	186	5	10	162	9	58	128
Sporting Public	74	8	10.8	10	2	4	16	1	2	13	0	4	12

high rate in athletes, the highest being in weightlifting (40.4%), crewing (33.3%) and gymnastics (27.8%). Therefore we surmised that lumbar disorders were caused by repeated movements under conditions of excessive heavy loading in these sports. Moreover, in this study, no significant difference was found between the young athletes and athletic people who were under 20 years of age and whose bony maturation had stopped (Table V).

Table V. Spondylolysis of Athletes Under 20 Years of Age
(13 to 20, Average 18.4)

List of Sports	No. of Examinees	Spondylolysis		Location				Clest type	Pseudo-arthrotic type	Lysis (+)	
		No. of Persons	%	L₃	L₄	L₅	L₆			lumbago(+)	lumbago(−)
Rugby	16	4	25.0			4		2	6	1	3
Judo	32	9	28.1		2	17		4	15	8	1
Kendo	4	1	25.0			2			2	0	1
Boxing	39	10	25.6			16		3	13	6	4
Am.Football	14	1	7.2			2			2	0	1
Weight-lifting	24	10	41.7		2	18		10	10	6	4
Gymnastics	17	5	29.4			6	2	2	6	4	1
Crewing	0	0	0							0	0
Total	146	40	27.4	0	4	65	6	21	54	25 (17.1 %)	15 (10.3 %)
Sporting Public	4	0	0							0	0

Discussion

From these results we have concluded that there is the possibility that spondylolysis can first occur even in adulthood depending upon the intensity and frequency of sports activity. Concerning the mechanism of spondylolysis development, we established the hypothesis as shown in Figure 5. As for the noncongenital causes, there are the cases of fatigue fracture and fracture due to abnormal

Etiological Factors of Spondylolysis (Hypothesis)

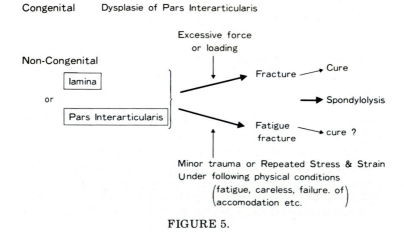

FIGURE 5.

external forces. But even when a fracture occurs at the pars interarticularis, it does not always cause severe dysfunction of the spinal column. It may be overlooked as a simple low back pain which often occurs in athletes. The causes of such fracture may be fatigue, carelessness, excessive speed, disharmony of motion, ground condition, etc. Attempts should be made to prevent such accidents by preventive orthopedic and physical medicine, including regular check-ups, proper progressive training, adequate warm-up and avoidance of overfatigue.

Experimental Observations on the Development of Spondylolysis with a Resin Model

The purpose of this experiment was to determine the stress and strain points and to determine critical destructive loading to position.

Experimental Method

A model of the fifth lumbar vertebra and the first sacral was molded to simulate those of an average person. This model was fixed on a platform, as shown in Figure 6, and was used to simulate the lumbar spine in flexion and extension as in the human body. Lateral roentgenograms of the lumbar spine of an adult were used to measure the angle between the horizontal plane and the upper

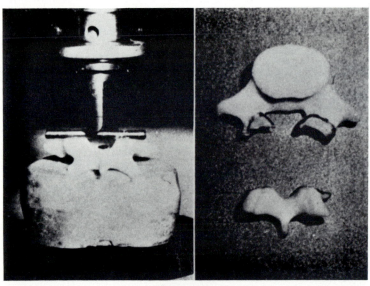

FIGURE 6.

surface of the 5th lumbar vertebra (Fig. 7). These angles in vivo are +15° in neutral position, +70° in maximum flexion and −10° in maximum extension. Three destructive experiments on the spine model were performed with a universal compression testing machine. A load was imposed upon the superior articular processes of the spine model fixed at three different Θ angles (0°, +15°, +35°) (Table VI). One-axis strain gauges were affixed at four locations on the pars interarticularis (dorsal, ventrolateral and two ventrals). The axes of the gauges were aligned in the direction perpendicular to the expected line of fracture. Strains were measured for loads of 8 kg and 10 kg at Θ angles ranging from −10° to +65° (Fig. 8).

Experimental Results

With the load imposed on the superior articular processes in this model, a fracture occurred at the pars interarticularis, which was considered to be the "locus minoris" mechanically. The relationship between the angle Θ and the load required to cause fracture is shown in Table VI: as Θ decreases, the critical load for a fracture decreases.

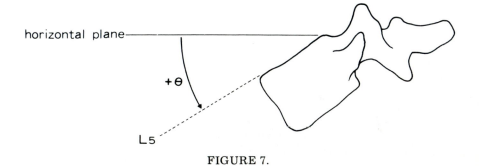

FIGURE 7.

Table VI.

No.	$\theta°$	load at fracture (kg)
1	0	110
2	+15	120
3	+35	140

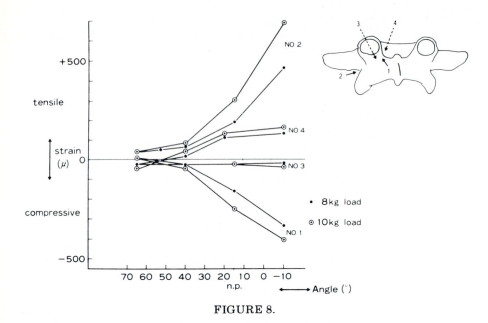

FIGURE 8.

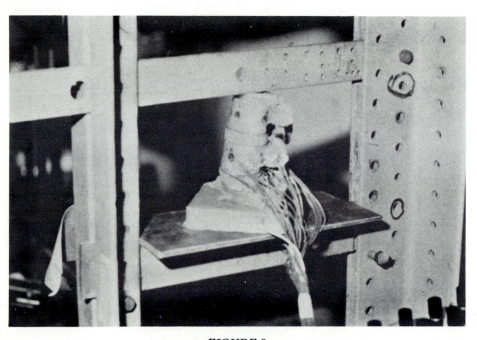

FIGURE 9.

When strain in the pars interarticularis were measured by a one-axis strain gauge, an increase of Θ angle which corresponded to an increasing flexion resulted in a decrease of strain. On the other hand, a decreasing Θ angle corresponding to an increasing extension resulted in an increasing strain. A concentration of tensile stresses was observed at the ventrolateral (No. 2) aspect of the pedicle, and a large compressive stress was detected at the dorsum (No. 1) (Fig. 8). In the last part of the experiment, a possibility of the fatigue fracture in the pars interarticularis was investigated. The spine model was fixed at the Θ angle of −10° corresponding to the maximum extension, and a load of 100 kg was applied intermittently. A fracture occurred after 2100 applications. With the Θ angle of +20° and otherwise identical conditions, no fracture was observed even after 3500 applications.

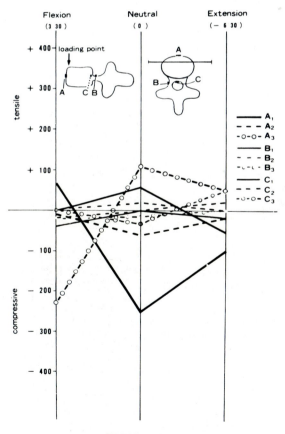

FIGURE 10.

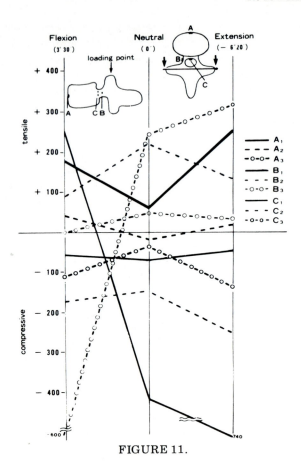

FIGURE 11.

Experimental Conclusion (Fig. 9)

1. The anterior portion of the vertebral body sustains a medium level of compressive or tensile stresses depending upon the loading position and the loading direction (Fig. 10).

2. The posterior portion of the vertebral body receives large compressive stresses when a load is applied at the superior articular processes (Fig. 11).

3. Spondylolysis was artificially produced in the spine model (Fig. 6).

Descriptive Analysis of Selected Alignment Factors of the Lower Extremity in Relation to Lower Extremity Trauma in Athletic Training

J. M. Lilletvedt and E. F. Kreighbaum

Introduction

The purposes of the following study were (1) to determine whether the alignment of the lower extremity, as defined by selected measurements, varied between persons who had never had shin splints, persons who had had shin splints previously and persons who had shin splints currently and (2) to determine the relative importance of selected measurements of the lower extremity and which of these measurements, if any, could be used to predict the occurrence of the shin splint syndrome. All future references to the shin splint syndrome will refer to it as it occurs on the medial side of the tibia. Scientific parameters considered were the ranges of inversion and eversion at the subtalar joint, dorsiflexion at the ankle joint/knee flexed and extended, external and internal rotation of the femur/hip flexed and extended, flexibility of the hamstring muscle groups and the positions of the forefoot in relationship to the rearfoot/subtalar joint neutral, frontal plane of the tibia/subtalar joint static and neutral, calcaneous in relationship to the floor/subtalar joint static and neutral and the malleoli/subtalar joint neutral.

Methods and Procedures

Thirty-two women athletes from Montana State University and surrounding area high schools were subjects. Ages ranged from 14 to 26 years with height and weight ranging from 5'1" to 5'9" and 98 pounds to 160 pounds, respectively. Subjects were interviewed by the investigator; symptoms and treatments were recorded; selected

J. M. Lilletvedt and E. F. Kreighbaum, Health, Physical Education and Recreation Department, Montana State University, Bozeman, Mont., U.S.A.

measurements of the lower extremity were taken; and the data from each measurement were recorded. The existence or nonexistence of shin splints was verified by the athletic trainer at Montana State University. Subjects' legs were then classified into the following groups.

Group 1: No Shin Splints. Legs that had never been afflicted with shin splints or other trauma were placed in this group. If an individual had one leg that was injury free, while the other leg was experiencing or had experienced some trauma such as sprained ankles or knee injuries, only the injury-free leg was included in this group. The other leg was eliminated from the study (N = 18).

Group 2: Current Moderate Shin Splints. Subjects who were diagnosed as having shin splints in both legs, but who complained of one leg hurting more than the other, had the less severe leg placed in group 2 and the more severe leg placed in group 3. Legs placed in group 2 were those that gave the subjects less pain as compared to the other leg (N = 5).

Group 3: Current Severe Shin Splints. Subjects who were diagnosed as having shin splints in both legs and who did not distinguish between the severity of the ailment, i.e., they did not complain of one leg hurting more than the other leg, had both legs placed in group 3. Subjects who did distinguish between the severity of the ailment from one leg to the other had the more severe leg placed in group 3 and the less severe leg placed in group 2 (N = 19).

Group 4: Previous Shin Splints. Subjects who had been previously diagnosed as having shin splints but who, at the time of this examination, were not suffering from any trauma of the lower extremity were placed in this group. If an individual had had shin splints in one leg but not in the other, only the afflicted leg was used.

Group 5: Current Shin Splints. Group 2 and group 3 were combined to form this group (N = 24).

Note that by definition of the nature of group 2 and group 3 it was possible for a subject to have one leg placed in each of the two groups. Verification of the existence or nonexistence of the shin splint syndrome by the athletic trainer at Montana State University was used to place the legs of each subject within the various groups.

Measurements of each of the specific parameters to be considered were taken by the investigator with a manual biometer developed by Phillips* using measurement techniques described by Lilletvedt [1]. A pilot study was conducted to determine the reliability of the investigator's use of the biometer for each of the measurements. The

---

*Robert Phillips, D.P.M., Phillips Podiatry Center, Great Falls, Montana.

coefficients of reliability for 13 of the 15 measurements were significant at the .01 level. The measurement of the degree of external rotation of the femur/hip extended and the measurement of the position of the calcaneous in relationship to the floor/subtalar joint neutral were significant beyond the .05 level.

An analysis of variance served as the basis for determining whether the alignment of the lower extremity, as defined by the selected measurements, was significantly different between groups 1, 4 and 5. A Duncan's test was used to determine which of the measures between the various groups were significantly different.

A step-wise regression analysis was performed to compare the data from groups 1, 2 and 3. The step-wise regression provided the basis for determining the relative importance of the selected measurements of the lower extremity to the relative severity of the shin splint syndrome and which of the measurements, if any, could be used to predict the occurrence of the shin splint syndrome.

The analysis of variance, the Duncan's test and the step-wise regression were done with computer programs written by a member of the Testing and Counseling Department at Montana State University.

Analysis of Variance

An analysis of variance between groups 1, 4 and 5 indicated that there were significant alignment differences (p <.05) between each of the above-mentioned groups. The analysis of variance is shown in Table I.

Differences Between Measures

The results of Duncan's test indicated which means of the variables were significantly different among each of the three groups. Results are presented in Table II.

Six of the fifteen measurements taken were significantly different (p <.05) between each of the three groups. These measure-

Table I. Summary of the Analysis of Variance

Source	df	SS	MS	F Ratio
Groups	2	77.5189	38.7594	15.966*
Treatment	14	26555.9	1896.85	78.382*
Group X treatment	28	203.175	7.25623	2.989†
Error	795		2.42730	

*Significant beyond p < .01
†Significant beyond p <.05

Table II. Summary of Duncan's Test Analysis

Variables	$\bar{X}$	$\bar{X}$	$\bar{X}$	Sig. Diff. (p < .05)
1. External rotation of femur/hip extended	51.39	57.64	64.96	abc
2. Dorsiflexion of ankle/knee flexed	16.56	17.79	20.33	abc
3. Inversion of subtalar joint	16.61	15.86	19.96	bc
4. Position of tibia/subtalar joint static all measurements varum	3.833	5.643	5.667	ab
5. Dorsiflexion of ankle/knee extended	31.61	33.00	31.08	ac
6. Position of calcaneous/subtalar joint static all measurements inversion	2.333	2.071	2.071	
7. Flexibility of hamstrings	7.444	2.357	9.542	abc
8. Position of tibia/subtalar joint neutral all measurements varum	.5000	.7857	.7500	abc
9. Internal rotation of femur/hip extended	67.44	61.50	72.17	abc
10. Internal rotation of femur/hip flexed	64.06	61.93	66.04	abc
11. Eversion of subtalar joint	13.83	13.50	14.75	c
12. Position of calcaneous/subtalar joint neutral all measurements inversion	2.278	.3571	2.042	ac
13. External rotation of femur/hip flexed	51.11	54.79	62.17	abc
14. Position of malleoli/subtalar joint neutral all measurements external	17.06	16.36	14.62	bc
15. Position of forefoot to rearfoot/subtalar joint neutral	−.2222	2.643	2.042	ab

−.2222 refers to vagum — other measurements varum

a Significantly different between groups 1 and 4 (p < .05)
b Significantly different between groups 1 and 5 (p < .05)
c Significantly different between groups 4 and 5 (p < .05)

ments included the ranges of external and internal rotation of the femur/hip flexed and extended, dorsiflexion of the ankle/knee flexed and flexibility of the hamstring muscle group.

In addition, those subjects who had no shin splints differed from those who currently had shin splints in the ranges of inversion at the subtalar joint, and the positions of the forefoot in relationship to the rearfoot/subtalar joint neutral, malleoli/subtalar joint neutral and frontal plane of the tibia/subtalar joint static.

Also, those with no shin splints differed from those with previous shin splints in the range of dorsiflexion of the ankle joint/knee extended and the position of the forefoot to the rearfoot/subtalar joint neutral; frontal plane of the tibia/subtalar joint static; calcaneous in relationship to the floor/subtalar joint neutral.

Finally, those with previous shin splints differed from those with shin splints in the ranges of inversion and eversion at the subtalar joint, dorsiflexion at the ankle joint/knee extended, and the positions of the malleoli/subtalar joint neutral, and the calcaneous in relationship to the floor/subtalar joint neutral.

The measurements of the position of the calcaneous in relationship to the floor/subtalar joint static and the position of the tibia/subtalar neutral showed no significant difference $(p < .05)$ between any of the three groups.

Step-wise Regression

Comparing the data from groups 1, 2 and 3, six of the 15 measurements included in the examinations significantly contributed to the regression $(p < .05)$. These measures were suggested as possible predictors of the severity of the shin splint syndrome on the medial side of the tibia. Table III presents the variables as they relate to the multiple regression.

The first six measures significantly contributed to the regression and are listed in order of contribution. These six factors appear to significantly predict the severity of shin splints. Other measurements did not significantly appear to increase the predictability of shin splints.

Discussion

Results of the study indicated that there were significant differences between the alignments of the lower extremity of those subjects who had no shin splints, those who had previously had shin splints and those who had current shin splints. This suggests that realigning the lower extremity in persons who had had shin splints

Table III. Summary of Step-Wise Regression Analysis

Step Number	Variable Entered	Multiple R	RSQ	Increase in RSQ	F Value to Enter
1.	External rotation of femur/hip extended	.4110	.1689	.1689	10.977*
2.	Dorsiflexion of ankle/knee flexed	.5830	.3398	.1709	13.7200*
3.	Inversion of subtalar joint	.6680	.4462	.1064	9.9892*
4.	Position of tibia/subtalar joint static	.6928	.4800	.0338	3.3164*
5.	Dorsiflexion of ankle/knee extended	.7133	.5088	.0288	2.9303*
6.	Position of calcaneous/subtalar joint static	.7333	.5377	.0289	3.0657*
7.	Flexibility of hamstrings	.7470	.5581	.0203	2.2065
8.	Position of tibia/subtalar joint neutral	.7576	.5740	.0159	1.7543
9.	Internal rotation of femur/hip extended	.7588	.5758	.0019	.2048
10.	Internal rotation of femur/hip flexed	.7645	.5845	.0087	.9387
11.	Eversion of subtalar joint	.7652	.5855	.0010	.1073
12.	Position of calcaneous/subtalar joint neutral	.7658	.5865	.0009	.0984
13.	External rotation of femur/hip flexed	.7663	.5872	.0008	.0790
14.	Position of malleoli/subtalar joint neutral	.7663	.5873	.0000	.0041
15.	Position of forefoot to rearfoot/subtalar neutral	.7663	.5873	.0000	.0004

*Value significant $p < .05$

and in persons who had current shin splints so that it approximates the alignment described in the no shin splint group may be helpful in treating or preventing the ailment.

Significant differences between each of the groups (Table II), whether the difference is an increase or a decrease in the range of motion or relative position, can be controlled or limited by the application of an external force, i.e., strapping, orthotics, etc. These ranges of motion and/or positions may be controlled or limited provided there are no physical defects that prevent such control. For example, the position of the frontal plane of the tibia/subtalar joint static and the position of the calcaneous in relation to the floor/subtalar joint static are significantly related to shin splints. Also, the degree of inversion at the subtalar joint and the degree of dorsiflexion at the ankle/knee flexed are significantly related to the syndrome. Both positions, that of the tibia and that of the calcaneous, as well as the degree of inversion present at the subtalar joint and the degree of dorsiflexion at the ankle/knee flexed may be controlled or limited by the application of an external force. Thus, using tape or orthotics to realign the tibia and the calcaneous and to limit the amount of inversion present at the subtalar joint and the amount of dorsiflexion at the ankle/knee flexed may be helpful in treating or preventing shin splints.

Excessive stretching of the plantarflexors of the foot and/or excessive strengthening of the dorsiflexors of the foot should be avoided. Such stretching and/or strengthening of these muscle groups may increase the degree of dorsiflexion at the ankle joint and, since increasing degrees of dorsiflexion at the ankle joint is related to shin splints, may increase the possibility of shin splints occurring. The degree of dorsiflexion at the ankle may be controlled and/or reduced through strengthening of the plantarflexors and stretching of the dorsiflexors. As the plantarflexors become stronger, they will limit the degree of dorsiflexion possible and consequently may decrease the possibility of shin splints occurring.

Excessive stretching of the internal rotators of the hip and excessive strengthening of the external rotators of the hip may increase the degree of external rotation of the femur when the hip joint is extended and should be avoided. Although some degree of external rotation is desirable and, in fact, necessary for normal ambulation, excessive increases in external rotation should be avoided since it seems to be related to the occurrence of shin splints.

The degree of external rotation of the femur may be controlled and/or reduced by strengthening the internal rotators of the hip, consequently stretching the external rotators. As the internal rotators become stronger, they will limit the degree of external rotation possible and so may decrease the possibility of shin splints occurring.

Note that any change in the hip position or in the external and/or internal rotation of the femur will cause changes throughout the alignment of the lower extremity since the extremity is a linked system. Likewise, changes in the alignment at any other points in the lower extremity will bring about a change at the hip.

Results of the study further indicated that six of the 15 measurements taken could be used to predict the occurrence of shin splints on the medial side of the tibia. Hence in attempting to predict and hopefully then prevent the occurrence of the shin splint syndrome, coaches and athletic trainers should be aware of the six warning signs. These include increasing degrees of external rotation of the femur/hip extended, dorsiflexion at the ankle/knee flexed, inversion of the subtalar joint, varum of the frontal plane position of the tibia/subtalar joint static, and decreasing degrees of dorsiflexion at the ankle/knee extended and of inversion of the calcaneous/ subtalar joint static. A coach or trainer may protect athletes from shin splints by detecting these above warning signals and adopting a program to adjust the necessary measurements.

Summary

Measurements describing the alignment of the lower extremities of 32 women athletes were taken. Data recorded were classified into five separate groups and were analyzed through the use of an analysis of variance, Duncan's test and a step-wise regression.

An analysis of variance found that there were significant alignment differences (p <.05) between those subjects who had no shin splints, those subjects who had had shin splints prior to the examination and those subjects who had shin splints at the time of the examination.

The Duncan's test indicated the variables which were significantly different (p <.05) between each of the above-mentioned groups.

The step-wise regression indicated that six of the 15 measurements taken could be used to predict the occurrence of shin splints on the medial side of the tibia. These six factors included in descending order of importance: the degree of external rotation of the femur/hip extended, the degree of dorsiflexion at the ankle joint/knee flexed, the degree of inversion at the subtalar joint, the frontal plane position of the tibia/subtalar joint static, the degree of dorsiflexion at the ankle joint/knee extended, and the position of the calcaneous in relationship to the floor/subtalar joint static.

Reference

1. Lilletvedt, J.M.: Descriptive Analysis of Selected Alignment Factors of the Lower Extremity in Relation to Lower Extremity Trauma in Athletic Training. Unpublished Master's thesis, 1976.

Mechanical Problems of Marathoners and Joggers: Cause and Solution

Karl K. Klein and Charles A. Roberts

The increasing emphasis on running as a means to fitness has brought with it a number of problems, notably low back pain, knee, ankle and foot injuries. The development of Iso-Ropo* (or body balance) seems to be a solution to many of these problems.

Many runners continue on the assumption that pain is a part of the process. Some obtain temporary relief with prescribed medication while the main causes, i.e., muscle imbalance, lack of flexibility and lateral pelvic imbalance (tipping), remain overlooked.

Recently Ryan [14] pointed to the many failures observed in the evaluation of low back pain in athletes. In the evaluation of this problem he listed a variety of treatment approaches that were of questionable value and emphasized that mechanical inefficiencies were the chief cause of stress.

Running is primarily a function of the hip flexor/extensor mechanism and lower leg musculature. The major hip flexor is the iliopsoas muscle. The psoas attaches to the lower five vertebrae and the iliacus to the inside rim of the pelvis. They combine, cross the lower rim of the pelvis and attach to the inside of the upper leg just below the pelvis. Basically, this is a strong and short muscle which in standing tends to pull the low back forward, tips the pelvis downward, causing a "sway" back. The rectus femoris on the front of the thigh, a part of the quadriceps mechanism, attaches to the anterior iliac spine of the pelvis and lower leg just below the knee and also tends to tip the pelvis forward while acting as a hip flexor. It is also active in knee extension.

When exercised as in running, straight leg sit-ups and even bent knee sit-ups, double leg raising or just prolonged sitting, these muscles tighten and shorten. They need to be stretched daily in order

---

Karl K. Klein, Department of Health, Physical Education and Recreation, Rehabilitation Laboratory, The University of Texas at Austin, and Physical Rehabilitation, U.T. Student Health Center and Charles A. Roberts, Foot Posture Controls, Waxahachie, Texas, U.S.A.

*A concept of body balance developed by Dr. Roberts.

to maintain normal flexibility. The iliopsoas muscle is the major muscle involved in low back stress [8].

The runner's leg is extended at the hip joint by the gluteus maximus ("fanny") muscle as well as the hamstrings which are also active extensors of the knee joint when the foot is in contact with the ground during the last 15° to 20° of knee extension.

When the hip flexors are tight and the pelvis is tipped forward, the hamstrings are actually in a state of "overstretch" because the origin of attachment on the pelvis is lifted upward and the normal distance between the origin and insertion of the muscle is lengthened. It is anticipated that this action will account for *early hamstring fatigue as well as one of the fundamental causes for hamstring injury.* The forward tilted pelvis is positively related to the shortening of the forward and extension stride of the distance runner. A flat pelvis is vital to the runner's efficiency.

The calf muscle (gastrocnemius) is also involved in running, and its overtightness can add to the problem of low back stress, "shin splints," ankle pronation (turning inward of the ankle) and knee stress (runner's knee) [3].

Muscle flexibility by daily stretching and improvement of foot mechanics are also important by daily activity inclusive of *before and after* running.

In order to make a self-evaluation for excessive muscle tension, refer to Figure 1. These are self-testing procedures, although you can have someone else help you to evaluate the tests. The results can pinpoint where the tension or short muscles are and the exercises in Figure 2 will show you what to do in correction of the problem. All of the stretching exercises should be done only to the point of comfort [2]. You may stretch to the point of discomfort (pain), *then back off and hold for a sustained period* one minute or more and repeat.

Lateral tipping of the pelvis ("the short leg syndrome" — one hip high, one low) is a significant part of the total problem and studies have shown it to be highly related to the issue of low back stress [1, 4, 6, 7] and is highly related to the problem in runners. If there are no medical findings to show cause for the problem, then it undoubtedly has been there since early childhood [5]. Some of the more common causes may de due to unilateral pronated ankle, one leg slightly short, one arch low and/or one knock knee (valgus knee). The problem here is to make a correction that puts the body into lateral balance. There are a number of ways to make corrections as follows:

Muscle tests usable for determining the state of muscle flexibility or lack of flexibility as a basis for prescribing the exercise prescription.

Tests for Psoas Muscle Tension

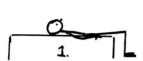

With back on table and lower legs hanging over edge of table, the knees free from table edge as in #1. Pull one knee to chest as in #2.

If opposite leg raises off of the table, the psoas is tight on that side. Also, if the lower leg starts to straighten, the rectus femoris of the upper leg shows tension. Repeat test to the opposite side.

Test for Gastroc (Calf Muscle) Tension

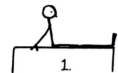

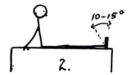

"Long" sitting on table with support of trunk with hands as in #1, pull foot (dorsal flex ankle) toward the knee as in #2.

If ankle cannot be dorsal flexed 10°-15° from a right angle of the foot on the leg tested, the gastroc is tight on that side. Repeat test on opposite side.

Test for Hamstrings Tension

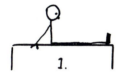

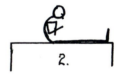

"Long" sitting on table as in #1, support trunk with hands, attempt to sit up straight and arch the lumbar spine. If the lower back cannot arch and

the lumbar curve is rounded as in #2, then the hamstrings muscles are tight and the pelvis is tipped backward thus preventing the lumbar spine to arch.

Tests for Rectus Femoris Muscle

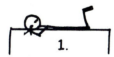

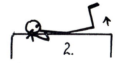

"Prone" lying on table with flexed knees as in #1. The tester places one hand beneath the bent knee and one on the subject's buttocks to hold the hips down. The tester then lifts upward

on the flexed knee. *No assistance* from the subject. If it is difficult to lift the leg, rectus femoris tension is present. Repeat the test on the opposite side.

These tests are a subjective clinical evaluation procedure. Experience in the testing process soon enables the evaluator to make accurate decisions regarding excess tension of the involved musculature.

Along with the exercise program, emphasis must be placed on good posture with abdominal flatness and pelvis control.

FIG. 1. Muscle flexibility tests.

Exercise Instruction:

1. Precede exercise program with an evaluation for muscle tension and lateral postural evaluation. Record findings.
2. Teach exact exercise technique. *Emphasize moderate sustained stretching only to point of comfort.*
3. Do all exercises four to five times. Alternate sides where indicated.

Exercise Explanations:

1. *Abdominal Strengthener* — Roll up head, neck and shoulders. Keep low back on floor. Hold 8-10 counts. Relax. Repeat.
2. *Pelvic Flattener* — Contact abdominals and gluteal muscles. Force low back to floor. Hold 8-10 counts. Relax. Repeat.
3. *Back Stretcher* — Pull knees to chest and squeeze, 8-10 counts. Relax. Repeat. On relaxation hold on to knees but extend arms.
4. *Psoas Stretcher* — Have foot in front of knee on forward leg — rear leg straight. Keep hips level. Push hips downward to *point of tension* in groin area of rear leg. Hold. Release (hips up). Repeat. Do same procedure other side, 8-10 counts for each stretch.
5. *Hamstring Stretch* — Stand with one leg extended sideward, heel on bench. Press hip downward on elevated leg side to point of mild stretch of hamstrings and leg adductors. Hold 30-40 seconds. Release. Repeat. Do same procedure for other side.
6. *Single Leg X-Overs* — On back, arms sideward on mat, legs straight. Swing right leg across toward left hand. *Keep knee straight*, roll at hips. The ultimate objective is to reach the foot to the opposite hand but this will take some time to gain the necessary flexibility.
7. *Gastroc and Plantaris Stretcher* — Stand near wall, toes slightly inward, weight on outer borders of feet. Reach forward to wall. Bend arms, lean forward. *Keep heels on floor* to a *MILD STRETCH* of calf muscle. Hold 50-60 seconds. Release. Repeat four to five times two to three times daily.
8. *Rectus Femoris Stretcher* — Top of one foot on low stand. Hands grasp back of chair. *TRUNK ERECT* pull abdominals up — back flat. Push hips forward to stretch rectus. Bend forward knee to increase tension. *MILD STRETCH ONLY.* Hold 50 to 60 seconds. Release. Repeat. Same to opposite side. Repeat two to three times each leg.

FIG. 2. Special exercise for low back and flexibility (partial William's series).

1. *Pronated ankle.* Use the Robert's Rear Foot Controls (or some other orthotic device) to correct the pronation [9-13]. Although one control can be used, it is suggested that the pair be used in the running shoes. They should also be transferred to the regular street shoes for general use. (A tie shoe is necessary for best results.) Figure 3 shows the bone structure of the ankle in a normal, pronated and corrected position with use of the control.

2. *"Short leg syndrome."* This can be a self-analysis procedure (standing in front of a mirror to check for the lateral pelvic tilt). Have blocks measuring 1/4", 3/8", 1/2" or more available for use. A more accurate approach is to have someone assist, i.e., team physician or athletic trainer, by sitting behind you to place sufficient block or blocks under the heel until the hips are level. Once this

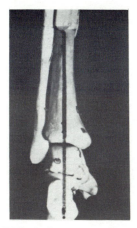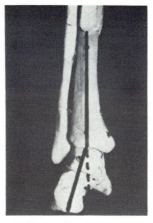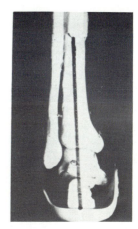

FIG. 3. Bone structures. *Left*, Normal ankle position in standing. *Middle*, Ankle pronated in standing. *Right*, Ankle position with use of the Robert's Rear Foot Control to lift the navicular (scaphoid) into a corrected position.

determination is made, then a heel lift of that thickness should be used on the running shoe as well as the regular street shoes. Refer to Figure 4 to see how this can be attached to the running shoe. A very small lift can be placed inside of the shoe, but it is better as illustrated. Figures 5 and 6 are included to give you a concept of what lateral pelvic tilt looks like before and after correction.

3. In *"runner's knee"* stress beneath the knee cap (chondromalacia) is more than likely caused by lateral tipping of the hips, knock knee (valgus) and/or ankle pronation. When lateral tipping exists, the knee on the short leg side tends to turn in and the foot tends to point outward (slufoot). This causes the muscles that extend the knee (quadriceps) to pull the knee cap to the lateral side of the

FIG. 4. Heel lift correction for lateral postural asymmetry on running shoes.

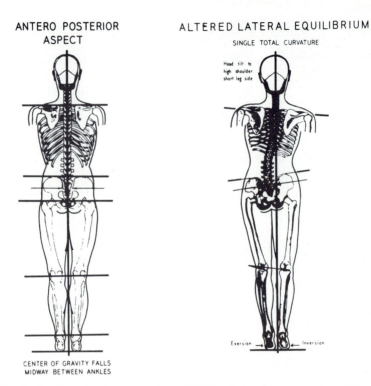

ANTERO POSTERIOR ASPECT

ALTERED LATERAL EQUILIBRIUM

SINGLE TOTAL CURVATURE

Head tilt to high shoulder short leg side

Eversion → ← Inversion

CENTER OF GRAVITY FALLS MIDWAY BETWEEN ANKLES

FIG. 5. *Left*, Structural symmetry. *Right*, Lateral asymmetry (short leg syndrome left).

knee joint when the lower leg extends and the lower leg and foot turn out on the runthrough. The patella is not working in its normal channel and pain results. Corrective efforts by use of the heel lift, rear foot controls and correction of running mechanics through concentrated practice aid in solution of the problem of stress and pain.

In conclusion, these are usable techniques in an effort to assist runners and joggers who come to the U. T. Rehabilitation Laboratory for assistance. The emphasis is on muscle flexibility and postural balance to improve running mechanics. To date the results have been highly successful. A few case studies are illustrative.

1. A young lady running 25-mile marathons came in with runner's knee pain. Postural measurements and a treadmill test for running mechanics indicated correction was needed: a 3/8″ heel lift and rear foot controls. She is running pain free at under three hours at marathon distance.

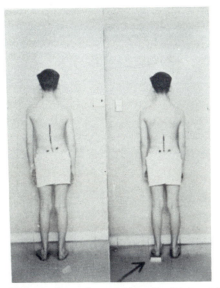 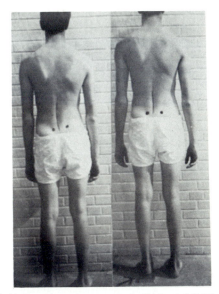

FIG. 6. Short leg syndrome. *Right*, 7/8" (2.2 cm) and corrected. *Left*, 1-1/16" (2.56 cm) and corrected.

2. A faculty runner with low back stress. Postural measurements showed lateral imbalance. Daily flexibility exercises and heel lift of 1/2" was placed on his shoe (Fig. 4). He is running 10 to 15 miles per week free of stress and competing in age group races.

3. A faculty jogger with low back stress. Lateral imbalance corrected with a heel lift and daily flexibility exercises. One year later he returned with ankle pain. Bilateral ankle pronation had been overlooked. Rear foot controls were applied. Ankle pain subsided in two to three days. Now running well, no more problems.

4. A U.T. trackman, miler. Knee stress, postural evaluation showed lateral imbalance and ankle pronation. A heel lift and rear foot controls seemed to solve the problem. He stated that he couldn't believe running could be so comfortable with the adjustments. He's in the four-minute miler class.

The above procedures have been helping those in need, but one has to recognize that other approaches and procedures have been successful. The simplicity of the Flexibility Exercises and Postural Balancing with the Heel Lift and use of the Robert's Rear Foot Controls seems to be simplicity personified in helping runners and joggers to make their exercise more pleasant.

As an added thought, by balancing the leg length, the step patterns will be equalized and the long-short leg pattern of one long and one short stride will be replaced with equal step strides which should get you there sooner. Now, visualize the possibility of setting some new world records!

References

1. Beal, M.C.: A review of the short leg problem. J. Am. Osteopathic Association, 1:3, 1950.
2. deVries, H.A.: Physiology of Exercise for Physical Education and Sports. Dubuque, Iowa:William C. Brown Co., 1966.
3. James, S.L. and Brubaker, C.E.: Running mechanics. JAMA 221:9:1014, 28 August, 1922.
4. Klein, K.K.: Progression of lateral asymmetries of growth: Comparison of boys elementary through high school with adults with chronic low back symptoms. The D. O. 11:2:107, October 1970.
5. Klein, K.K. and Buckley, J.C.: Asymmetries of growth in the pelvis and legs of growing children, summation of a three year study 1964-1967. Am. Correct. Ther. Assoc. 22:2:53, March-April 1968.
6. Kraus, H.: The Cause, Prevention and Treatment of Backaches, Stress and Tension. New York:Simon and Schuster, 1965, p. 183.
7. Lovett, R.W.: Lateral Curvature of the Spine and Round Shoulders. P. Blakiston's Sons and Co., 1912.
8. Michele, A.A.: Orthotherapy. New York:M. Evans and Co., 1971, p. 223.
9. Roberts, C.A.: Foot balance and athletic achievement. Texas Coach, April 1961, p. 15.
10. Roberts, C.A.: Rear foot controls. Texas Coach, August 1961, p. 14.
11. Roberts, C.A.: Isoropo-body equilibriums-body balance-body posture. Texas Coach, 1962, p. 22.
12. Roberts, C.A.: Isoropo (iso-Equal + Robo-Body) inequality of leg length. Texas Coach, November 1962, p. 12.
13. Roberts, C.A.: Isoropo-heel valgus. Texas Coach, February 1963, p. 12.
14. Ryan, A.J.: What causes low back pain. Physician and Sports Med. 2:9:37, 1973.

Bibliography

Clancy, W.G. Jr.: Lower extremity injuries in the jogger and distance runner. Physician Sports Med. 2:6:47, June 1974.
Green, W.T.: Discrepancies in leg length of the lower extremities, Instructional Course Lectures VIII. Am. Acad. Orthopaed. Surg. 1951.
Lowman, C.L., Colestock, C. and Cooper, H.: Corrective Physical Education for Groups. New York:A. S. Barnes, 1937.
Sheehan, G.: The pain of distance runners. Physician Sports Med. 2:5:31, May, 1974.
Wright, R.M.: The role of Manipulation in the Rehabilitation of the Athlete. J. Am. Osteopath. Assoc. 73, October 1973.

Strength and Flexibility in Relation to Hamstring Strains

Wendell Liemohn

Introduction

Klafs and Arnheim [7] have indicted uneven muscle strength and inflexibility as precipitators of hamstring strains. Burkett [2], utilizing Clarke's [4] strength measurement procedures and a bilateral hip-joint flexibility test, found that strength imbalance between (1) the hamstring pairs, (2) the quadricep pairs and (3) the contralateral hamstring-quadricep pairs were all specific factors that determine susceptibility to hamstring strains. Fried [5] noted that if there were a marked difference of strength between the hamstrings and quadriceps, then the weaker muscle group was liable to strain.

The hamstrings are directly antagonistic to the quadriceps during the first 160 to 165° of leg extension [8]; during the last few degrees of knee-joint extension, however, the hamstrings augment the diminishing effectiveness of the quadriceps and assume a paradoxical extensory action concurrent with foot strike. This sudden change from a stabilizing-flexion action to one of active extension has been cited by Slocum and James [10] as possibly being related to hamstring strains. Carlsoo and Molbech [3] found that the exact timing of this paradoxical functioning of two-joint muscles may vary from individual to individual. The aforementioned, coupled with the variance in force generated by these muscles with respect to joint angle [9], suggests advantages to measuring the strength of these two muscle groups at more than the two angles suggested by Clarke [4].

It also appeared that there may be other factors, particularly in track athletes, that should be examined in addition to the aforementioned. It seemed logical to expect bilateral imbalance with respect to hip-joint flexibility by the unilateral requirements of some of the activities in which track participants perform (e.g., one lead leg in hurdling, one take-off leg in long jumping); for this reason

Wendell Liemohn, Department of Physical Education, Indiana University, Bloomington, Ind., U.S.A.

unilateral hip flexibility measurements appeared desirable. Of course, it should also be kept in mind that some of the event specific characteristics, such as those mentioned, may also be responsible for muscle imbalance. Therefore, the purpose of this study was to compare select physical characteristics including strength and flexibility and to examine these factors in relation to event/athlete idiosyncrasies.

Method

The subjects were 27 members of the 1975 Indiana University track and field team who were competing in events in which hamstring injuries had been relatively prevalent. The number of subjects and their events were ten sprinters, five hurdlers, six long and/or triple jumpers and six pole vaulters. The measurements made included four cable-tension strength tests; these tests were administered prior to and during the 1975 indoor track season. In addition to measuring quadricep and hamstring strength at $115°$ and $165°$, respectively (Fig. 1), as suggested by Clarke [4], the strength of each muscle group was also measured at its antagonist's purported strongest angle (Fig. 2). Unilateral hip-joint flexibility measurements were made with a goniometer utilizing the procedure suggested by Kendall et al [6] (Fig. 3). Three measurements were made bilaterally for all strength and flexibility tests; the means of the repeated measurements were used in the analysis. The strength data were converted to ratios to obviate extremes in scores and to facilitate comparisons. The data collected also included the determination of (1) the forward leg in block starts, (2) the lead leg in hurdling, and (3) the take-off leg in the long jump, triple jump and pole vault.

Results

Seven* of the 27 subjects sustained hamstring strains subsequent to the collection of the data; three additional track men sustained hamstring strains in the 1974 track season. The ten instances were further categorized as either being a mild or a moderate strain. The American Medical Association [1] has defined a mild strain as a slightly pulled muscle and a moderate strain as a moderately pulled muscle. To put this in a time perspective, the athletes in this study who sustained mild strains were competing within one month; and

---

*One subject sustained bilateral hamstring strains; however, only the one classified as moderate is reflected in the data presented.

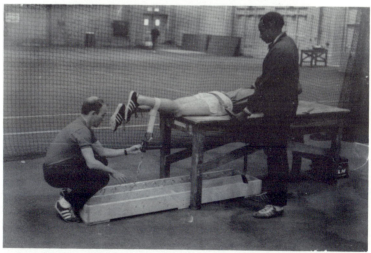

FIG. 1. Measuring quadricep and hamstring strength at 115° and 165°, respectively.

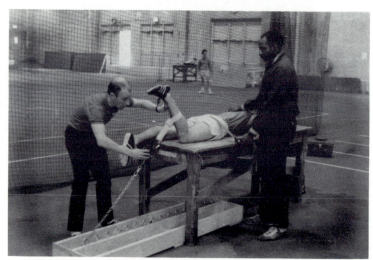

FIG. 2. Measuring strength of each muscle group at strongest angle.

FIG. 3. Hip-joint flexibility measurements made with goniometer.

those sustaining moderate strains were out of competition one month or longer. This categorization procedure facilitated making four experimental/control group comparisons, namely, comparing data on the following: (1) five individuals sustaining moderate strains in 1975 (E5) with the remainder (C22); (2) seven individuals sustaining mild or moderate strains in 1975 (E7) with the remainder (C20); (3) ten individuals sustaining mild or moderate strains in either 1974 or 1975 (E10) with the remainder (C17); and (4) six individuals sustaining moderate strains in either 1974 or 1975 (E6) with the remainder (C21).

The data are more graphically presented (Figs. 4-10). Generally speaking, the individuals in this study tended to have stronger right thigh than left thigh musculature. Conversely, for all group analyses, more flexibility was noted for left hip joint flexion than for right hip joint flexion.

Strength Ratio Comparisons and Flexibility Comparisons

    1. Ipsilateral Antagonists
        a. Leg Flexion/Leg Extension at 115° and 165° (Figs. 4 and 5)

            A discernible difference was noted for right thigh musculature in that the right leg flexors were proportion-

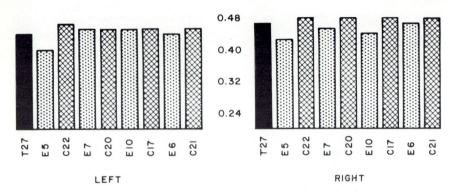

FIG. 4. Leg flexion/leg extension 115°.

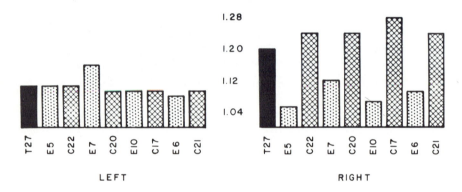

FIG. 5. Leg flexion/leg extension 165°.

ately stronger in the control groups than in the experimental groups. However, similar differences were not noted for the strength of the left thigh musculature.

b. Leg Flexion 165°/Leg Extension 115° (Fig. 6)
    Although the figure does not permit definitive inferences, it does indicate that, utilizing Clarke's standard measuring techniques, in the population studied the flexor-extensor ratio averages .585. This approximates the .60 ratio which Klein and Allman [8] recommended for college football players to enhance knee joint stability.

2. Contralateral Agonists

a. Right Leg Extension/Left Leg Extension (Fig. 7)
    At 115° in both groups the extensors of the right leg

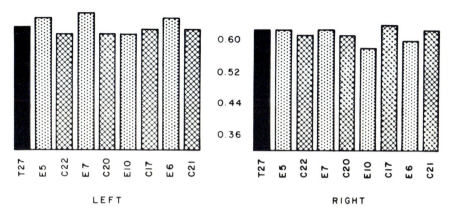

FIG. 6. Leg flexion 165°/leg extension 115°.

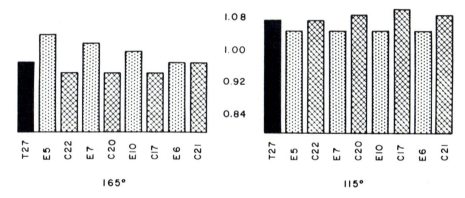

FIG. 7. Right leg extension/left leg extension.

were stronger than those of the left; surprisingly, the difference was greater in the control groups. At 165° the right leg extensors tended to be stronger than those of the left leg in the experimental groups; however, at this angle in the control group the left leg extensors were slightly stronger.

b. Right Leg Flexion/Left Leg Flexion (Fig. 8)
    At both angles measured the flexors of the right leg in the control groups were stronger than those of the left; surprisingly, the same measurements for the experimental groups reveal more bilateral balance.

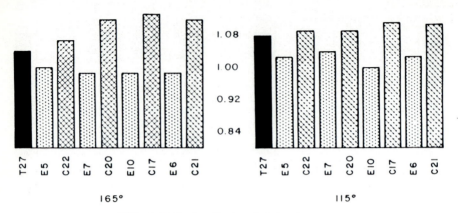

FIG. 8. Right leg flexion/left leg flexion.

3. Bilaterality (Fig. 9)

    In basically all group comparisons the leg flexor-extensor strength composite was stronger in the right leg than in the left; again, the greatest bilateral balance slightly favored the experimental groups.

4. Flexibility (Fig. 10)

    Greater flexibility was noted for both the experimental and control groups in left hip joint flexion than in right hip joint flexion. Furthermore, the mean flexibilities for the control groups and for the experimental groups were 91.6° and 87.1°, respectively. The difference between left and right hip joint flexibility was also greater in the experimental groups than in the control groups.

Discussion

Bilateral strength imbalance was noted frequently; however, a relationship between this factor and factors such as leg injured,

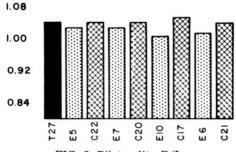

FIG. 9. Bilaterality R/L.

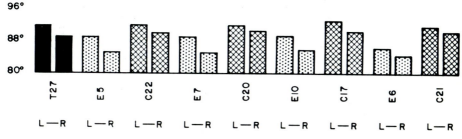

FIG. 10. Hip-joint flexibility.

take-off leg, etc., was not seen. Although the ratio of leg flexion/leg extension strength was higher in the control groups than in the experimental groups, the fact that this was only noted for the right leg reduces the value of this observation.

The leg flexor-extensor strength composite in all groups was found to be stronger in the right leg than in the left; this is not readily explainable although the dominance factor might have some significance. Six of the seven hamstring strains occurring during the 1975 track season were to the nondominant leg (i.e., leg ipsilateral to the nondominant hand). Furthermore, the one individual sustaining a moderate strain to the dominant leg also sustained a mild strain to his nondominant leg, so in reality seven of the eight strains occurring were to the nondominant leg. The right knee flexor-extensor strength composite was greater than the left for 19 of the 27 athletes. When this was examined relative to handedness, 15 of the 22 right handers and 4 of the 5 left handers were found to have stronger right leg flexor/extensor strength composites than left. Perhaps something so nominal as running around tracks counterclockwise contributes to this asymmetry. If this were true, indoor track would appear to have the most deleterious effect.

Perhaps the most definitive precipitator of hamstring strains suggested in this study relates to hip-joint flexibility. It can be seen in Figure 10 that the control groups always tended to be more flexible than the experimental groups; furthermore, a greater degree of bilaterality was also noted in the control groups relative to flexibility. However, although bilaterality with respect to flexibility may be a factor, the data in this study did not show that the least flexible limb was the one that was usually injured.

It is possible that the ideal flexibility range for track and field athletes may not be known. Kendall et al [6] state that 80 to 85° is the normal hip-joint flexibility range; only two of the athletes in this study failed to reach this. One of these athletes sustained a moderate strain to his left hamstring; his hip-joint flexibility was 78° for the injured limb and 80° for the noninjured one. The fact that most of the athletes examined exceeded 85° in hip-joint flexibility may support the contention that some of these individuals are deficient in hamstring development.

It is conceivable that either age and/or years in track could also be factors which are related to hamstring strains. Those individuals sustaining strains tended to be underclassmen; it is possible that the training regimen followed at Indiana University may have provided a greater degree of protection to the upperclassmen. Asymmetry relative to flexibility was noted in that the athletes were usually more flexible in the left hip joint than in the right. Perhaps something in our "right-handed world" is a factor, e.g., a student's desk usually permits the left leg to be crossed over the right but not vice versa.

Perhaps a few additional inferences may be drawn by examining the data with respect to the events in which the athletes competed. Three of the ten sprinters sustained hamstring strains; in each case the injury was to the "up-leg" (which was also the nondominant leg for these three) in block starts. Furthermore, the flexor-extensor strength ratio of the three injured sprinters averaged .20 less for the four strength measurements than the ratios for the seven sprinters who did not sustain an injury. A similar disproportionate strength differential was noted by Burkett [2] in individuals having hamstring strains. As a group, the sprinters were the most bilateral relative to flexibility (i.e., ratios averaged .97).

The one hurdler sustaining a hamstring strain in 1975, as well as the one sustaining a hamstring strain in 1974, injured his lead leg; in both instances the lead leg was his dominant leg. The one long jumper as well as the two pole vaulters sustaining a hamstring strain injury in the 1975 season injured his take-off leg which also happened to be his nondominant leg. The same was true for the one pole vaulter injuring his leg in the 1974 season. The one long jumper having a hamstring strain in 1974 also injured his take-off leg; however, in this case it was the dominant leg. The bilaterality ratios relative to flexibility were .95 for the hurdlers and the long and triple jumpers, and .94 for the pole vaulters.

Conclusions

There are a host of factors that either singly or synergistically precipitate and/or potentiate hamstring strains. The possibility exists that strength and flexibility ratios are most important considerations;

however, factors such as leg dominance, lead leg in hurdling, take-off leg in jumping events and counterclockwise running of turns may also have importance. Needless to say the specific causes of hamstring strains, whether they be anatomical, physiological, and/or environmental, need to be further elucidated. Although the task may be most imposing, it would appear that a cooperative extensive data collection on a large number of subjects followed by a stepwise regression analysis could explicate many of the more controllable precipitators of hamstring strains.

References

1. American Medical Association: Standard Nomenclature of Athletic Injuries. Chicago:American Medical Association, 1966.
2. Burkett, L.N.: Causative factors in hamstring strains. Med. Sci. Sports 2:39-42, 1970.
3. Carlsoo, S. and Molbech, S.: The functions of certain two-joint muscles in a closed muscular chain. Acta Morphol. Neerl. Scand. 6:377-386, 1966.
4. Clarke, H.H.: Muscular Strength and Endurance in Man. Englewood Cliffs:Prentice-Hall, Inc. 1966.
5. Fried, T.S.: Soccer. In Taylor, A.W. (ed.): The Scientific Aspects of Sports Training. Springfield:Charles C Thomas, 1975.
6. Kendall, H.O., Kendall, F.P. and Wadsworth, G.E.: Muscles — Testing and Function. Baltimore:The Williams and Wilkins Co., 1971.
7. Klafs, C.E. and Arnheim, D.D.: Modern Principles of Athletic Training. St. Louis:C. V. Mosby Co., 1973.
8. Klein, K.K. and Allman, F.L.: The Knee in Sports. Austin:Pemberton Press, 1969.
9. Reid, D.C. and Kelly, R.: Selected problems of the thigh and knee to illustrate some basic techniques of rehabilitation. In Taylor, A.W. (ed.): The Scientific Aspects of Sports Training. Springfield:Charles C Thomas, 1975.
10. Slocum, D.B. and James, S.L.: Biomechanics of running. JAMA 205:97-104, 1968.

Biomechanics of the Human Patellar Tendon

H. Krahl

Introduction

Our knowledge of the functional properties and the load limit of human tendons is insufficient, despite increasing experience in the clinical and theoretical field. Generally, a previous damage is supposed to be the cause of a rupture. On the other hand, results of recent research do not exclude the possibility of an entire traumatic procedure.

In sports the tendopathies of the patellar tendon are of special interest, besides the injuries of the Achilles tendon. The pathogenesis and therapy are not well known, because of insufficient knowledge of the basis.

The patellar tendon represents the passive transmitter of the strongest human muscle, the quadriceps femoris. It is used in all dynamic movements, especially in getting up from a sitting position, in running, climbing and jumping, as well as in cushioning or slowing down the body weight with bended knees. In sports mainly jump events, with vertical components like high jump, basketball, volleyball, pole vaulting and weightlifting, an extraordinary strain is involved for the tendon.

Mathematically in ordinary conditions a tension load of 300 to 600 kp is assumed (Frankel, 1971; Groh and Weinmann, 1962, 1965), which may increase under extreme dynamic conditions up to 2000 kp.

Methods

We tried to find out through experiment the mechanical properties of the patellar tendon. We took the material, which consisted of the patella, the patellar tendon and the head of tibia, from dead bodies, generally within 24 hours after death. It was

H. Krahl, Orthopaedic Clinic and Policlinic of the Heidelberg University, Federal Republic of Germany.

embedded and fixed in a special construction, consisting of a divisible light metal mold, constructed in the coarse form of a patella and with a conical interior space, and of another metal mold to fix the head of tibia, which was connected to a metal plate by screws. Between the implant and the metal mold we put an unsaturated polyester material. This method of fixation provides the possibility for stretching the tendon as a whole and its bony insertion, in contrast to the methods described in other experiments. These methods of fixation by metal wire, clamps of metal, only allow the investigation of a part of the tendon, because the fixed end of the tendon cannot be used for the investigation.

The extension tests were done with two machines, like those used for testing synthetic or other materials in industry. These machines allow different speeds of deformation. A storage oscillograph makes it possible to record the diagram of load and elongation.

Results

Ninety-eight knee joints were investigated and analyzed. At first we found that there was a decrease of cross-section in relation to the age and the sex statistically significant: the cross-section of tendons of older people is lower than that of young people, and the data of women are lower than those of men.

The point of rupture of the bone-tendon-bone system was situated in the region of the apex patella, i.e., with three exceptions there was no tendon rupture but an avulsion fracture of the distal patella pole. This discrepancy to the localization of clinical ruptures is explained by the different mechanical or morphological facts. In clinical cases mainly, a previous degenerative damage of the tendon tissue is responsible for the rupture, which often occurs spontaneously.

The load of rupture is considered as a rough description of strain property of tendon. We found a dependence of the age, the velocity of deformation and the sex; therefore, the average values of young people (20 to 39 years) with 505.5 kp differ clearly from those of older people (420.9 kp at 40 to 59 years) and those of oldest people of more than 60 years with an average value of 313.3 kp.

A higher velocity of tension is connected with higher values of load of rupture. Remarkable also is the maximum value of 1180 kp, which is equivalent to the load of a passenger motor car.

Comparing the average values of men and women we notice a difference of up to 28.8%.

It is possible to compare the values of the patellar tendon with those of the Achilles tendon (Wilhelm, 1972, 1973), which is supposed to be the strongest tendon of the human body.

The relation of the rupture load to the cross-section of the material is the stress, in the dimension of kp/mm^2. We found an average value of 5.08 kp/mm^2, which is to be compared with the results of other authors (Wertheim 1847; Triepel 1902; Stucke 1950; Tittel and Otto 1970; Langhoff 1973). The value of stress also depends upon age and velocity of tension which at a higher velocity amounts to more than 20%. In one case we found a value of 16 kp/mm^2, which means a higher dimension that those of the metals brass or copper.

The elongation of the tendon means the amount of length at the breaking point. We found again a dependence upon the velocity of deformation: when the speed is low, the values for elongation are high and vice versa (about 20%). Furthermore, we discovered a decrease of about 20% with older people.

The shape of our diagrams belongs to group A of Viidik. This sigmoid type is found at all fibers with helical structure of the molecule. These materials have the properties of creeping or relaxation and they are called "visco-elastic" and "visco-plastic." They are caused by the dependence upon time of the delayed equilibration of the long-chain molecules. It can be made clear by the so-called Maxwell-Model.

Unphysiological strain in the tendon tissue or its insertion can be prevented by these deadening elements, which are able to destroy energy by its structural properties.

Many others regard the perfect elasticity of the tendon only in an area of 3% or 4% of elongation (Abrahams 1967; Vidiik 1966; Hirsch 1974). That means we are able to reproduce the diagrams only in the area up to 3% to 4%. We call the behavior beyond 4% an elastic imperfection. This phenomenon is to be regarded as cyclic, that means repeated, strain. Our material had been stretched six times up to a load of 50 kp, or more than 4% elongation. After every loading we fixed the new value of elongation of the material. We observed a decrease of the elongation, because the tissue was unable to restitute its molecular structure.

If we transfer this fact into clinical conditions, it is possible to explain the painful tendopathies, which occur especially in those sports in which the patellar tendon is exposed to high dynamic, cyclic strain (by example, in the training of the jumping force with weights, without sufficient recreation). This cyclic stress means a loss of elongation and therefore a loss of the ability of deadening. Like stress fractures of the bone the tendon tissue may fail, at first with micro-ruptures. Later, spontaneous ruptures may occur.

Conclusion

It is possible to test the patellar tendon as a whole with its bony insertions and to fix the weakest point of the functional unit by our method as described before. The results of breaking load and stress are comparable with the values of the Achilles tendon. The maximal load of 1180 kp was up to now only presumed mathematically, but not verified by experiments.

The influence of higher velocity of deformation leads to an increase of load and stress, to a decrease of elongation and to alteration of the load-elongation diagram.

The influence of age leads to alterations of the structure and therefore to decreasing results of load, stress and elongation. A dependence upon the sex is only to be seen in the results of breaking load which decrease in female tendon tissue.

Cyclic strain leads to a decrease of the elongation as a result of the elastic imperfection.

Generally, the patellar tendon has visco-elastic properties with an extraordinary solidity which is necessary for its task as a passive transmitter of strength. The bone-tendon-bone system only will fail when high loads arise. Normally, avulsion fractures of apex patella occur, real tendon ruptures will only originate at degenerated tendon tissue, or at traumatic conditions, when different forces at the same time affect the tendon, as we observed with a basketball player who had been attacked by the knee of another player at the moment of the beginning of a high-jump movement.

Analyse cinétique de la grande flexion des jambes avec charge

Pierre P. Lagassé et Clermont P. Simard

Introduction

Le développement physique spécifique, dont l'objectif principal est l'amélioration des qualités organiques, musculaires et perceptivo-cinétiques nécessaires à la performance, constitue l'un des principaux éléments de la préparation du champion. Tout système d'entraînement visant à améliorer les qualités musculaires doit solliciter la participation des mêmes groupes musculaires que ceux qui sont responsables de l'exécution de l'activité physique en cours [2].

Plusieurs activités physiques font appel aux extenseurs des genoux et la grande flexion des jambes avec charge (squat) constitue l'un des exercices couramment utilisés pour développer la force, la résistance et l'endurance de ces groupes musculaires. Toutefois, les travaux de recherche de Kotani et al [7] et ceux de Troup [10] indiquent une haute incidence de traumatismes au niveau de la région lombaire non seulement chez les haltérophiles d'expérience, mais également chez des athlètes qui utilisent l'haltérophilie pour améliorer leurs qualités musculaires.

Notre recherche visait à analyser et à comparer les moments de force aux différentes articulations, de même que les pressions intervertébrales au niveau de la région lombaire, chez des haltérophiles d'expérience et des sujets novices lors de l'exécution de la grande flexion des jambes avec charge.

Méthodologie

Deux groupes d'athlètes de sexe masculin servirent de sujets dans cette étude. Le premier groupe se composait de dix haltérophiles confirmés pratiquant la grande flexion des jambes avec charge depuis au moins cinq ans. Leurs poids et taille étaient, en moyenne, de 77.6 kg et de 172 cm respectivement. Le deuxième groupe se composait

Pierre P. Lagassé et Clermont P. Simard, Département d'éducation physique, Université Laval, Québec, Canada.

de sept sujets novices en haltérophilie. Leurs poids et taille moyens étaient de 66.2 kg et de 169 cm respectivement.

La cueillette des données se divisait en deux parties. Chaque athlète s'adonnait d'abord à une période de réchauffement dont le but principal était de déterminer sa charge maximale. La deuxième partie était consacrée à la prise des donnés cinématographiques. Chaque sujet exécutait une grande flexion des jambes avec 80% de sa charge maximale. Il devait fléchir les jambes au maximum et maintenir cette position de flexion maximale pour une durée de deux secondes. Une caméra à haute vitesse (Photosonics), placée perpendiculairement au sujet et tournant à une vitesse de 100 images/seconde, servit d'instrument pour capter les données cinématographiques.

L'analyse des données, exécutée à l'aide d'un projecteur analytique (Lafayette) et d'un analyseur de films (Graph-Pen), consistait à déterminer, lors de la position de flexion maximale, l'emplacement horizontal et vertical des articulations de l'épaule, de la hanche et des chevilles de chacun des sujets. Le poids et la longeur des segments de chaque sujet, de même que la location du centre de gravité de chacun des segments ont été déterminés à l'aide des données de Dempster [4]. Les moments de force aux articulations de la hanche, du genou et de la cheville ont été compilés selon le modèle suggéré par Plagenhoef [8].

On retrouve à la figure 1 le diagramme des forces qui ont servi à déterminer les moments de force. La force musculaire des extenseurs dorsaux (Fm), la pression intervertébrale (Fu) au niveau de l'articulation L4 — L5 et ses composantes de dislocation (Fs) et de compression (Fc) ont ensuite été déterminées en suivant le modèle suggéré par Hayes et Wood [6] et présenté en figure 2.

Résultats et discussion

Le tableau I présente les résultats moyens obtenus chez les haltérophiles et chez les novices. La force musculaire (Fm) des "*erectores spinae*" est environ trois fois plus grande chez les haltérophiles que chez les novices. Il faut noter que le calcul de cette force musculaire a été fait à partir du moment de force à l'articulation intervertébrale L4 — L5 en assumant que ce groupe musculaire se situe parallèlement à la colonne vertébrale et à une distance de 6.0 cm de celle-ci [6]. Le résultat est attribuable, premièrement, à une plus grande charge portée par les haltérophiles et, deuxièmement, au fait que l'inclinaison du tronc est plus marquée chez ceux-ci que chez les novices.

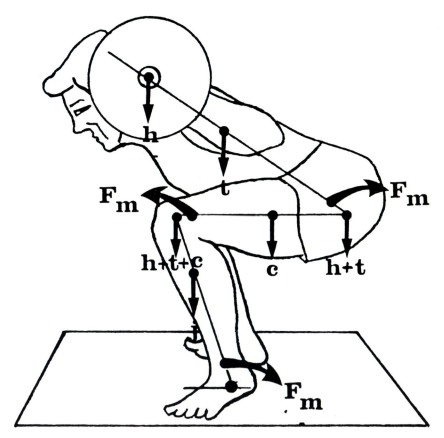

FIG. 1. Position d'analyse du sujet et diagramme des forces utilisées pour le calcul des moments de force aux articulations de la hanche, du genou et de la cheville.

Des études de Evans [5] et Sonoda [9], réalisées sur des cadavres, ont déjà démontré que la pression intervertébrale maximale que l'être humain peut soutenir avant que les cartilages ne subissent des micro-traumatismes se situe aux environs de 700 kg [6]. Les résultats de cette étude démontrent que la pression intervertébrale, à 80% de la charge maximale, a dépassé ce seuil chez les haltérophiles (Fu = 1,146 kg), mais qu'elle est demeurée inférieure chez les novices (Fu = 495 kg).

Nos résultats tendent à démontrer que l'utilisation des grandes flexions par des novices ne semble pas contre-indiquée, du moins en ce qui concerne les pressions intervertébrales. Toutefois, il faut envisager la possibilité que ces exercices engendrent des modifica-

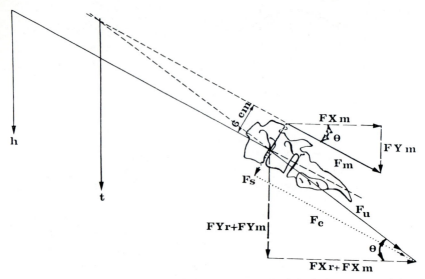

FIG. 2. Diagramme des forces utilisées pour le calcul de la force musculaire des extenseurs dorsaux (Fm), de la pression intervertébrale (Fu) et des composants de dislocation (Fs) et de compression (Fc).

Tableau I. Force des extenseurs dorsaux (Fm), pression intervertébrale (Fu), force de dislocation (Fs), force de compression (Fc) et moments de force aux articulations de la hanche (MOH), du genou (MOG) et de la cheville (MOC) chez les haltérophiles et chez les novices

Variable	Haltérophiles (N = 10)	Novices (N = 7)
Fm(Kg)	910	382
Fu(kg)	1,146	495
Fs(Kg)	135	52
Fc(Kg)	1,137	492
Fs/Fc	0.118	0.106
MOH(Kg/m)	31	14
MOG(Kg/m)	10	13
MOC(Kg/m)	19	7

tions chroniques au niveau des cartilages chez les haltérophiles d'expérience.

La force de dislocation dont la valeur est de 135 kg chez les haltérophiles et de 52 kg chez les sujets novices, revêt une importance particulière puisqu'elle est une des causes principales des hernies discales. Tel que mentionné par Hayes et Wood [6], l'intégrité de l'articulation L4 − L5 dépend principalement du rapport entre la force de dislocation et la force de compression. Ce rapport diminue lorsque la charge est plus lourde et augmente lorsque la position du tronc se rapproche de l'horizontale. Les résultats de la présente étude démontrent que le rapport entre la force de dislocation et la force de compression est semblable chez les deux groupes. Ceci peut être attribué aux deux facteurs mentionnés plus haut, puisque les haltérophiles portaient une charge plus lourde tout en inclinant le tronc davantage.

Les moments de force aux articulations de la hanche et de la cheville sont considérablement plus élevés chez les sujets haltérophiles que chez les novices et ceci peut être attribué à la charge plus lourde et à l'alignement des segments des haltérophiles. Toutefois, les résultats démontrent un moment de force plus élevé à l'articulation de genou chez les novices (13 kg/m), comparativement aux haltérophiles (10 kg/m). Ce résultat revêt une importance capitale puisque, tel que mentionné par Ariel [1], le moment de force est le principal élément qui contribue à la dislocation du genou. La probabilité de dislocation au niveau de genou nous apparaît donc plus grande chez les novices que chez les haltérophiles.

Conclusion

Cette étude entreprise dans le but d'investiguer les moments de force et les pressions intervertébrales au niveau de la région lombaire chez des sujets experts en haltérophile et chez des sujets novices, nous permet de tirer deux conclusions:

1. la grande flexion des jambes avec 80% d'une charge maximale exécutée par des sujets novices en haltérophilie ne semble pas atteindre un seuil dangereux pour la région lombaire;

2. la grande flexion des jambes peut entraîner des traumatismes au niveau du genou et possiblement une dislocation chez les sujets novices.

Remerciements

Des remerciements sont exprimés à Jean-Yves Dionne et aux haltérophiles pour leur aide precieuse dans la realisation de ce projet.

Références

1. Ariel, B.G.: Biomechanical analysis of the knee joint during deep knee bends with heavy load. *In* Nelson, R.C. and Morehouse, C.A. (eds.): Biomechanics IV. Baltimore:University Park Press, 1974.

2. Brunelle, J., Poirier, G., Descheneaux, R. et Bérubé, G.: Le développement physique spécifique (Dps). *Dans* Bouchard, C., Brunelle, J. et Godbout, P. (eds.): La Préparation d'un Champion. Québec:Editions du Pélican, 1973.

3. Chaffin, D.B. and Park, K.S.: A longitudinal study of low-back pain as associated with occupational weight lifting factors. J. Am. Indust. Hyg. Assoc. 34:513, 1973.

4. Dempster, N.T.: Space Requirements of the Seated Operator. W.A.D.C. Technical Report, 1955.

5. Evans, F.G. and Lissner, H.R.: Biomechanical studies of the lumbar spine and pelvis. J. Bone Joint Surg. 41A:218, 1959.

6. Hayes, K.C. and Wood, G.A.: A kinetic model of intervertebral stress. *In* Proceedings of the Canadian Society of Biomechanics, 1973.

7. Kotani, P.T., Ichikawa, N., Wakabayashi, W. et al: Studies of spondylolysis found among weightlifters. Br. J. Sports Med. G:4, 1971.

8. Plagenhoef, S.: Patterns of Human Motion, Englewood Cliffs, N.J.:Prentice-Hall, 1971.

9. Sonoda, T.: "Studies on Compression, Tension and Torsion Strength of the Human Vertebral Column", Journal of Kyoto Prefect. Medical University, 71:659, 1962.

10. Troup, J.D.G.: Relation of lumbar spine disorders to heavy manual work and lifting. Lancet 1:857, 1965.

Bilan radiologique de la région lombo-sacrée chez l'haltérophile débutant et expert

Hugues Archambault, E. Michel Azouz et Clermont P. Simard

Introduction

La pratique de l'haltérophilie peut-elle provoquer des modifications dégénératives des structures lombo-sacrées? . Si oui, existe-t-il des facteurs morphologiques qui peuvent favoriser le développement de ces lésions? .

Matériel

Telle était l'idée directrice de cette étude où nous avons fait un bilan radiologique de 10 sujets qui pratiquent l'haltérophilie depuis au moins 5 ans et que l'on appellera les "experts" par comparaison à 7 sujets qui commencent dans ce sport, c'est-à-dire les "novices." Nous avons donc réalisé chez chaque suject des clichés radiologiques de face sans charge, et de profil avec et sans charge. Le cliché avec charge a été tiré alors que le sujet supportait 80% de sa capacité maximale.

Méthode

Il est évident que le fait de lever régulièrement des poids très lourds impose à la région lombo-sacrée un "stress" considérable qui met à rude épreuve la stabilité de cette portion du rachis.

Quels sont les critères radiologiques qui permettent d'évaluer cette stabilité du rachis?

L'angle de Ferguson

C'est l'angle que fait le plateau supérieur du sacrum avec l'horizontale (Fig. 1). Il dépend de la forme et de la position

Hughes Archambault et E. Michel Azouz, Service de radiologie, Centre hospitalier de l'université Laval, Sainte-Foy, et Clermont P. Simard, Département d'éducation physique, Université Laval, Québec, Canada.

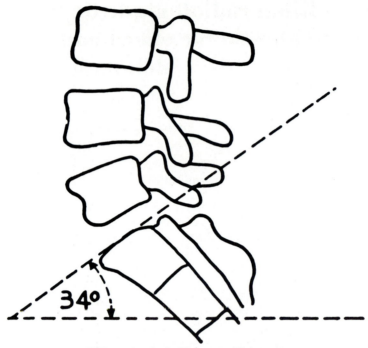

FIG. 1. Angle de Ferguson (Schéma).

anatomique du sacrum. Selon Ferguson, il se lit normalement à 34°
(Fig. 2) [4]. En pratique, on dit qu'il est franchement anormal s'il est
plus grand de 40°. On peut déduire facilement les répercussions de
cet angle sur les vertèbres lombaires susjacentes. En effet, plus il sera
ouvert plus la courbure lombaire sera accentuée.

L'axe du support pondéral

    C'est une perpendiculaire à l'horizontale abaissée, tel un fil-à-
plomb, du centre du corps vertébral L3 (Fig. 3).

    Si cette perpendiculaire tombe sur le plateau sacré, on dit que la
statique est normale. En effet, la ligne de force se trouve à appuyer
sur son support anatomique naturel que constitue le sacrum. Si au
contraire, cette ligne tombe en avant du bord antérieur du sacrum,
ceci constitue un facteur d'instabilité du rachis puisque les muscles
lombaires doivent compenser pour cette force qui tombe dans le
vide. Pour plus de précision, on peut mesurer en millimètre la
distance de cette ligne avec le bord antérieur du sacrum.

    La figure 4 illustre des variantes possibles de cet axe de support
pondéral par rapport au sacrum.

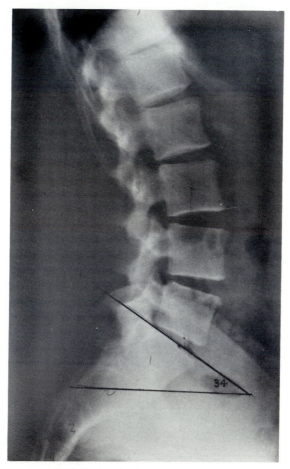

FIG. 2. Angle de Ferguson normal.

L'asymétrie des facettes articulaires postérieures

Un autre critère d'instabilité est constitué par l'asymétrie des facettes articulaires postérieures L5-S1 (Fig. 5 et Fig. 6). Il s'agit d'une anomalie congénitale qui compromet la stabilité du rachis lombaire par rapport au sacrum puisqu'elle constitue un porte-à-faux qui, à la suite d'un *stress* répété [2], (constitué par l'imposition d'une très grande force à cet endroit) pourrait favoriser sinon un glissement d'une des facettes articulaires, du moins une réaction arthrosique précoce. On a retrouvé cette anomalie chez un seul des sujets étudiés.

Existe-t-il d'autres modifications qui peuvent compromettre la stabilité du rachis?

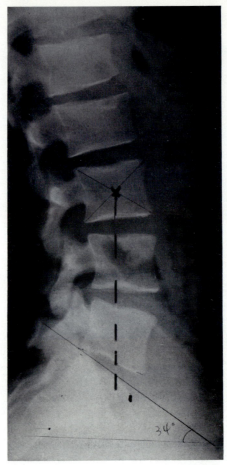

FIG. 3. Axe de support pondéral chez un sujet dont l'angle de Ferguson est aussi normal.

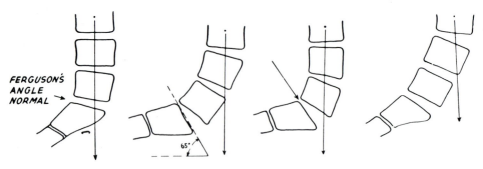

FIG. 4. Schéma de Meschan illustrant des variantes d'axe de support pondéral anormal.

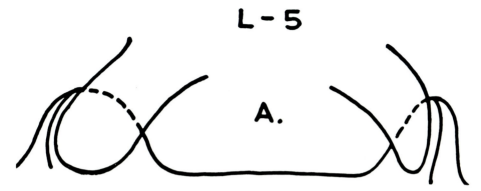

FIG. 5. Illustration schématique de Meschan d'une asymétrie dans l'orientation des facettes articulaires postérieures de L-5 — S-1.

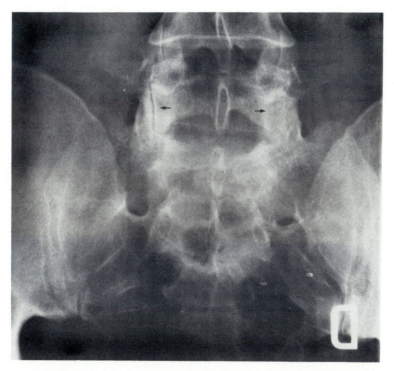

FIG. 6. Asymétrique: La facette gauche qui a une orientation sagittale se présente comme une ligne verticale radiotransparente alors que la droite qui est dans le plan coronal n'est pas visible sur le cliché.

D'abord des anomalies congénitales.

Certaines n'ont probablement aucune répercussion comme la spina-bifida occulta ou une anomalie transitionnelle symétrique [1]. Par ailleurs, il est incontestable qu'une anomalie asymétrique pourra réagir à un stress très fort et répété par une dégénérescence prématurée. Il en est de même d'une forte scoliose congénitale ou acquise où les forces imposées au rachis créeront sûrement à plus ou moins brève échéance des répercussions néfastes sur les surfaces articulaires qui ont à supporter un poids supplémentaire.

Résultats

L'angle de Ferguson

L'étude comparative de l'angle de Ferguson chez les 10 experts avec le groupe témoin de 7 novices nous montre que chez les novices 50% ont au départ un angle normal comparativement à 30% chez les experts.

La constatation la plus intéressante est que chez 60% des experts (6/10) l'angle de Ferguson est fortement anormal (soit $> 40°$) lors des clichés avec charge alors que chez les novices on n'en compte que 2 sur 7. Ces deux sujets sont les mêmes qui étaient déjà anormaux sans charge, alors que le nombre double chez les experts.

L'axe de support pondéral

On constate au tableau II et III que les experts rétablissent à l'effort leur axe du support pondéral même si trois d'entre eux

Tableau I. Angle de Ferguson

	Novices (7)		Experts (10)	
	Sans charge	Avec charge	Sans charge	Avec charge
$-34°$	4	3	3	1
$35° - 39°$	1	2	4	3
$+40°$	2	2	3	6

Tableau II. Axe de support pondéral

	Novices (7)		Experts (10)	
	Sans charge	Avec charge	Sans charge	Avec charge
N	5	5	7	6
-10 mm	–	–	–	1
$+10$ mm	2	2	3	3

Tableau III. Comparaison A°F et A.S.P. anormaux

	Novices (7)		Experts (10)	
	Sans charge (-)	Avec charge (+)	Sans charge (-)	Avec charge (+)
AF 40°	2	2	3	6
ASP + 10 mm	2	2	3	3

avaient un angle de Ferguson très anormal (> 40°) alors que chez les novices, le nombre reste identique.

Ceci porterait à croire que les experts compenseraient, grâce à une technique adéquate, un handicap morphologique initial.

La pratique de l'haltérophilie occasionne-t-elle des processus dégénératifs au rachis lombo-sacré? .

Discussion

Contrairement aux constatations de Kotani et collaborateurs [3], nous n'avons pas trouvé chez les sujets que nous avons étudiés de spondylolyse ou de modification majeure au rachis lombo-sacré.

Chez deux sujets, on a observé une très légère scoliose de cet ordre. De plus, on retrouve bien chez les deux experts les plus âgés (47 et 53 ans) des réactions ostéophytiques, mais il est vraisemblable que ces signes sont imputables autant à l'âge qu'à l'haltérophilie.

Toutefois, la mesure de la hauteur de l'interligne L5-S1 chez les novices et chez les experts, avec toutes les restrictions dues à l'acuité de ces lectures en raison du flou cynétique des clichés pris avec effort, tend à démontrer que cet espace L5-S1 est en moyenne 1 mm plus petit chez les experts.

A noter de plus, que tous ceux dont la hauteur de L5-S1 est inférieure à cette moyenne de 7.1 mm sans effort et 6.3 mm avec effort ont aussi, sauf un, un angle de Ferguson anormal.

Tous ces critères réunis soulèvent la possibilité de signes radiologiques suggestifs d'un début de dégénérescence discale L5-S1 chez les athlètes qui pratiquent l'haltérophilie depuis plus de 5 ans.

Tableau IV. Hauteur (mm) de l'interligne L5-S1

	Novices (7)		Experts (10)	
	Sans charge	Avec charge	Sans charge	Avec charge
Moyenne	8.57	7.43	7.10	6.30

Conclusion

Il se degagé de notre étude deux corollaires d'ordre pratique:

1. L'importance d'établir, grâce à un bilan radiologique, des critères de sélection pour les candidats qui se proposent de pratiquer l'haltérophilie. On peut alors mettre en évidence des anomalies ou déformations qui peuvent constituer une contre-indication stricte à ce sport. Une scoliose importante et une spondylolyse avec glissement vertébral constituent deux exemples.

2. L'importance d'alerter l'entraîneur sur l'existence de certains critères d'instabilité du rachis lombo-sacré; c'est là que le bilan radiologique peut s'avérer le plus utile.

Nous illustrons ce fait par un exemple concret tiré de notre étude. Un sujet qui, au départ, a un angle de Ferguson nettement anormal à 40° (Fig. 7), ramène, grâce à une bonne technique, son

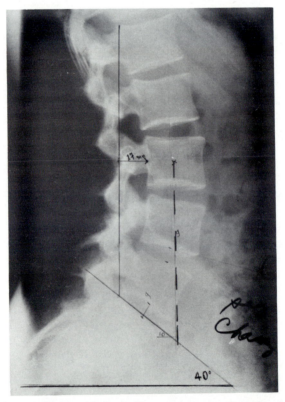

FIG. 7. Cliché sans charge. Angle de Ferguson anormal (40°). Axe de support pondéral anormal (10mm) en avant du bord antérieur du sacrum.

angle à 35° et son axe de support pondéral à la normale (Fig. 8). Inversement, (Fig. 9) un autre athlète part d'un angle presque normal à 38° et au cours de l'effort le porte à 52° avec un axe de support pondéral très anormal (Fig. 9), imposant ainsi aux structures de la charnière lombo-sacrée un effort anormal.

L'entraîneur peut donc aider, par une technique appropriée, une morphologie qui, sans être nettement pathologique, risque à la longue d'accélérer des modifications dégénératives résultant de l'imposition de charges très importantes sur une colonne instable.

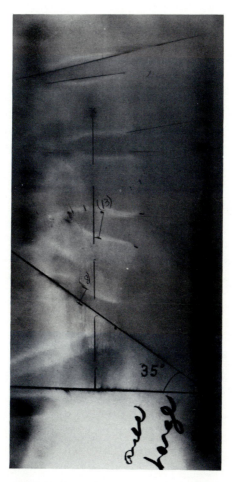

FIG. 8. Même sujet qui à l'effort corrige l'angle de Ferguson à 35° et ramène l'axe de support pondéral à la normale.

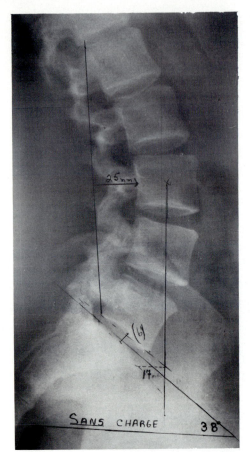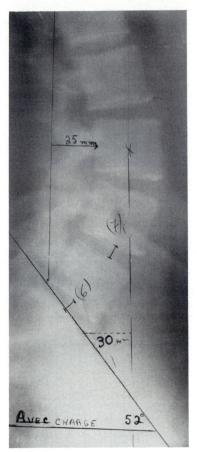

FIG. 9. Axe de support pondéral déjà anormal sans charge (+17mm). Il est
amplifié à l'effort par ouverture de l'angle de Ferguson (52°).

Remerciements

Nous tenons à souligner la collaboration indispensable de
Messieurs P.P. Lagassé, J.Y. Dionne, S. Cloutier ainsi que des dix-sept
haltérophiles qui ont rendu cette étude possible. Nous remerciens
également Mme Nicole Dionne et Mlle Sylvie Alain pour leur aide
dans la rédaction du manuscrit.

Références

1. Fischer, F.J., Friedman, M.D. et Van Demark, R.E.: Roentgenographic
   abnormalities in Soldiers with low back pain: A comparative study. Am. J.
   Roentgen. 79:673-676, 1958.

2. Henry, G.W., Larsen, I.J. et Stewart, S.F.: The roentgenologic criteria for appraising the human back as an economic asset or liability. Am. J. Roentgen. 79:658-672, 1958.
3. Kotani, P.T., Ichikawa, N., Wakabayashi, W. et al: Studies of spondylolysis found among weightlifters. Br. J. Sports Med. 6:4-8, 1971.
4. Meschan, I.: Roentgen Signs in Clinical Practice. W.B. Saunders Company, Vol. I, 1966.

Les accidents sportifs chez des anciens compétiteurs

L. Dec et J. Slezyński

Introduction

Le sport de performance pose de hautes exigences à l'organisme de l'individu et surtout aux organes de mouvement. La participation à la compétition ainsi que l'entraînement oscillant souvent à la frontière des possibilités maxilales de l'organisme constituent souvent un risque potentiel de subir un trauma [5, 6, 8]. Malgré une amélioration de l'assistance médicale et des conditions d'entraînement et malgré un perfectionnement de la technique des exercices, le nombre des accidents dans le sport augmente [1, 4, 7]. Les sollicitations précédentes n'ont pas mené à une élaboration de formes efficaces de prophylaxie. Selon plusieurs auteurs, les traumatismes constituent près de 10% de tous les accidents [3]. On dit que plus de 25% d'anciens et actuels footballeurs jouaient ou bien jouent encore avec un trauma psychique consécutif à une contusion donnée. On peut donc admettre que le trauma est selon toute vraisemblance un facteur inhibitoire de leur développement sportif [2]. Les raisons qui précèdent nous ont incités à effectuer une étude rétrospective des traumatismes parmi les anciens sportifs. Il s'agissait pour nous de vérifier nos opinions à ce sujet en prenant pour base les accidents survenus au cours de la pratique sportive chez des anciens sportifs encore vivants.

Méthodologie

Nous avons examiné 418 anciens sportifs âgés de 40 à 81 ans parmi lesquels se trouvaient: 109 participants des jeux olympiques et du championnat du monde ou d'Europe, 212 représentants du pays ou finalistes du championnat de la Pologne et 97 anciens compétiteurs-représentants de district ou de club. Les examens ont consisté à analyser des données assemblées à l'aide d'un questionnaire spécial.

L. Dec et J. Slezyński, Institut de médecine du sport de l'Ecole supérieure d'éducation physique, Katowice, Pologne.

Nous avons pris en considération une lésion du corps causant une incapacité de pratiquer le sport au moins au cours de quelques semaines et par conséquent influant, même temporairement, sur l'état de santé du compétiteur.

Résultats

Parmi 418 cas examinés, 323 personnes (77.3%) ont subi une lésion du corps liée avec la pratique du sport de performance; 95 personnes (22.7%) n'ont pour leur part subi aucun accident sérieux au cours de leur carrière sportive (Tableau I).

Notre analyse a montré que parmi les anciens compétiteurs, la carrière sportive était plus longue dans le groupe des plus âgés et qu'il y avait aussi moins d'accident sportif dans ce même groupe (Fig. 1).

Il semble que chez les sportifs, les lésions étaient autrefois moins nombreuses que maintenant. Dans notre étude, les lésions sont les plus élevées (80.6%) chez les sportifs âgés de 40 à 49 ans. Dans ce groupe d'âge, le nombre de personnes qui n'ont pas subi de lésions n'est que de 19.4%; dans les groupes plus âgés, ces pourcentages sont de 25.8 ct 30.4. Cette tendance suggère que malgré une meilleure assistance médicale et une amélioration considérable des conditions de jeu, le sport pratiqué de nos jours semble favoriser plus que jamais l'occurrence des blessures.

Les traumatismes ne sont pas identiques dans les diverses disciplines sportives (Tableau II). Nous en avons observé un plus grand nombre dans les jeux collectifs tels que le football, le hockey

Tableau I. Les lésions chez les anciens sportifs pendant leur carrière sportive

Groupe d'âge des anciens sportifs	40-49 ans n = 242		50-59 ans n = 120		60-81 ans n = 56		Total n = 418	
	n	%	n	%	n	%	n	%
Sportifs sans lésion corporelle	47	19,4	31	25,8	17	30,4	95	22,7
Sportifs avec lésions corporelles	195	80,6	89	74,2	39	69,9	323	77,3
Lésions des tendons, articulations	297	152,3	98	110,1	46	117,9	441	136,5
Fractures des os	140	71,7	48	55,1	27	69,2	215	65,5
Lésions des muscles	94	48,2	28	32,1	17	43,5	139	43,0
Autres lésions*	69	35,3	20	22,9	8	20,5	97	30,0

*lésions intérieures, cérébrales, etc.

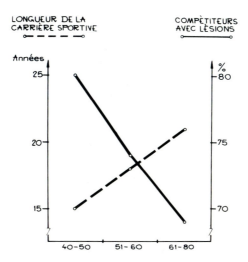

LONGUEUR DE LA CARRIÈRE SPORTIVE
ET LES LÈSIONS TRAUMATIQUES DU CORPS

FIGURE 1.

sur glace et la boxe (Fig. 2). Chez les footballeurs, les lésions des articulations et des ligaments, ainsi que les fractures des os de la jambe semblent dominer. Nous avons constaté relativement peu de traumas chez les escrimeurs.

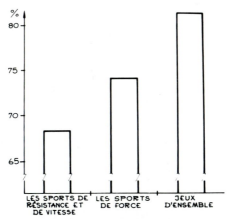

DISCIPLINE SPORTIVE ET LES LÉSIONS
DU CORPS
/COMPÉTITEURS AVEC LÉSIONS DU CORPS/

FIGURE 2.

Dans la catégorie "autres lésions" (Tableau II), figurent 15 anciens footballeurs et hockeyeurs qui ont subi un accident de type commotion cérébrale.

Nous avons remarqué que les traumatismes n'avaient pas tendance à diminuer avec l'augmentation du calibre des sportifs (Tableau III).

Cependant, parmi les anciens compétiteurs de la plus haute classe sportive, c'est-à-dire parmi les anciens compétiteurs olympiques, nous avons observé des lésions en plus petit nombre que chez les représentants du pays et les représentants de région (Fig. 3).

Les compétiteurs représentant un niveau sportif médiocre sont probablement les plus susceptibles d'accidents.

Bien que la fréquence des lésions chez les athlètes appartenant à la plus haute classe sportive soit proportionnellement plus petite, leur pourcentage n'en suscite pas moins l'inquiétude. Parmi nos 418 cas, on a souvent constaté des lésions réitérées, surtout de l'organe du mouvement, lesquelles ont souvent des conséquences d'invalidation.

Le cas 1

Un ancien compétiteur, né en 1929, champion de la Pologne de Cross-Country et aux distances de 1,500 à 10,000 m. A l'âge de quinze ans il a développé un ulcère duodénal. Il a été traité pour cette raison plusieurs fois. Au cours de sa carrière sportive de quelque vingt années, il a subi plus de 80 différentes contusions, y compris 11 contusions des articulations du pied et de nombreuses lésions des

Tableau II. Les disciplines sportives et les lésions corporelles

	Les sports de force n = 94		Les sports de ré- sjstance et de vitesse n = 106		Sports collectifs n = 218	
	n	%	n	%	n	%
Sportifs sans lésion corporelle	25	26,5	34	32,1	36	18,5
Sportifs avec lésions corporelles	69	73,4	72	67,9	182	81,5
Lésions des tendons, articulations	75	108,6	93	129,1	285	156,5
Fracture des os	57	82,6	37	51,3	123	67,6
Lésions des muscles	24	34,7	37	51,3	55	30,2
Autres lésions*	21	30,4	23	31,9	62	34,0

*lésions intérieures, cérébrales, etc.

Tableau III. Le niveau sportif et les lésions corporelles
lors de la carrière sportive

	Participants des Jeux olympiques, Championnats du monde ou d'Europe n = 109		Représentants du pays n = 212		Représentants régionaux n = 97	
	n	%	n	%	n	%
Sportifs sans lésion corporelle	29	26,6	45	21,3	21	21,7
Sportifs avec lésions corporelles	80	73,4	167	78,7	76	78,3
Lésions des tendons, articulations	126	157,8	231	138,3	95	125,0
Fractures des os	56	70,0	130	77,8	36	47,3
Lésions des muscles	30	37,5	65	38,9	23	30,2
Autres lésions*	31	38,7	50	22,9	19	25,0

*lésions intérieures, cérébrales, etc.

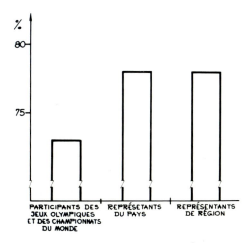

NIVEAU SPORTIF ET LES LÉSIONS
DU CORPS

FIGURE 3.

ligaments et des muscles des membres inférieurs. Un déchirement du
muscle droit de l'abdomen lui a causé des affections durant sept
années. Il a fini sa carrière sportive à l'âge de 33 ans. Il poursuit
aujourd'hui une carrière dans une profession.

Le cas 2

Un ancien cycliste, né en 1915, plusieurs fois participant à la victoire d'équipe dans la Course de la Paix et au championnat de la Pologne. Il fut également vainqueur à des courses internationales. Au cours de sa carrière cycliste, jusqu'à 1948, il a subi plusieurs fois des contusions sans graves conséquences. Une chute pendant une course cycliste en 1948 lui valut une fracture de la colonne vertébrale lombaire avec perte de mobilité. Il porte actuellement un corset. Malgré son invalidité, il est devenu entraîneur.

Le cas 3

Un ancien athlète, né en 1919, international de la Pologne et champion olympique. Au cours de sa carrière sportive il a subi plusieurs contusions, entre autres, une fracture des côtes, une fracture du péroné, des lésions de l'articulation du genou et du pied, sans graves conséquences. Vers 1950, sa vue diminue progressivement. En 1956, il se retire de la pratique active de l'athlétisme et doit être traité plusieurs fois dans les cliniques ophtalmologiques. En plus d'une lésion dégénérative de la rétine (retinitis, degeneratio retinae pigmentosa), on a constaté une opacification progressive du cristallin qui dut être retranché opérativement en 1969. Aujourd'hui, il voit peu, ne gardant que le sens de la luminosité. Il a maîtrisé le métieur de masseur et est un spécialiste apprécié dans ce domaine.

Conclusion

Parmi 892 lésions sportives accidentelles étudiées par nous, près de 80% concernaient l'organe de mouvement. Ces lésions traumatiques constituent hors de tout doute un danger considérable; elles causent l'élimination d'un très grand nombre de sportifs talentueux de la pratique du sport. Les sportifs de haute performance ne sont pas à l'abri des lésions corporelles, bien que certaines formes soient chez eux moins fréquentes. Il convient de travailler à développer une prophylaxie qui prenne en considération la gravité des lésions en tant que telles ainsi que leurs conséquences psychologiques et sociales.

Références

1. Achoubi, R.: Traumatologie et sport. A-propos de 535 lésions traumatiques du membre inférieur chez le footballeur. Méd. Sport 2:55, 1973.
2. Dec, L. and Prochaczek, F.: Urazowość w sporcie pilkarskim w ocenie samych pilkarzy. Rocz. Nauk. WSWF Katowice 4:203, 1974.
3. Fischer, H.: Sportverletzungen (Kritische Literaturübersicht). Sportarzt Sportmed. 12:328, 1972.

4. Hornof, Z. and Napravnik, C.: Vergleich der bei indivuduellen un kollektiven betriebenen Sportarten auftretende Unfälle nach Ursache und Mechanismus. Sportarzt Sportmed. 10:260, 1972.
5. Konaszewska, Z.: Z problematyki urazowości w sporcie. Rocz. Nauk. WSWF Gdánsk 2:54, 1973.
6. MacIntosh, D.J., Skrien, T. and Shephard, R.J.: Physical activity and injury. J. Sports Med. Phys. Fitness 2:224, 1972.
7. Schweisheimer, W.: Besonder gefährdete Stellen im menschlichen Körper. Turnen und Sport 7:146, 1973.
8. Worobjew, G.P.: Zur Prophylaxe der Sportverletzungen. Leistungssport 4:286, 1973.

Injuries in a Soccer Tournament in Boys 11 to 18 Years of Age (Norway Cup 1975)

S. Nilsson, I. Teige and S. Maehlum

Since its start four years ago, "Norway Cup," which is an international youth soccer tournament, has become one of the world's largest tournaments for soccer-playing adolescents. Last year more than 10,000 boys and girls from 11 to 18 years of age participated.

The physical surroundings of the tournament comprises a large recreation area and 18 soccer fields situated on a hill overlooking Oslo. Soccer was played continuously from 8 a.m. until 8 p.m. for five consecutive days, a total of 1,332 matches. The five finals were played in Bislet Stadium on the sixth day.

The type, frequency and severity of injuries occurring in soccer in adult players is relatively well known [1, 2]. However, little is known about this in adolescents. Therefore, the medical service for the 1975 Norway cup tournament was organized so as to study this problem.

All teams visiting Oslo were lodged in schools in the area. Every school had a first aid station and in the playing area four stations covered all the soccer fields. All stations were manned by staff from one of the voluntary health organizations in Norway, all trained in first aid. Three physicians were stationed in the main station located in the center of the area. All minor injuries were treated at the nearest first aid station, while all the others were referred to the main station.

During the tournament 879 injuries or cases of disease were treated (Table I). Sixty-two injuries or cases of disease occurred among soccer-playing girls. The tournament has been open to female soccer teams for the last two years. However, since these teams play in one group (covering the ages from 11 to 18 years), while the boys play in four age groups, the injuries among the girls cannot be

S. Nilsson, I. Teige and S. Maehlum, Oslo City Hospital, Emergency Department, Oslo, Norway.

Table I. Number of Consultations

Age Group	Matches	Training	Others	Disease	Total
		Injuries			
A	85	14	43	14	156
B	174	28	63	38	203
C	130	25	52	28	235
D	50	14	38	21	123
E	33	12	12	5	62
Total	472	93	208	106	879

A = (17-18 years); B = (15-16 years); C = (13-14 years); D = (11-12 years); E = female players (11-18 years).

compared with the injuries among the boys. Hence these injuries are omitted from this study.

The distribution of the 439 injuries occurring in boys during matches is shown in Table II. Almost 80% of the injuries are located in the lower extremities and only 11% in the upper extremities. This is the same distribution as previously found in adult soccer players [2].

Type of injury is shown in Table III. There were 212, or 48.3%, small wound or minor skin abrasions. Contusions claim another 31.7%. Among these we have included six cerebral concussions, of which four were hospitalized from one to six days. All recovered completely. Fifty sprains of the knee and ankle joint were mostly minor, and only one torn meniscus was found. Nine fractures occurred, of which four were located in the distal radius. All were treated as outpatients.

Table II. Distribution of Injuries

Localization of Injuries	Number of Injuries		Percent of Total
Lower extremities			
Foot/toes	90		
Ankle	35		
Calf	40		
Knee	111		
Thigh	69	345	78.6
Trunk	14		3.2
Head/face	32		7.3
Upper extremities	48		10.9
Total	439		100.0

Table III. Type of Injury

Type of Injury	Number	Percent of Total
Abrasions	212	48.3
Contusions	139	31.7
Sprains	50	11.4
Strains/tendinitis	25	5.7
Fractures	9	2.0
Others	4	0.9
	439	100.0

During the tournament the temperature was high. Oslo had a bout of tropical climate for the first time in many years during that week. Therefore, we anticipated patients with heat exhaustion or heat stroke, especially during the last two days when the winning teams played as many as three matches per day. When four cases of heat exhaustion occurred suddenly at noon on the fourth day, within minutes they were taken to a "cooling area," where their body temperature was lowered with crushed ice. All recovered completely, but further playing was prohibited.

During the qualifying rounds groups of four teams were matched against each other. The two best teams in each group qualified for the final rounds, whereas the losing team in each match was eliminated from the tournament. The winning teams played as many as three matches per day until the end of the fifth day when there were only two teams left in each age group, ready for the final.

As can be seen in Table IV more injuries were seen in the final rounds. This was probably due to the increased number of matches per day together with higher intensity when playing. In the qualifying rounds we found an injury rate per 1000 hours of play of 26.5, and this increased in the final rounds to 34.2. Closer examination revealed that this was true in all age groups.

Table IV. Number of Injuries per 1000 Hours
of Play During Qualifying (Q)
and Final Matches (F)

	Q	F	Total
Playing time (hr)	11,182	4,184	15,366
Number of injuries	296	143	439
Injuries/1000 playing hours	26.5	34.2	28.6

Table V. Frequency of Injuries in Different Age Groups,
Totally (T) and Excluding Minor Skin Abrasions (M)

Age Group (yr)	Playing Time (hr)	Total	Number of Injuries Per 1000 Playing Hours	
			T	M
A (17-18)	3,179	85	26.7	13.5
B (15-16)	5,063	174	34.4	18.4
C (13-14)	4,521	130	28.8	14.8
D (11-12)	2,603	50	19.2	10.8

As mentioned earlier, 212 of the injuries were minor wounds and skin abrasions mostly affecting knee, heel, leg and thigh in that order. These injuries would normally not be registered as soccer injuries. If these were excluded the total number of injuries was lowered to 227. As Table V makes clear, this lowers the injury rate in all age groups. The lowest injury rate (10.8/1000 hr) was found in the 11- to 12-year age group, whereas the highest rate of 18.4 was found in the 15- to 16-year group. The overall injury rate was lowered from 28.6 to 14.8. Two hundred seventy-seven other injuries occurred during training and free play. Some of these injuries were more severe than the soccer injuries.

Studies involving adult soccer players indicate a much higher injury rate. Bass [1] found an average injury rate of one injury per player per season in an English team of professional players. Our own observations from Norwegian soccer indicate the same rate. This will give a higher injury rate per 1000 hours of play than in this study.

Injuries among adults are also more severe presumably due to the greater physical impact at the moment of injury. Our study indicates that adolescents playing soccer suffer few, and mostly minor, injuries. Therefore, we conclude that soccer is a relatively safe sport for boys.

References

1. Bass, A.L.: Rehabilitation after soft tissue trauma. Proc. R. Soc. Med. 59:653-656, 1966.
2. Nilsson, S., Roaas, A. and Maseide, T.: Fotballskader (Soccer injuries). T. Norske Laegeforen. 93:377-381, 1973.

Incidence et gravité des blessures et des maladies lors des jeux du Québec

H. Lavallée, M. Rajic, R.J. Shephard, R. LaBarre,
J.C. Jéquier, L. Plamondon et C. Beaucage

Introduction

Depuis quelques années, l'incidence croissante des compétitions sportives pour des enfants de plus en plus jeunes et leurs répercussions possibles sur la santé physique et psychique des participants préoccupent davantage les professionnels de la santé et en particulier les médecins [11].

En accord avec quelques auteurs [1, 17, 18], nous reconnaissons que jusqu'à maintenant, la médecine sportive a mis davantage l'accent sur le traitement et la réhabilitation et peu sur la prévention. Il y a peu de statistiques disponibles sur les critères qui permettent d'établir des modalités de participation à des compétitions sportives pour un enfant ou un adolescent qui, en période de croissance, est soumis à de multiples adaptations physiques, psychologiques et sociales [1, 6, 14].

La médecine sportive et préventive exige d'abord la connaissance des mécanismes étiologiques des blessures dont l'incidence et la gravité peuvent être influencées par le type de compétition, les règlements, l'environnement, l'équipement protecteur individuel et les caractéristiques physiques et psychiques des participants (Tableau I).

Matériel et méthode

Sujets

Lors des Jeux du Québec en 1973—74—75, nous avons fait une étude épidémiologique des blessures et des maladies survenues lors de

H. Lavallée, M. Rajic, R.J. Shephard, R. LaBarre, J.C. Jéquier, L. Plamondon et C. Beaucage, Département des sciences de la santé, Université du Québec à Trois-Rivières et Department of Preventive Medicine and Biostatistics, University of Toronto, Canada.

Tableau I. Facteurs qui influencent l'incidence et la gravité des blessures

Type de compétition	—Règlements —Niveau de compétition —Organisation des compétitions —Compétence des arbitres —Nombre et comportement des spectateurs
Environnement	—Qualité du terrain et de l'équipement de base —Conditions climatiques —Qualité des services physiques
Equipement protecteur individuel	—Utilisation et qualité de l'équipement —Adaptation aux risques
Caractéristiques physiques et psychiques des participants	—Compétitions entre équipes de même caractère physique (poids- taille- sexe- âge) —Entraînements physiques et psychologiques adéquats
Caractéristiques de surveillance	—Examen médical préventif —Surveillance médicale —Entraînement élémentaire des officiels en hygiène et sécurité.

ces compétitions sportives. Les Jeux du Québec regroupent de 3,500 à 4,000 athlètes parmi 20,000 participants aux compétitions régionales. Les sujets sont âgés de 10 à 18 ans et des deux sexes. Ces athlètes sont sélectionnés en fonction de leur performance lors des jeux régionaux (Tableau II).

Supervision médicale

La supervision médicale était organisée en pyramide (Fig. 1). Chaque terrain d'activité était doté soit d'un poste primaire où des para-médicaux entraînés dispensaient les premiers soins soit de postes secondaires, sur les terrains où les activités athlétiques présentaient plus de risques de blessures. Ces postes étaient sous la responsabilité d'infirmiers (ères). Si les cas pathologiques dépassaient leur compétence ou exigeaient un traitement plus complexe, ils étaient référés au poste central où une équipe médicale, composée de médecins,

Tableau II. Participants au Jeux du Québec

Participants	1973	1974	1975
Garçons	2,330	2,302	2,216
Filles	1,338	1,380	1,674
Total	3,668	3,682	3,890

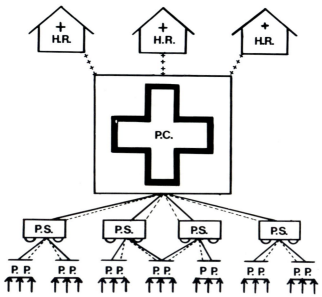

LEGENDE:

P.C.: poste central.

H.R.: hôpital régional.

P.P.: poste primaire.

P.S.: poste secondaire.

——: transfert obligatoire d'athlètes malades et/ou blessés au poste plus spécialisé.

----: ligne de communication pour avis et directives médicales pour les cas bénins.

+++: transfert pour traitements spécialisés s'il y a lieu.

N.B.: chacun des sites de compétition aura à sa proximité soit un poste(s) primaire(s), soit un poste(s) secondaire(s) selon les risques inhérents à la compétition en cours et selon le nombre des participants.

FIG. 1. Organigramme du Service de santé.

d'infirmières et de physiothérapeutes, assurait la permanence de soins 24 heures par jour.

Gravité des blessures

Quelques auteurs ont classifié la sévérité des blessures selon soit la région atteinte, soit la durée et l'intensité du traitement ou la durée et le pourcentage d'incapacité temporaire ou permanente [12, 13, 23]. Nous avons adopté un indice de gravité des blessures ou des maladies qui tient compte à la fois de l'atteinte fonctionnelle et/ou anatomique des différents systèmes et de l'incapacité temporaire ou permanente (Tableau III).

Tableau III. Indice de gravité des accidents et maladies

	Atteinte fonctionnelle		Atteinte anatomique	Incapacité
Grade I	X m		X a	—
Grade II	X	et	X	—
Grade III	X	et/ou	X	temporaire
Grade IV	X	et/ou	X	permanente
Grade V	X	et/ou	X	décès

m = maladie
a = accident

Les grades I et II font référence à des blessures et des maladies mineures n'entraînant pas d'incapacité. Les grades III et IV pourraient être précisés en tenant compte du nombre de jours d'incapacité temporaire et du pourcentage d'incapacité temporaire ou permanente.

Résultats

Les Jeux du Québec, qui ont débuté en 1971, comprennent plusieurs disciplines sportives et socioculturelles; sauf quelques modifications, on retrouve dans l'ensemble les mêmes à chaque année. Le Tableau IV montre le nombre de participants par discipline sportive en 1973—74—75.

Taux de blessures et de maladies

Le nombre absolu des incidents (blessures et maladies) en 1973—74 est sensiblement le même mais a diminué d'une façon significative en 1975 à Trois-Rivières (χ^2 = 74). Il en est de même pour les blessures (χ^2 = 6.5) et maladies (χ^2 = 96.2) si on les considère séparément (Tableau V). La fréquence relative des incidents (blessures et maladies) en rapport avec le nombre de participants a également diminué progressivement de 1973 à 1975 (16% (73), 15.5% (74), 8.6% (75)).

Cette diminution n'est pas due au hasard, elle est la conséquence directe de l'adoption d'un règlement préventif plus strict. Le point majeur de ce règlement consistait à accorder au Service de Santé le droit d'interrompre la participation d'un athlète blessé ou malade. Ce règlement a pour effet la modification relative de l'indice de gravité et par conséquent une augmentation considérable du taux d'arrêt de compétition.

Tableau IV. Participation au Jeux du Québec

Discipline	1973 Nombre	1974 Nombre	1975 Nombre
Athlétisme	726	720	720
Balle molle	262	–	231
Baseball	291	262	–
Crosse	210	207	234
Cyclisme	186	205	183
Golf	119	–	137
Natation	576	574	572
Parachutisme	51	–	–
Plongeon	166	138	126
Ski nautique	158	161	119
Soccer	260	264	267
Tennis	180	142	136
Tir à l'arc	123	83	125
Tir à la carabine	60	–	65
Voile	105	78	102
Water polo	195	195	211
Danse	–	–	109
Handball	–	217	245
Gymnastique	–	160	176
Equitation	–	–	36
Canot kayac	–	144	96
Aviron long parcours	–	24	–
Pétanque	–	108	–
TOTAL	3,668	3,682	3,890

Tableau V. Taux des blessures et des maladies aux Jeux du Québec, 1973, 1974 et 1975

Année	Nombre de participants Total (T), Garçons (G) Filles (F)	Incidents pathologiques	Blessures	Maladies	Arrêt de compétition Blessures	Arrêt de compétition Maladies	Sexe Filles	Sexe Garçons
1973	3668T 2330G 1338F	589	284	305	30	23	224	365
1974	3682T 2302G 1380F	572	245	327	35	17	206	366
1975	3890T 2216G 1674F	338 $x^2 = 74.0$	213 $x^2 = 6.5$	125 $x^2 = 96.2$	38 $x^2 = 1.6$	19 $x^2 = 0.5$	194	144

Niveau de gravité des blessures et des maladies

On observe une diminution absolue et significative du nombre de blessures et de maladies, mais une augmentation relative des arrêts de compétition en regard du nombre de pathologies observées. En effet le taux d'arrêt de compétition par rapport à l'incidence de blessures se situe à 10.5% (1973), 14.3% (1974) et 17.8% (1975) et pour les maladies 7.8% (1973), 5.2% (1974) et 15.2% (1975) (Tableau VI).

Il n'y a pas eu de blessures de grade IV ou V indiquant soit une invalidité permanente soit un décès. De plus nous avons remarqué que des blessures et des maladies n'ont été rapportées au Poste central que 24 à 48 heures après l'incident et qu'elles étaient aggravées par le retard du diagnostic et du traitement.

Le nombre de maladies grade I a sensiblement diminué en 1975 (χ^2 = 73.0). Le nombre de maladies grade II a aussi diminué d'une façon significative en 1975 (χ^2 = 50.3). Cependant, en proportion avec le nombre total de maladies, le nombre de maladies grade III est relativement plus élevé en 1975 (χ^2 = 29.57) (Fig. 2). Le nombre de blessures grade I a diminué significativement en 1975 (χ^2 = 13.2). Le nombre de blessures de grade II n'a pas changé significativement au cours des années mais le nombre de blessures de grade III est relativement plus élevé en 1975 (χ^2 = 8.4) (Fig. 3).

L'influence du sexe sur l'incidence des blessures et des maladies

En 1973 et 1974, le taux d'incidents est approximativement le même pour les deux sexes. Toutefois en 1975 nous avons remarqué un taux plus élevé de blessures et de maladies chez les filles en rapport avec le nombre total des participants (Tableau VII) et aussi par rapport au nombre total d'incidents (Fig. 4).

Localisation des blessures

Le système le plus atteint chez les garçons est le système musculo-squelettique (Fig. 5). Ceci s'explique par le fait que les garçons participent davantage aux sports de groupe avec mise en échec. Les autres systèmes sont peu atteints, sauf la peau et les

Tableau VI. Taux d'arrêt de compétition par rapport au total des blessures et maladies

	1973	1974	1975
Blessures	10.5%	14.3%	17.8%
Maladies	7.8%	5.2%	15.2%

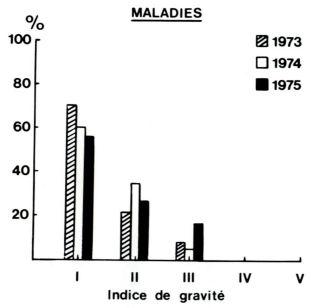

FIG. 2. Indice de gravité des maladies aux Jeux du Québec, 1973, 1974, 1975.

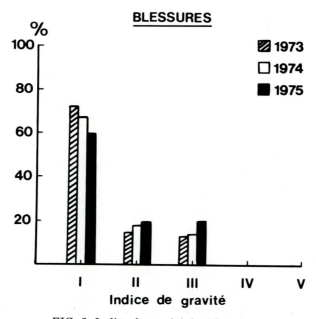

FIG. 3. Indice de gravité des blessures.

Tableau VII. Taux des blessures et maladies selon
le sexe en rapport avec le nombre de participants

	1973	1974	1975
Garçons	15.6%	15.9%	6.5%
Filles	16.5%	14.9%	11.5%

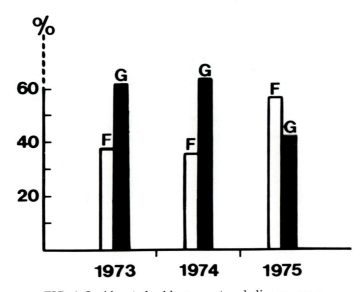

FIG. 4. Incidence des blessures et maladies par sexe.

phanères qui montrent un taux relativement élevé de blessures. Chez
les filles la peau et le système musculo-squelettique subissent un taux
à peu près égal de traumatisme. Les autres systèmes chez les deux
sexes ont un taux de blessures peu élevé.

Regroupement des maladies par système

Les troubles digestifs et les infections des voies respiratoires
supérieures, les otites internes et externes demeurent les maladies les
plus souvent rencontrées dans un regroupement de 10 à 15 mille
personnes, si l'on inclus les entraîneurs, les parents et les visiteurs
(Fig. 6).

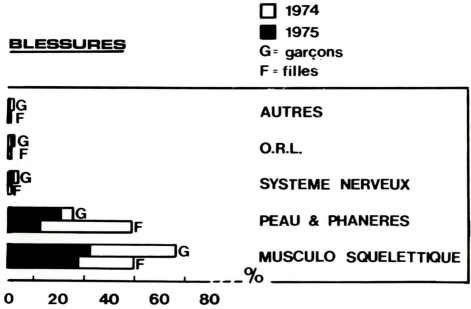

FIG. 5. Type des blessures, Jeux du Québec, 1974, 1975.

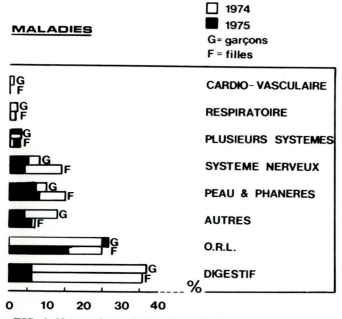

FIG. 6. Nature des maladies, Jeux du Québec, 1974, 1975.

Les maladies au niveau de la peau et des phanères consistent surtout en réaction allergique et en infections superficielles. Le taux relativement élevé des maladies du système nerveux provient du fait que nous avons classé dans cette catégorie certains symtômes et syndromes tels que la céphalée, les étourdissements et les réactions psychopathologiques.

L'influence des disciplines sportives

Si l'on considère le taux d'incidence des blessures par discipline et par sexe, on constate que la danse, le water-polo et le tennis sont des disciplines sportives où les risques sont minimes (Fig. 7). Par contre, le soccer (football), la crosse, la gymnastique et l'athlétisme constituent des disciplines où les risques sont plus élevés.

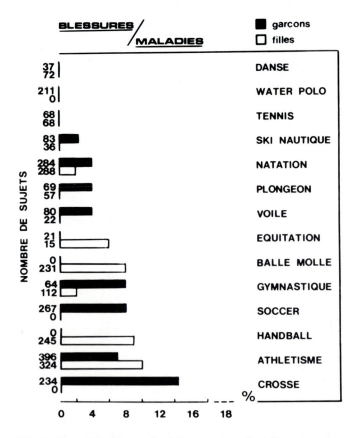

FIG. 7. Taux d'incidence des blessures par discipline et par sexe.

Discussion

La fréquence relative du nombre de blessures a diminué progressivement de 1973 à 1975, mais les arrêts de compétition pour les blessures plus sérieuses ont proportionnellement augmenté. La baisse du nombre de blessures pourrait s'expliquer par de meilleures méthodes de prévention, par des examens médicaux pré-compétition et des règlements adaptés; mais l'augmentation concomitante de la gravité exigeant un arrêt de compétition selon les mêmes critères, nous suggère que les participants ont caché leurs blessures et leurs maladies pour ne pas être pénalisés dans leur participation. Cette hypothèse nous apparait vraisemblable puisque plusieurs blessures nous ont été rapportées 24 ou 48 heures après les incidents et se sont trouvées de ce fait aggravées par le retard de diagnostic et de traitement. Des règlements spécifiques devraient être adaptés au degré de risques inhérents à chaque sport; ces règlements devraient tenir compte des équipements protecteurs et de l'âge biologique des participants.

Les raisons pouvant expliquer les accidents varient selon les disciplines sportives. La crosse est un sport de contact; la plus grande partie des blessures rapportées à ce sport sont dues à un défaut d'équipement protecteur adéquat, aux règlements inadaptés et à l'agressivité particulière des joueurs. En ce qui regarde la gymnastique, il est possible que les épreuves exigées soient trop sévères pour des enfants trop jeunes.

Cependant, d'autres sports comme le hockey, le football américain et le ski qui ne sont pas au programme des Jeux d'été du Québec, comportent des risques de blessures encore plus élevés. D'autres rapports ont fait état de la question au Canada et aux Etats-Unis [3-6, 8, 9, 12, 13, 15-18, 21-23].

Il est déjà connu que l'incidence et la gravité des blessures sont en rapport avec le niveau de compétition [12]; nous notons que les garçons pratiquant l'équitation, de même que les filles qui participent à la voile, à la gymnastique et au ski nautique subissent moins de blessures, probablement en raison du niveau de compétition ou ils se trouvent.

Il est important de préciser davantage l'étiologie des blessures et les facteurs qui peuvent contribuer à la prévention. Beaucoup d'informations et de collaboration seront nécessaires entre les fédérations sportives, les missions régionales, les athlètes et les responsables de l'hygiène et de la sécurité pour que le service de supervision médicale des compétitions ne soit plus un service de dépannage mais un veritable service de prévention.

Références

1. American Association for Health Physical Education and Recreation. Desirable athletic competition for children of elementary school age. A.A.H.P.E.R., Washington, D.C., 1968.
2. Bellow, D.G. et al: An investigation into the evaluation of hockey helmets. Med. Sci. Sports 2:43-49, 1970.
3. Clarke, K.S.: Calculated risk of sports fatalities. JAMA 197:172-174, 1966.
4. Encausse, P.: Sport et santé — Précis de médecine sportive. Paris:Baillière et Fils, 1969.
5. Fekete, J.F.: Severe brain injury and death following minor hockey accidents: The effectiveness of the "safety helmets" of amateur hockey players. Can. Med. Assoc. J. 99:1234-1239, 1968.
6. Garrick, J.G.: Prevention of sports injuries. Postgrad. Med. January, 125-129, 1972.
7. Ilfeld, W. and Field, S.M.: Treatment of tennis elbow. Use of a special brace. JAMA 195:111-114, 1966.
8. Kraus, J.F. et al: The effectiveness of a special ice hockey helmet to reduce head injuries in college intramural hockey. Med. Sci. Sports 2:162-164, 1970.
9. Kraus, J.F. et al: The quality of officiating as an injury prevention factor in intramural touch football. Med. Sci. Sports 3:143-147, 1971.
10. Larivière, G., Lavallée, H. and Shephard, R.J.: A simple skating test for ice-hockey players. In Lavallée, H. and Shephard, R.J. (eds.): Frontiers of Physical Activity and Child Health. Québec, P.Q.:Pelican Press, 1976.
11. Lavallée, H., Rajic, M., Shephard, R.J. et al: Supervision médicale des compétitions sportives: Résultats obtenus aux Jeux du Québec, 1973—1975. En préparation.
12. MacIntosh, D.L., Skrien, T. and Shephard, R.J.: Athletic Injuries at the University of Toronto. Med. Sci. Sports 3:195-199, 1971.
13. O'Donoghue, D.H.: Treatment of injuries to athletes. Philadelphia:W.B. Saunders, 1970.
14. Rivard, G., Lavallée, H., Rajic, M. et al: Influence of competitive hockey on physical condition and psychological behaviour of children. In Lavallée, H. and Shephard, R.J. (eds.): Frontiers of Physical Activity and Child Health. Québec, P.Q.:Pelican Press, 1976.
15. Robey, M. and Blytil, C.S.: Athletic Injuries. Application of epidemiologic methods. JAMA 217:184-189, 1971.
16. Rontal, E. et al: Maxillofacial injuries in football players. An evaluation of current facial protection. J. Sports Med. 11:241-245, 1971.
17. Ryan, A.J. and Allman, F.: Sports Medicine. Toronto:McGraw Hill, 1974.
18. Shephard, R.J.: New perspectives in sports medicine. Can. Fam. Physician, April, 1974.
19. Shephard, R.J., Lavallée, H., Beaucage, C. et al: La capacité physique des enfants canadiens-français, canadiens-anglais et esquimaux. III. Psychologie et Sociologie des enfants canadiens-français. Union Med. 104:1131-1136, 1975.
20. Shephard, R.J.: In Lavallée, H. and Shephard, R.J. (eds.): Frontiers of Physical Activity and Child Health. Québec, P.Q.:Pelican Press, 1976.
21. Siffert, R.S. et al: Athletic injuries in children. Pediatr. Clin. N. Am. 12:1027-1037, 1965.

22. Snook, G.A.: Head and neck injuries in contact sports. Med. Sci. Sports 1:117-123, 1969.
23. Tucker, W.E.: Injury in Sport — The physiology, Prevention and Treatment of Injuries Associated with Sport. London:Staples Press, 1964.

Problems of the Differential Nutrition in Sport

P. Slantchev and J. Afar

The contemporary records in "top sports" were achieved due to a complex of factors. Some of them are of great importance to the adaptation of organisms to physical loadings of great volume and intensity. Such a factor is the differential and rational nutrition. It exercises not only the functions of energetic equivalent of physical efforts and a source of plastic material for the adaptive structural changes in organism, but it is also a biological stimulator for increasing the working capacity, for its maintenance at a high level, as well as for the fast recovery of the homeostatic constants after training and sports loadings.

Different kinds of sports and events have a various character, volume and intensity of training and sports loading. They are distinguished from one another by their character, volume and intensity in the separate periods of the training cycles as well. The adaptive mechanisms to physical loadings are also different depending upon sex, body weight, age and climatic peculiarities. All these facts require the nutrition of sportsmen to be strictly differential. The understandings of the Bulgarian sports medicine of the problems of differential nutrition in sports are based on the principal workings of the Soviet school of N. N. Jakovlev and on the achievements of Bulgarian dietetics especially those of academician T. Taschev and collaborators. The problems of differential nutrition in sports are related mainly to the caloricity and the qualitative composition of the accepted food.

As a matter of principle rational nutrition is striving for the establishment of the energetic balance of the organism, e.g., the calories adopted by the organism to be equivalent to the expended ones. In theory as well as in practice of rational nutrition the practice exists that the supply of calories from food exceeds the 24-hour energy output in order for the percentage of the nonassimilation of

P. Slantchev and J. Afar, Higher Institute of Physical Culture, Sofia, Bulgaria.

the nutritive products to be filled up and a series of plastic processes to be assured with raw materials. These create a peculiar "energetic comfort" which, from our point of view, is not quite expedient under sports conditions. On the basis of numerous biochemical researches it is established that by way of reverse connection the excess of a formed product of the metabolic processes leads to a decrease of its following production, while the insufficiency stimulates its creation.

On the basis of this biological regularity, we think that nutrition in sports has a greater effect if a "relative physiological energetic deficit" (5% to 10% lower caloricity from the actually expended calories) is established. Such a relative incomplete energetic satisfaction of the energetic needs of the organism is a biological stimulant for maintaining a higher level of the metabolic processes, which improves the adaptive metabolic processes and increases the coefficient of the useful effect from the food consumed. We assume an exception to this rule only in the heavy and superheavy categories of wrestling and heavy athletics.

The "relative physiological deficit" may be compensated with the supply of food preparations composed by different metabolites in the days of recovery, only in the periods of superintensive training and competitive activity.

On the basis of our understandings mentioned above, and our researches on the energetic expenditure in the different kinds of sports, we propose our work-scheme for differential nutrition depending upon the caloricity of the food for sportsmen. The different kinds of sports and events are divided into four groups:

First group. Caloricity of food from 3800 to 4200 K calories (from 70 to 50 kcal/kg body weight). The group includes:

1. Women — sports games (volleyball, basketball, handball), court tennis, sprints, jumping and throwings from light athletics, short-distance swimming.

2. Men and women — gymnastics, sports shooting, table tennis, and court tennis.

3. Men — lightweight categories in wrestling and boxing.

Second group. Caloricity of food from 4200 to 4600 K calories (from 80 to 60 kcal/kg body weight). The group includes:

1. Women — long-distance swimming.

2. Men and women — middle-distance running, alpine-ski events, track-cycling, short-distance rowing.

3. Men — sports games (football, basketball, volleyball), sprints and jumpings in light athletics, wrestling, boxing in middle-weight

categories, heavy athletics in lightweight categories, short-distance swimming.

Third group. Caloricity of 4600 to 5200 K calories (from 80 to 60 kcal/kg body weight). The group includes long-distance runnings in light athletics, throwing and shot-putting in light athletics (for men), walking to 20 km, long-distance swimming up to three hours, alpinism, ski-running up to 30 km, long-distance rowing, the heavyweight categories in wrestling and boxing, the middle-weight categories in heavy athletics.

Fourth group. Caloricity of food from 5200 to 6000 K calories (from 90 to 70 kcal/kg body weight). This group includes marathon running, 50-km walking ski runnings, road-cycling, marathon swimming, the heavyweight categories in heavy athletics.

The second basic problem of differential nutrition in sports is related to the qualitative composition of food. We do not support the view that this differentiation has to be applied to every particular kind of sport and event. Our opinion is that the differences in the technical methods, typical of every kind of sport, are not the factors to define the differentiation in nutrition. Our conception is that differential nutrition has to be guided by the character, volume and intensity of the physical loading. The purposes and aims set up to the sportsman in the definite period of his training must also be taken into consideration.

The changes in the volumetric processes, caused by the sport and training loadings, are different in character and direction, depth and duration. These changes are determined by the physical loadings, differing from one another by volume, intensity and duration. According to these facts we differentiate the *qualitative composition* of the received food into three main groups.

First group. It is transient in training regimens, but with maximal and submaximal power requires high adaptive possibilities of the organism to deep anaerobic oxidation processes. This imposes to increase the carbohydrate component (9 to 10 gm/kg body weight), the protein ration being the same (2.0 to 2.2 gm/kg body weight), on account of the limited acceptance of fats (1.5 gm/kg body weight). The anaerobic character of the oxidation processes requires an additional quantity of vitamins included in the food such as C, B, B_1, B_6, B_{12}, B_{15} — substance-rich products — predecessors of the enzymes' systems of the tissue breathing.

Second group. These are connected during training regimens with the accumulation of muscular mass and development of the muscular power and typical with maximal and submaximal dynamic and static muscular effort. The differential nutrition in this group differs from the previous one only by the priority of the protein nutrition 2.2 to 2.5 gm/kg body weight, but the 250 gm have not to be exceeded with view to the protection of the liver function.

Third group. This group is characterized by training regimens with great duration of the physical effort, but at a relatively low power. There is almost complete satisfaction of the oxygen needs and a prevailing aerobic oxidation in actively working tissues.

The considerable caloricity of the food requires a total increase of carbohydrates (from 10 to 11 gm/kg body weight), and especially that of proteins (2.0 to 2.5 gm/kg body weight). Thus, an opportunity is given for a more considerable inclusion of lipids in food (2.0 to 2.5 gm/kg body weight). The lipids have to be rich in nonsaturated fatty acids and phosphatides, which will facilitate the function of the liver to a great extent. In the food and the substance-rich mineral and microelements components a varied number of vitamins (C, B_1, B_2, PP) is provided, in order for the mineral-salt exchange to be maintained, which is of great importance for the preservation of the osmosis regulation and the alkaline-acid balance.

We considered it useful to limit our attention only to the two abovementioned basic problems of the differential nutrition in sports, thus sharing our experience and opinion in that scientific sphere. The correct decision of these problems will allow to a greater extent, by means of differential nutrition, the creation of optimal conditions for adaptation and physiological balance of the organism, which will help prevent fatigue during physical efforts, as well as accelerate the recovery processes.

Significance of Medical Studies in Sports Prognosis of Young Biathlonists

N. M. Ledovskaya and N. S. Konchits

Biathlon or modern winter sport combination is one of the youngest Olympic ski sports. Effectiveness in biathlon is composed of high-speed ski race qualities and accurate target shooting at the fire lines of the distance (Savitsky, 1970; Sergeyev, 1970; Tuzov, 1975; Timonov, Romanin, 1976). The work done by biathlonists during the race essentially influences the target shooting. The more intensive the skiing the more probable the deterioration of the shooting. At the same time the fire lines approach and shooting break the rhythm and tempo of the race (Sergeyev, 1970). Such a combination makes a number of specific demands on the athletes and creates many complicated tasks for coaches and sports physicians.

This presentation contains the results of many years' medical supervision of 465 biathlonists aged from 10 to 18 visiting the children's sport centre "Lokomitiv" in the city of Novosibirsk.

In the group of beginners (the first two years of training) the main task of the coach was to make all the children physically fit and developed in all-round way. Later against the background of general physical education and improving the main athletic qualities the percentage of specific biathlon actual loads such as cross-country ski-running of various intensity and shooting with or without any load was doubled. Individual plans for training the most promising athletes have been developed.

Those under observation had their anthropometric indices, respiratory and cardiovascular systems condition studied, their physical working capacity determined in accordance with Physical Working Capacity (PWC$_{170}$)test. To make a comparison analogous findings of 168 persons of the same age not engaged in sports were taken. The group "leaders"- athletes taking first through third in the competitions were chosen from among the biathlonists.

The leaders did not differ sufficiently from other biathlonists as to body proportions. Their active body mass calculated in accord-

N. M. Ledovskaya and N. S. Konchits, Novosibirsk State Medical Institute and Regional Sporting Medicine Centre, Novosibirsk, U.S.S.R.

281

ance with the results of measuring of the skin fat fold as is recommended by Parzhiskova (1962) is somewhat higher, that is, their muscular system is better developed as compared with other studied athletes. They exceeded sufficiently in muscular tension as well, hands tensile force in particular; in respiratory system indices vital capacity of the lungs, pneumotachometer figures. The pulse of the leaders at rest is somewhat rarer in younger persons and later on it becomes equal to that of the biathlonists of the main group. PWC_{170} is noticeably larger in its absolute meaning as well as evaluated per kilogram of body weight. The differences are statistically significant.

The noted differences become evident in young athletes at age 10 to 12 when real and special training does not begin as a matter of fact. Therefore, to choose biathlonists as well as ski racers one should attach vital importance to the functional state of the respiratory and cardiovascular systems. Taking into consideration the specific features of biathlon, one must apparently reckon with the important role of the musculus palmaris tension required for the safe fixation of the rifle while shooting.

It is also confirmed by means of calculation of correlative relations between the results of the race and various facts studied. No highly reliable factors of correlation between the data of cardio-respiratory system and physical development, on the one hand, and with the speed of the ski race, on the other hand, have been found in athletes of the main group of biathlonists aged 10 to 11. At the age of 17 to 18 9 or 10 factors of correlation of the high degree of reliability have been found of the total amount of 62 calculated factors.

Thus, with age correlative relations tend to grow. The number of significant factors of correlation increases. All this probably depends upon the level of training of the investigated persons.

Medico-sporting investigation and thorough analysis of the results obtained are an important source of information for prognosing the results of an athlete for the years to come in this kind of sport. An expert medical consultation can play an important role in choosing young promising biathlonists.

Researches With Rose Bengal ^{131}I Regarding Liver Function on High Performance Sportsmen

I. Dragan and T. Pop

Introduction

In another paper [4, 7] we studied the colloidopexic function of the liver by determining the clearance with ^{198}Au in healthy sportsmen, at rest and after effort. The conclusions of that study indicated a decrease of the coloidopexic function after effort in sportsmen who had had a viral hepatitis.

That is why we carried on new studies in order to establish the hepatocyte function in high performance sportsmen who have had a viral hepatitis in their history. We chose for this study the determination of the clearance with Rose Bengal ^{131}I.

Subjects and Method

We investigated 30 sportsmen, all male, aged 23.6 ± 2.4 years; height = 183.4 ± 4.8 cm; weight = 80.700 ± 2.300 kg, all being in good condition and fit for competitions. We determined the clearance with Rose Bengal ^{131}I and divided them into three groups:

1. *Group I:* 10 healthy sportsmen, without an hepatic history, for whom we determined the clearance at rest;

2. *Group II:* 10 healthy sportsmen, without an hepatic history, for whom we determined the clearance at rest and seven days after submaximal effort (200 W, 10 min on a cycloergometer);

3. *Group III:* 10 sportsmen with viral hepatitis in their past, clinically in good condition and having normal biochemical tests, for whom we determined this clearance at rest and seven days after submaximal effort (200 W, 10 min on a cycloergometer).

We injected 75 μCi Rose Bengal ^{131}I, the subject being seated in an armchair. The detector of the radiations, with a crystal of Na I$_2$,

I. Dragan and T. Pop, Sports Medicine Centre and Hospital, Panduri, Bucharest, Romania.

was placed over the temporal-mastoid region, in order to avoid the radiation coming from the heart or liver. The registration was made on "Modular System for Physiological Application Packard." The epuration curve was obtained from the results registered automatically on a "teletype." The calculation of T 1/2 (half-time) allows the determination of the clearance by using the formula:

$$C = \frac{0.693 \times 100}{T \ 1/2}$$

where C represents the relative liver clearance for Rose Bengal [131]I. Normal values for our method = 12% to 14%.

We have chosen the external clearance method [2] because it is comfortable for sportsmen, very precise and the results obtained are similar to the other methods.

Results and Discussion

We can see the results in Table I. Healthy sportsmen have normal values at rest and after submaximal effort, a fact which confirms the good condition of these sportsmen, well trained and without an hepatic history. These data are similar to those obtained in healthy sportsmen without an hepatic history, by the clearance with [198]Au. The third group, sportsmen who had suffered from a viral hepatitis, presented normal values at rest but after effort the values decreased significantly, a fact also remarked on the [198]Au clearance. That is why we should consider these low values of both clearances as a decrease of the hepatic function in sportsmen who have had viral hepatitis, which becomes evident only during effort. (This decrease

Table I.

Group I (at Rest)	Group II (After Effort)		Group III (After Effort)
N = 10	N = 10		N = 10
X = 13.76%	X = 13.05%		X = 11.20%
D.S. = 0.7719	D.S. = 0.6566		D.S. = 0.3620
c.v.% = 5.6138	c.v.% = 5.0316		c.v.% = 3.2329
e = 0.2440	e = 0.2076		e = 0.1144
		s = 0.5302	
		t = 7.8021	
		p < 0.001	
		r = 0.8318	

seems to be induced by circulatory, metabolic and neurohormonal factors.)

Conclusions

The evaluation of the clearance with Rose Bengal ^{131}I, on high performance sportsmen, seems to be a useful test for hepatic investigation, especially for strength sports.

Recovery after a viral hepatitis must occur not only in connection with biochemistry tests but also after the determination of the two clearances evaluated at rest and after effort.

Especially in resistance sports, in high performance sportsmen who have suffered from a viral hepatitis, the evaluation of these clearances at least every year, at the end of the season and only after effort, could call our attention to some liver dysfunctions which become evident only during effort, a fact which requires practical means (liver protection by medicines, recovery after effort, diet) during training and allows us sometimes the precocious detection of a chronic hepatitis, a disease which calls for a total elimination of sports participation.

Summary

The authors investigated the metabolic liver function at rest and after exercise by determining the clearance with Rose Bengal ^{131}I on 30 high performance sportsmen. The results obtained at rest (normal values) and immediately after a submaximal effort on a cyclo-ergometer (200 W) were equal, except for the sportsmen who had suffered from a viral hepatitis. They presented lower values after effort.

The authors suggest the isotope liver investigation of sportsmen with a history of viral hepatitis in order to evidence eventual hepatic dysfunctions appearing under the condition of sports stress (not detected by standard biochemical tests) which call for therapeutic and other special means to be taken for the protection of sportsmen.

Bibliography

Brown, C. and Glasser, D.: J. Lab. Clin. Med. 48:454, 1956.
Burkle, J.S. and Gliedman, M.L.: Gastroenterology 36:112, 1959.
Ciobanu, V. and Zalaru, M.: Investigatia hepatica. In Elemente de investigatie în practica medico-sportiva. Ed. Stadion, Bucuresti, 1970.
Dragan, I., Pop, T. and Ionescu, C.: Contributii la studiul functiei coloidopexice a ficatului în effort. Rev. EFS, 12:38-41, 1968.
Dragan, I. et al: Patologie Sportiva. Ed. Stadion, Bucuresti, 1972.

Dragan, I. et al: Medicina Sportiva. Ed. Stadion, Bucuresti, 1974.

Dragan, I. and Ionescu, C.: Cercetari radioizotopice cu [198]Au privind unele aspecte ale functiei hepatice la sportivi de performanta. Rev. EFS 11:33-38, 1970.

Gheorghescu, B. and Brasla, I.: Diagnosticul cu radioizotopi în clinica. Ed. Medicala, Bucuresti, 1964.

Hamilton, W.F.: The hepatic circulation. In Handbook of Physiology, vol. II. Washington, 1964.

Meredith, O.M., William, C., Jane, P. and Holmes, I.: Am. J. Physiol. 202:1, 1962.

Sotgiu, G., Lubisch, T. and Barbieri, I. Med. dello Sport (Roma) 53:14-19, 1960.

Taplin, G.V., Meredith, O.M. and Kade, H.: Lab. Clin. Med. 45:665, 1955.

Vetter, H., Faltner, R. and Numayer, A.: J. Clin. Invest. 3:1602, 1954.

Gerovital H₃ Effects Upon Physiological Parameters in Physical Effort

Gerovital H_3 Effects Upon Physiological Parameters in Physical Effort

Andrei Demeter, Adrian Gagea,
Ariade Claudian and Bragarea Georgeta

Introduction

Unpublished experimental data, extensively proceeding from the Geriatrical Institute from Bucharest, emphasize the procain-therapy eutrophic-anabolical effects, especially in cases of severe cell damage caused by illness, old age or intense physical and neuropsychic stress.

The multiple, favorable effects of GH_3 upon the body, established practically and in the gerontological field particularly by Aslan and collaborators, draw attention to the usage of GH_3 for the improvement of the sportsmen's physical effort output and for the hastening of the body's recovery after physical effort.

The assumption of the thesis that GH_3 properly and conveniently administered to sportsmen influences favorably the principal physiological functions involved in the physical effort is based on scientific data related to general eutrophic activity, improvement of nervous system activity, general metabolic effects, directly influencing glycolysis, the Krebs' cycle and oxidative phosphorylation, improvement of blood circulation velocity, increased vascular response, proteinic alternations, etc., and is generated by the question as to whether the effects are systematically and significantly related to the voluntary physical effort.

Subjects and Method

Twenty-four male students (average age 20 years) at the Physical Education and Sports Institute, who practiced sports systematically and were clinically healthy, served as subjects. The subjects possessed similar daily physical and mental activities (belonging to the same student group).

Andrei Demeter, Adrian Gagea, Ariade Claudian and Bragarea Georgeta, Institute of Physical Education and Sports, Bucharest, Romania.

The heterogenous batch was divided randomly into two groups of 12: group A (experiment) and group B (control).

To group A subjects 200 mg GH_3 was administered daily according to a schedule, while the B group subjects received placebo daily.

The experiment lasted 68 days, but during the last 24 days the groups were reversed with the B group subjects given GH_3.

During the entire period, the experiment was conducted by the double-blind method.

By means of these particularities of the method we have excluded the possibility of physiogenic factor influencing the results, excluding as well the effort response differences initially and accidentally existing between the groups. This aspect is supported by the results' interpretation method as well as by means of calculating the indices relative modifications, for each subject separately.

The body's physiological response indices to physical effort have been selected according to the following two criteria (with contra-dictory, antagonistic dynamic): (1) they detect easily the immediate, significant motor alterations both at the level of the muscular effector, related to the neuromuscular command and the locomotory apparatus adaptation and (2) they are easily and practically recorded, applicable to effort and recovery conditions.

The practical, adequate and acceptable significant solution comprised in this study the following indices, gathered before and immediately after performing a five-minute physical effort, graded at 200 w by pedaling on a cycloergometer:

1. Maximal force of the palm flexor.
2. Maximal velocity of the arm flexion-extension movement.
3. Maximal duration of the isometric contraction of the palm's flexors (at one-half maximum force).
4. Degree of instability of the isometric contraction.
5. Latency of the digital motor reaction in case of light stimulation.
6. Maximal O_2 consumption and the relative one, related to kp/body.
7. Fusion frequency in intermittent light stimulation.
8. Heart rate.

The experiment included 16 recordings in identical conditions with those of the above-mentioned physiological parameters during the whole 68-day period, out of which four recordings were obtained while both groups of students were practicing winter sports at an altitude of 1700 m (14 days).

The recordings (6528 values) have been graphically analyzed, having in view the individual's average relative variations for each of the 16 recordings.

Results and Discussion

Fusion Frequency in Intermittent Light Stimulation

The light stimulus energy has been of 25 J and it lasted 50 ms, features which allowed the subject's retina affecting, through the eyelids, from a distance of 50 cm.

Immediately after the effort the fusion threshold lowered from 30.80 (impulses/minute) to 29.60 for the experimental group and from 33.00 to 28.40 for the control group (Fig. 1).

The relative dynamic variations emphasize to a smaller extent the differences between the groups. Although, from Figure 2 a synchronization of the features' reversals and the administration of GH_3 may be observed.

The decrease of the impulses fusion threshold is a high intensity physical effort normal effect, and the fact that for the experimental group the decrease is less emphasized could mean an increase in working capacity and a delay in the onset of fatigue.

Maximal Force of Palm Flexor at the Predominant Hand

Before the effort the representative average values have been thus classified: 92.80 (cm Hg. col.) for the A group and 98.00 for the B group (Fig. 3).

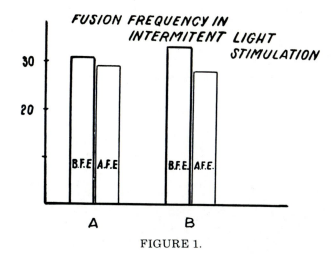

FIGURE 1.

A. DEMETER ET AL

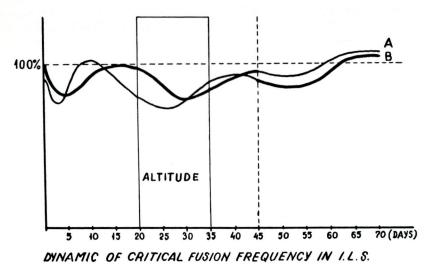

DYNAMIC OF CRITICAL FUSION FREQUENCY IN I.L.S.

FIGURE 2.

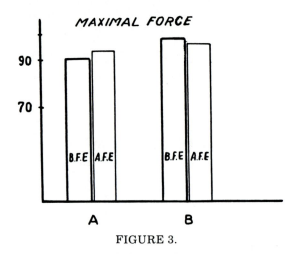

FIGURE 3.

After the effort the maximal force reached 94.00 for the experimental group while for the control group it decreased to 96.80 (Fig 3).

From Figure 4 it is obvious the features' reversal at the same time with the reversal of the groups regarding the administration of GH_3.

The GH_3 influence upon the muscular force is, in our mind, the most important aspect from all those observed, and it coincides, regarding the working mechanism, with the literature.

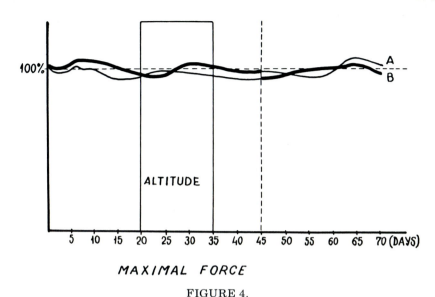

MAXIMAL FORCE

FIGURE 4.

Motor Reaction Latency in Light Stimulation

The digital limited reaction latency in light stimulation with a reduced inertia has been made obvious by means of an electronic chronometer which had an error value of 10^{-4} sec.

Before the effort, group A had a central value of 180 ms and group B 183 ms. After the effort the motor reaction latency decreased for group A to 178 ms and for group B to 182 ms (Fig. 5).

Figure 6 represents the relative dynamic motor reaction (the counterpart of the latency) throughout the testing period. With the exception of a short altitude period the better situation of the batch to which GH_3 has been administrated is obvious.

The decrease of the motor reaction latency is due to the neuromuscular commands and cortical analyzer activation by means of indirect influences and is more acute for group A. It is likely for GH_3 to have a facilitating role for the motor reaction and probably for the complex motor activity.

The Maximum O_2 Consumption

The representative average values for groups A and B are 4.030 l and 3.950 l, respectively. Related to kp/body these represent 48.6 ml/kp for group A and 46.0 ml/kp for group B (Fig. 7). That means that the subjects who used GH_3 had a stimulated oxygen consumption, although not in significant quantities.

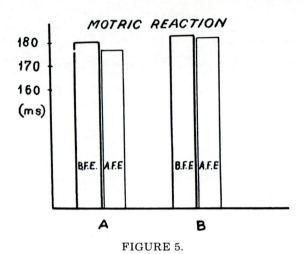

FIGURE 5.

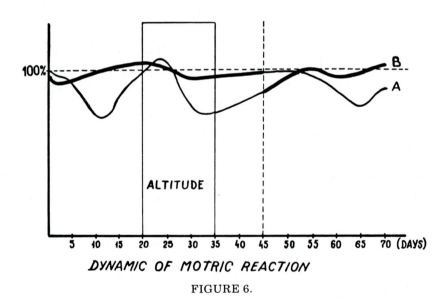

DYNAMIC OF MOTRIC REACTION

FIGURE 6.

*The Highest Speed in the Arm's Flexion-Extension Movement
From the Elbow Articulation, Without Load*

From the relative variations (Fig. 8) it is very clear that the speed after an effort does not change significantly for both group A and group B.

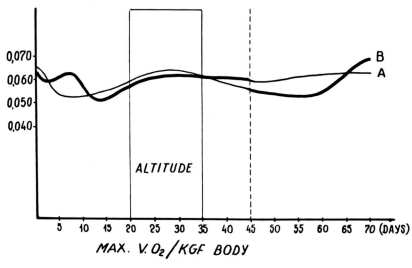

FIGURE 7.

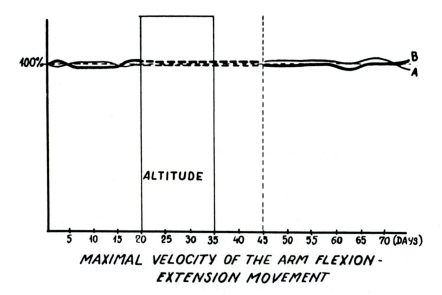

FIGURE 8.

Looking at this biomechanical parameter in the light of the contractile features of the movement of the involved muscles, it seems that it is not significantly altered through the GH_3 action.

The Isometrical Contraction Maximum Duration at Half of
the Palm Flexor Force Value

This is not significantly influenced by GH_3. The relative differences after the effort for both groups are disputable as dynamic (Fig. 9).

The Isometrical Contraction Instability Level

The relative variation dynamic for both groups is not convincing. It is possible that GH_3 has favored the stimulating-inhibitory equilibrium processes regarding the agonist-antagonist effector coupling, but this is not convincing from the experiment's results (Fig. 10).

Heart Rate

Although the heart rate relative increased differences for both groups is sometimes great during the testing period, yet on the basis of the profiles a systematic action of the GH_3 cannot be discerned (Fig. 11).

Conclusions

From the test results it may be observed that GH_3 influences favorably the main physiological functions involved in submaximal

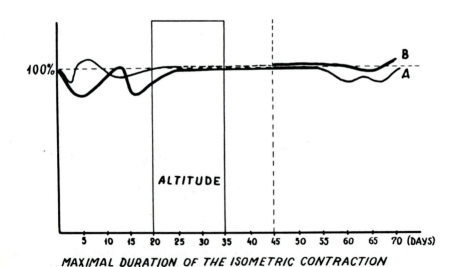

MAXIMAL DURATION OF THE ISOMETRIC CONTRACTION

FIGURE 9.

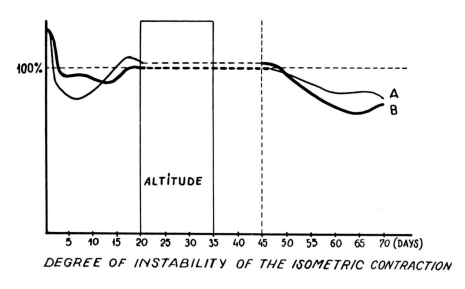

DEGREE OF INSTABILITY OF THE ISOMETRIC CONTRACTION

FIGURE 10.

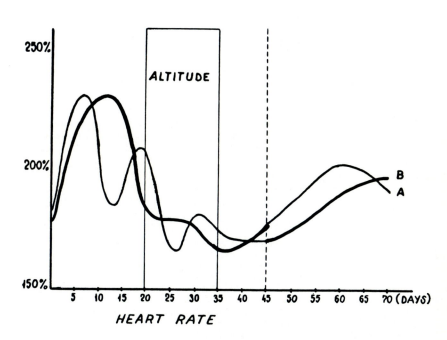

HEART RATE

FIGURE 11.

physical effort, improving the following physiological parameters: the fusion frequency in case of intermittent light stimulation; maximal force of the palm flexor for the predominant hand; the motor reaction latency in case of light stimulation; and the maximum O_2 consumption.

Regarding the maximal velocity of the flexion-extension movement of the arm from the elbow articulation, without load; maximal duration of the isometric contraction at half of the palm flexor maximum force value; instability level of the isometric contraction and heart rate, the GH_3 implied modifications are not significant. At any rate they do not work to a disadvantage.

Gerovital H_3 administrated under medical supervision to sportsmen can favor the sports result as well as the recovery after effort.

Bibliography

Aslan, A.: Procain therapy in old age and other disorders (Novocain-facteur H_3). Clin. Gerontol. No. 213, pp. 148-176, 1960.

Aslan, A., David, C. and Cimpeanu, S.: The procaintherapy metabolical effects. Norm. Patol. Physiol. 4:321, 1963.

Aslan, A. David, C. and Cimpeanu, S.: The patosclerosis and procainic therapy age influence upon the differential capilar permeability. Norm. Patol. Physiol. No. 1, pp. 35-47, 1960.

Aslan, A. and Vrabiescu, A.: Recherches oscillométriques chez les vieillards par l'épreuve à l'effort. St. Cercet. Endocrinol. 6/1-2:215-221, 1955.

Aslan, A.: Gerovital H_3. Edité par le Ministere de l'Industrie Chimique, IPAC-secteur rédactionnel, Bucharest, 1975.

Demeter, A.: The sportsmen's body recovering physiological basis. Physical Education and Sport Magazine, No. 10, Bucharest, 1973.

Demeter, A., Gagea, A. and Firea, E.: A complex and practical method for the body's reactivity transitory alterations study in case of the sport and physical education practicing pupils. Physical Education and Sport Magazine, No. 8, Bucharest, 1975.

Dragan, I,: The after effort recovering and the biological training for a contest. Physical Education and Sport Magazine, No. 10, Bucharest, 1973.

Partheniu, A., Neacsu, C., Jeflea, G. and Gagea, A.: An integrated and corelative standard of metabolical criteria — Endocrinical and nervous muscular functional consistent with the first rate sportive activity. Physical Education and Sport Magazine, No. 12, Bucharest, 1973.

Partheniu, A. and Gagea, A.: Method and way for the corelative and manysided nervous function researching, OSIM Invention No. 61358, Romania.

Effects of Tedral Upon Exercise Performance: A Double-Blind Crossover Study

Kenneth H. Sidney and Neville M. Lefcoe

Introduction

The combination of ephedrine with theophylline forms the basis of a commonly used anti-asthmatic medication, commercially known as Tedral. Apparently, the sympathomimetic and the methylxanthine act synergistically to elicit greater and more prolonged broncho-dilation than if either agent was administered separately [1].

Sympathomimetic amines, however, are specifically proscribed by the International Olympic Committee, even though it recognizes that medical treatment may demand the use of such therapeutic drugs. Unfortunately, although ephedrine and ephedrine-containing drugs are listed as "doping agents," there is little direct evidence that human physical performance is actually improved by such agents. In fact, recent work from our laboratory on fit young men showed that 24 mg of ephedrine had only a slight stimulating effect on blood pressure and heart rate and no effect on measures of muscle strength, muscle power, muscle endurance, anaerobic capacity and speed, cardiorespiratory endurance, reaction time, lung function and maximum oxygen intake [2]. Ephedrine, however, may have assisted the learning of a pursuit rotor tracking task although this effect was questionable.

The purpose of this experiment was to determine whether a single full therapeutic dose of the drug combination 24 mg ephedrine and 130 mg theophylline (T + E) has any effect on exercise performance.

Methods

Six male and five female university track athletes, aged 18 to 21 years, volunteered for this study. Values of maximum oxygen intake

Kenneth H. Sidney and Neville M. Lefcoe, Departments of Medicine, Victoria Hospital and the University of Western Ontario, Canada.

This study was supported in part by a grant from the Ontario Thoracic Society.

averaged 66.3 and 52.4 ml/kg/min for men and women, respectively. Each person was tested on three occasions within three weeks. On day 1, control data were collected, and on days 2 and 3, either T + E or a placebo was administered orally 45 minutes before testing commenced using a double-blind crossover design. Subjects were unable to tell whether they had received the drug or placebo and no side effects were observed. The test battery included determinations of lung function, reaction time, pursuit rotor tracking, agility, balance, muscle strength, static and dynamic muscle endurance, muscle power, anaerobic and aerobic performance times and predictions of maximum oxygen intake ($\dot{V}O_2$ max). Test items were administered in the same sequence on each day of testing and required about 2½ hours for their completion. Difference scores for drug vs. control were compared to difference scores for placebo vs. control using paired t-tests.

Results

Effects on Physical Performance and Work Capacity

T + E had no significant effect on handgrip strength, grip endurance (time to exhaustion at 50% grip strength), or muscle power (as measured by the jump and reach test). Relative to the placebo, the administration of the drug combination resulted in a 4% increase (P <.025) in the number of sit-ups completed in one minute (2/min).

T + E had no effect on the time to exhaustion for either the high speed, high slope anaerobic treadmill run or the progressive (2% increase in slope every two minutes) aerobic run. Maximum oxygen intake, predicted from individual heart rate − $\dot{V}O_2$ curves obtained during steady-state submaximal treadmill effort, was also not altered by drug administration.

Effects on Psychomotor Performance

Simple reaction time in response to a visual stimulus was not altered by T + E. Each subject was given ten trials on the pursuit rotor; tracking times, whether expressed as the average score or best score, were not significantly improved by the drug combination.

Conclusions

The drug combination, 24 mg ephedrine and 130 mg theophylline (Tedral minus phenobarbital), taken orally, has relatively little effect upon the exercise performance of fit young track athletes. This drug combination, however, may assist the performance of tasks requiring dynamic muscle endurance over a short period of time.

References

1. Cohen, B.M.: A double-blind crossover comparative study of ephedrine plus theophylline (Tedral) vs. ephedrine after single and multiple dosage. New Jersey:Warner-Lambert Research Institute, No. 950-0022, 1973.
2. Sidney, K.H. and Lefcoe, N.M.: The effects of ephedrine on the physiological and psychological responses to submaximal and maximal exercise in man. In preparation.

Examens anti-doping effectués in 1975 par la ligue vélocipédique belge

A. Dirix

Entre 1965 et 1975, les concours cyclistes de la ligue vélocipédique de Belgique ont été soumis à des examens anti-doping. Durant cette période, 3,812 examens ont été effectués. Le présent rapport a pour objet de présenter un certain nombre de données concernant ces examens.

Les examens anti-doping ont été effectués aux laboratoires de la Faculté de médecine vétérinaire, Chaire de pharmacologie et de toxicologie de l'Université de Gent.

De 1965 à 1972 (Tableau I), le nombre d'examens menés annuellement a oscillé entre 117 et 265. Ce nombre est porté à 471 en 1973, 619 en 1974, pour atteindre 1,149 examens en 1975.

Parallèlement à cet accroissement des contrôles anti-doping, on observe, durant cette décade, une réduction du pourcentage de cas positifs. En effect, de 25.59% de cas positifs en 1965, on passe à

Tableau I.

Année	Nombre de coureurs examinés	Cas positifs	Pourcentage (%) de cas positifs
1965	254	65	25.59%
1966	126	25	19.84%
1967	130	11	8.46%
1968	196	16	8.16%
1969	234	19	8.12%
1970	265	11	4.15%
1971	251	12	4.78%
1972	117	3	2.56%
1973	471	8	1.70%
1974	619	44	7.10%
1975	1,149	40	3.48%
Total	3,812	254	6.66%

A. Dirix, Commission médicale, Ligue vélocipédique belge; trésorier, Fédération internationale de médecine sportive, Sint Niklass, Belgique.

3.48% en 1975. A noter, cependent, une remontée des cas positifs en 1974, avec 7.10%.

Le tableau II présent la répartition des contrôles effectués en 1975, ainsi que le nombre de cas positifs, de fraude et de carence, par catégorie de coureurs. Au total, 40 cas positifs ont été détectés, dont 32 après examen de laboratoire, ainsi que 1 cas de fraude et 7 cas de carence (cas qui ne sont pas soumis à la réglementation) assimilés aux cas positifs. C'est dans la catégorie des sportifs amateurs étudiés que l'on retrouve le pourcentage le plus élevé de cas positifs (3.9%), alors que pour les professionnels, ce pourcentage n'est que de 2.58% dans notre échantillon.

Parmi les substances utilisées, ce sont les amphétamines qui sont identifiées le plus souvent (Tableau III), suivies, mais à un degré moindre, par l'éphédrine. Sur les 40 cas examinés, 6 coureurs

Tableau II.

Catégorie	Nombre de contrôles	Cas positifs	Cas de fraude	Cas de carence
Professionnels	155	4	1	1
Amateurs	459	18	–	6
Amateurs corporatifs	19	–	–	–
Amateurs étudiants	13	–	–	–
Amateurs militaires	6	–	–	–
Juniors	251	7	–	–
Débutants	163	3	–	–
Vétérans	6	–	–	–
Dames	27	–	–	–
Total	1149	32	1	7

Tableau III.

Substance	Professionnels	Catégories de coureurs Amateurs	Juniors	Débutants	Nombre de cas
Amphétamine	2	11	4	–	17
Méthyl-amphétamine	1	4	1	1	7
Fencamfamine	–	–	–	1	1
Méthylphénidate	–	–	–	–	–
Lévophacétopérane	–	–	–	–	–
Heptaminol	1	1	–	–	2
Ephédrine	2	3	2	1	8
Noréphédrine	1	3	–	1	5
Total	7	22	7	4	40

utilisaient plus d'une substance. Se sont présentés: deux cas d'éphédrine et de noréphédrine; 2 cas de méthylamphétamine et d'amphétamine, et 2 cas de méthylamphétamine, éphédrine, et noréphédrine.

Les stéroïdes anabolisants ne sont pas mentionnés dans la liste des produits interdits par l'U.C.I., mais seront interdits aux prochains Jeux Olympiques de Montréal qui auront lieu dans quelques jours.

Interrelationships Involving Selected Physical Fitness Variables and Attitude Toward Physical Activity in Elementary School Children

C. R. Meyers, D. R. Pendergast and D. L. DeBacy

Introduction

This investigation was directed to an examination of the interrelationships among selected physical fitness variables and attitude toward physical activity in elementary school children — an area that has seen little research despite its importance in understanding the growth and development of children. Subpurposes of the study were (1) to utilize refined instrumentation, such as electronic recording of static strength and heart rate (HR), and related procedural techniques in measuring certain variables in a school setting and (2) to explore promising directions for further research.

The study was conducted in a suburban elementary school in the Greater Buffalo, New York Area and involved all classes in grades 4 through 6 (N = 472, 251 boys and 221 girls, 9 to 12 years of age). All data were collected within an eight-week period in the spring of 1975. For variables in which it was not feasible to measure all subjects, the number that could be accommodated was randomly selected from the total number by classes. Informed consent forms were obtained with parental signatures for each child participating. For subjects selected and volunteering for treadmill testing, a special parental consent form was required relating information peculiar to this testing.

The variables included with their respective modes of measurement were (1) muscular strength — grip on Stoelting dynamometer

C. R. Meyers, D. R. Pendergast and D. L. DeBacy, Departments of Physical Education and Physiology, State University of New York at Buffalo, N.Y., U.S.A.

Supported in part by SUNY Interinstitutional Grant from BSSG/NSF Funds.

(n = 468) and LVDT (Linear Variable Differential Transformer) tests of knee extension at angles of 135° (n = 260) and 115° (n = 216); (2) muscular endurance — 60-second bent-knee sit-ups (n = 434); (3) muscular power — vertical jump (n = 451); (4) aerobic power — $\dot{V}O_2$/kg max as predicted from a three-stage intermittent progressive treadmill test (n = 41), HR response to 4-minute bench-stepping and 1½ minute recovery (n = 94), and HR regression on $\dot{V}O_2$ (n = 41); and (5) attitude — Children's Attitude Toward Physical Activity (CATPA) Instrument (n = 322) and Kenyon's ATPA Scales for parents (n = 83).

Testing protocol and initial reliability were established in a pilot study involving four third grade classes (n = 93). All consenting students with parental permission completed measures of height, weight, sit-ups, grip and vertical jump in the gymnasium during regular physical education class activity. The attitude inventory was administered in the classroom setting for children and by mail for their parents. Selected students participated in treadmill and knee extension testing on an individual basis in a separate room and performed bench-stepping in groups of four in another room. Boys and girls were tested separately in all instances, except for attitude assessment, and all testing was administered or directly supervised by one of the investigators. Some classes or subjects, as appropriate, were randomly selected for retesting to indicate reliability for sit-ups and knee extension tests.

Procedure

Bent-knee sit-ups for 60 seconds (reliability — .72, n = 100 boys; .82, n = 73 girls) were administered to half of each class at one time with partners supporting the feet and counting the number performed [2]. Height was recorded to the half inch and weight to the half pound. The better of two trials for preferred grip (reliability — .92, n = 40 boys; .89, n = 42 girls) and nonpreferred grip, performed in that order, was recorded to the 0.5 kg on the Stoelting hand dynamometer, grip span = 4.8 cm [2]. For the vertical jump the standing reach was determined by raising a movable jump board, graduated in one-half inch intervals, as high as possible with the finger tips of both hands, while facing the board [2]. The score was the highest of three jumps to the one-half inch made with a one-hand touch, preferred side facing the board.

The treadmill testing was performed on a Quinton Model 18-54 Treadmill, during which oxygen consumption ($\dot{V}O_2$) was measured by a closed circuit method with a 13.5 lieter Collins Respirator and

HR was recorded by a Model 7A Grass Polygraph. After a brief period of orientation to equipment and procedure, each subject had HR and $\dot{V}O_2$ recorded for two-minute standing rest period; five-minute period of treadmill walking at 3 mph 0° elevation; and two-minute recovery period. Following a five- to ten-minute standing rest, HR and $\dot{V}O_2$ were recorded for five-minute period of treadmill walking at 3 mph, 10° elevation and two-minute recovery.

Tests of knee extension at 135° (reliability — .85, n = 53 boys; .80, n = 50 girls) and 115° (reliability — .81, n = 40 boys; .90, n = 36 girls) were performed on different occasions using a specially constructed padded chair with adjustable seat depth to provide firm support behind the knee and a seat belt and two shoulder straps to control positioning. The pulling assembly consisted of a webbed strap loop secured on the ankle just above the malleoli, a Schaveitz LVDT transducer, Model FTA-IU-500, and adjustable chain to facilitate fixation at the prescribed knee angle with the line of pull perpendicular to the lower leg. The better of two trials was recorded to 0.5 kg for preferred and nonpreferred legs, in that order, with subject grasping the sides of the seat without exerting force. Peak readings were recorded on a Daytronic transducer amplifier-indicator, Model 300D-M-70.

Bench-stepping was done on a 14-in bench, 10 ft long, at a rate of 24 s/m with a handrail set at approximately shoulder level. Subjects performed in groups of four with HR recorded on a Model 7A Grass Polygraph continuously from one minute prior to the onset of exercise until two minutes after exercise. Testing instructions and stepping cadence were given by tape recorder.

The CATPA inventory [3] was administered in the classroom during a 45-minute period prescheduled on a class basis. Students identified by the school reading specialist as having reading problems did not participate in the attitude assessment. Upon completion of the instrument subjects were given the opportunity to ask questions relating to its content. The Kenyon ATPA Scales [1] were delivered in sealed envelopes to the parents and returned to the school office by the children. A coding scheme was used to permit matching of child and parent attitude responses as well as postal mail follow-up and return of delinquent responses.

Findings

The product-moment coefficients for the intercorrelation of selected fitness and attitude measures are presented in Table I, for boys and for girls, ages 9 to 12 years. Analysis reveals few meaningful

Table I. Intercorrelations Among Selected Measures
for Boys and Girls, Ages 9-12[1]

	1	2	3	4	5	6	7	8	9	10	11
1. Sit-ups	** **	.13 (231)		.11 (99)	.41 (229)	.12 (19)	-02 (43)	-05 (42)	-.24 (44)	.07 (163)	.06 (163)
2. Grip[2]	.13 (200)	** **				-30 (22)	.18 (48)	.57 (47)	.22 (48)	.15 (176)	.12 (176)
3. Knee 135°[2]			** **	.73 (88)	.33 (132)						
4. Knee 115°[2]	.22 (105)		.80 (84)	** **	.48 (105)						
5. Vertical jump	.37 (196)		.30 (123)	.50 (106)	** **	-.43 (22)			-.02 (47)		
6. $\dot{V}o_2$/kg max	.28 (18)	-.10 (19)			.42 (18)	** **	-27 (12)	-12 (11)	.13 (12)	.14 (14)	.31 (14)
7. HR-3 min of exercise	-.03 (39)	.13 (42)				-14 (8)	** **	.83 (46)	.54 (48)		
8. HR-5-15 sec post exercise	.22 (39)	.14 (42)				.13 (8)	.72 (42)	** **	.72 (47)		-.14 (32)
9. HR-60-90 sec post exercise	-.16 (42)	.10 (45)			.00 (44)	.14 (8)	.58 (42)	.65 (42)	** **		.00 (29)
10. Total CATPA	.04 (138)	-.06 (149)				.12 (15)				** **	
11. CATPA—Health Scale	.13 (138)	.00 (149)				.43 (15)		.14 (28)	-.08 (31)		** **

[1] Values in upper right sector are for boys and lower left—girls; n is given in parentheses.

[2] Preferred limb.

interrelationships among the selected measures. Understandably, the strongest correlations were found within the same family of tests, i.e., knee-extension tests and HR counts. Across variables, the correlation of grip and HR 5-15 seconds postexercise for boys reflects 32% common variance in contrast to 2% for girls. Another relationship that warrants mention is knee extension at 115° with vertical jump for boys and girls, in which approximately 25% of variance was shared as compared to approximately 10% for knee extension at 135° with vertical jump. It was noted that for the knee 115°-vertical jump relationship by ages for boys, $r = .91$ (n = 39) for 10-year-olds and $r = .43$ (n = 40) for age 11. An intriguing finding was observed in the relationship of vertical jump and $\dot{V}O_2$/kg max, wherein correlations of comparable size but opposite signs were obtained, boys showing a negative relationship. Overall, the inter-correlations in Table I indicate the specificity of the measures selected to represent the different physical fitness variables in this study. Examination of correlation coefficients calculated for each age showed no tendency for rs to increase with age, although it was found that 9-year-old boys and girls had somewhat stronger correlations for sit-ups with vertical jump and grip than at the other ages.

The descriptive statistics in Tables II and III are presented to disclose the pattern of gradual increase manifested from ages 9 to 12 years in the selected items, with some exceptions. Proportionately greater increases occurred in sit-ups from 11 to 12 years for boys and girls; in grip from 11 to 12 years for boys and 10 to 12 years for

Table II. Means and Standard Deviations of Selected Measures for Boys by Age

Measure	9			10			11			12			Total
	$\overline{X}$	SD	N	$\overline{X}$	SD	N	$\overline{X}$	SD	N	$\overline{X}$	SD	N	N
Height	54.3	2.05	37	55.1	2.76	89	56.9	2.87	88	59.1	3.32	36	250
Weight	70.7	10.01	37	74.4	17.29	89	83.9	18.24	88	97.1	23.31	36	250
Sit-ups	27.4	9.03	37	26.4	8.48	83	27.4	8.64	78	30.5	7.27	33	231
Grip—P	17.3	2.53	37	18.3	3.65	89	20.6	3.61	88	24.3	4.87	36	250
Grip—NP	16.2	2.80	37	17.2	3.68	88	19.1	3.65	88	23.0	4.86	36	249
Knee 135°—P*	43.3	6.94	21	50.4	11.41	51	58.2	13.81	44	62.7	16.63	17	133
Knee 135°—NP*	44.1	7.53	21	49.1	11.82	50	56.3	13.40	44	62.6	17.28	17	132
Knee 115°—P	60.2	8.41	13	69.5	14.47	38	78.3	15.49	40	75.3	13.89	14	105
Knee 115°—NP	53.3	9.43	13	68.8	11.67	33	72.2	15.19	34	76.7	15.78	13	93
Vertical jump	11.6	1.90	36	12.4	2.12	85	13.1	2.08	85	14.0	2.40	36	242

*P—preferred limb; NP—non-preferred

Table III. Means and Standard Deviations of Selected Measures for Girls by Age

Measure	9			10			11			12			Total
	$\overline{X}$	SD	N	$\overline{X}$	SD	N	$\overline{X}$	SD	N	$\overline{X}$	SD	N	N
Height	53.8	2.65	39	55.3	2.49	74	57.8	2.93	83	59.4	2.68	22	218
Weight	69.4	14.97	39	75.9	17.97	74	86.2	20.90	83	88.7	15.41	22	218
Sit-ups	22.2	9.39	37	22.6	6.06	68	23.8	6.87	79	26.0	7.95	20	204
Grip—P	14.6	4.01	39	15.5	3.21	74	18.4	4.40	83	21.1	5.44	22	218
Grip—NP	12.8	3.13	39	14.3	2.94	72	17.1	3.62	83	19.4	5.05	22	216
Knee 135°—P*	40.2	8.57	21	46.6	12.69	41	51.4	13.19	52	60.3	15.93	13	127
Knee 135°—NP*	41.0	8.44	21	45.9	12.22	41	51.4	14.15	52	59.3	15.70	11	125
Knee 115°—P	62.4	17.05	14	63.1	13.73	37	75.6	16.37	49	78.1	15.51	11	111
Knee 115°—NP	60.3	13.48	12	64.5	15.05	30	73.2	15.43	45	76.9	12.26	11	98
Vertical jump	11.1	1.95	36	11.8	1.76	67	12.8	1.88	85	13.7	2.01	21	209

*P—preferred limb; NP—non-preferred

girls; and in knee 115° from 10 to 12 years for girls. A slowed rate of increase appeared in knee 115° from 11 to 12 years for boys.

The most profound findings involved cardiopulmonary measurement. The electronic monitoring of HR during bench-stepping afforded a more accurate determination of HR at postexercise intervals than can be accomplished by conventional pulse counting. In addition, it was possible to obtain and correlate steady state HR (three minutes of exercise) with 5 to 15 and 60 to 90 second postexercise HR counts (Table I). The magnitude of the relationship between steady state HR and HR 5-15 seconds postexercise suggests that the former can be predicted from HR 5 to 15 seconds (69% common variance for boys, 52% for girls). Contrarily, the comparatively lower relationship between steady state HR and HR 60 to 90 seconds postexercise (shared variances of 29% and 33%) implies that steady state HR cannot be predicted from HR 60 to 90.

Analysis of HR data for 40 subjects (21 boys, 19 girls) tested on the treadmill divulged a rate of HR rise that was noticeably faster than HR data generally reported for adult subjects with a mean half-time of 12 seconds. This dramatic increase in HR was supported by HR recordings for the bench-stepping (n = 94). Little difference was apparent between the rate of HR rise in boys and girls. The data collected herein were observed over a HR range similar to that reported by other researchers, viz., rest to 150 b/m.

Analysis of $\dot{V}O_2$ max and $\dot{V}O_2$/kg max data by grade levels 4 through 6 and sex is presented in Table IV. The values for boys were higher in grades 4 and 5, while the girls were higher in grade 6. The range of correlations for the HR-$\dot{V}O_2$ relationship was .85-.99 for boys and girls. It was noted that $\dot{V}O_2$ max not only served as an indicator of aerobic fitness, but also of the overall HR-$\dot{V}O_2$ relationship. The HR-$\dot{V}O_2$ data for girls in grades 4, 5 and 6 (Fig. 1) reveal that for any given $\dot{V}O_2$ the older girls had a lower steady state HR, thus giving a better indication of aerobic power than $\dot{V}O_2$ max alone.

Focusing on attitude toward physical activity, only the correlation between $\dot{V}O_2$/kg max and CATPA-Health Scale exceeded .30 (Table I). The correlation of parental and children's attitude, based upon 18% parental response, resulted in rs of .24 (n = 36) for father-boy and .16 (n = 38) for mother-boy; and −.08 (n = 26) for father-girl, −.21 (n = 27) for mother-girl. The interparental relationship on ATPA Scales was somewhat stronger for parents of boys (32% common variance, n = 44) than for girls (18% common variance, n = 29); for the combined groups, $r−.52$, n = 83.

Table IV. Continuous Simple Linear Regression Data by Grade and Sex

	Slope	$\underline{y}$	$\underline{r}$	SE	x at y $\overline{200}$ $\dot{V}o_2$max	$\dot{V}o_2$/kg
Gr. 4 Boys	0.0584	78.12	0.9999	0.1443	2.09	67.16
Gr. 4 Girls	0.0613	80.06	0.9880	2.2802	1.96	52.57
Gr. 5 Boys	0.0634	73.90	0.9995	0.4811	1.99	54.71
Gr. 5 Girls	0.0646	88.79	0.9763	3.7174	1.72	47.36
Gr. 6 Boys	0.0619	70.71	0.9991	0.7213	2.09	52.29
Gr. 6 Girls	0.0499	85.13	0.9788	3.6450	2.30	61.77

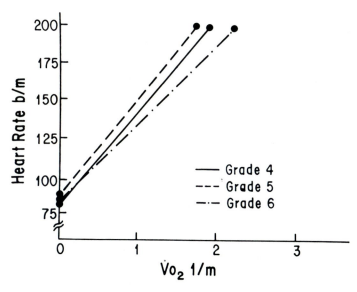

FIG. 1. Comparison of the linear slope for girls in grades 4, 5 and 6.

Implications

Careful consideration of the developmental pattern in the selected measures studied, together with close scrutiny of intercorrelations at each age, can provide a valuable basis for planning physical activity programs to enhance the growth and development of children. This investigation has disclosed that the measures selected to represent different variables of physical fitness appear to provide different (i.e., specific) information in the broad context of physical fitness for 9- to 12-year-old boys and girls. Accordingly, this specificity of measures makes it imperative that items representing all of the variables be included in order to present a total picture of the growth and development of children in physical fitness as a guide for informed program planning.

The findings of this investigation are suggestive of areas that warrant further research, illustrative of which are the following:

1. The procedure and instrumentation for determining knee extension strength warrant continued application to involve other knee angles and considered adaptation to other joint movements.

2. The methodology utilized in this study affords a feasible means of validating pulse counting after bench-stepping at various age levels.

3. The nature of the HR-$\dot{V}O_2$ relationship as a measure of aerobic fitness should be carefully examined, rather than continuing reliance upon $\dot{V}O_2$ max or $\dot{V}O_2$/kg max alone.

4. Based upon the strength of the respective interrelationships it appears that postexercise HR 5-15 seconds provides an adequate prediction of steady state HR, whereas postexercise HR 60-90 seconds does not predict steady state HR but would appear to indicate the rate of recovery from stress.

5. The negative parental-girl correlations suggest that further study may be fruitful in determining the attitude formation pattern characteristic of elementary age girls, especially in light of the rapid societal changes related to females.

References

1. Kenyon, C.: Six scales for assessing attitudes toward physical activity. Res. Q. 39:566-574, 1968.
2. Meyers, C.R.: Measurement in Physical Education, ed. 2. New York:Ronald Press Co., 1974.
3. Simon, J.A. and Smoll, F.L.: An instrument for assessing children's attitudes toward physical activity. Res. Q. 45:407-415, 1974.

Physical Fitness of the Czechoslovak 12- to 55-Year-Old Population

V. Seliger, M. Mácek, O. Skranc, J. Piric, P. Handzo,
J. Horák, J. Rous and Z. Jirka

Introduction

Within the framework of the section Human Adaptability of the International Biological Programme (IBP) we investigated the physical fitness of the average Czechoslovak population. The fitness of man may be considerably influenced by the environment in which he lives [24], and on the contrary a fit man possesses all prerequisites that could help him to influence rationally his environment. The knowledge of physical fitness of the average population enables one to ascertain the population norms.

The level of physical fitness in populations constitutes also a primary social and medical problem. An impaired physical activity (hypokinesis) causes a decrease of physical fitness of the organism, and together with the growing share of psychic stress, nervous overstrain, static muscular exertion, noise, vibrations, detriments in the environment of everyday life, the preconditions grow for the origin of so-called diseases of civilization. The following risk factors precede the attack of diseases of civilization: high blood pressure, high cholesterol level, diabetes, obesity, nicotinism, lack of physical movements, stresses and infectious diseases.

Physical activities, be it in the forms of organized physical education, sport or recreation, become a significant, objective and social need. The World Health Organization (WHO) arranged a seminar on optimal level of physical performance capacity in adults [26]. This seminar pointed out the importance of prevention of cardiac diseases especially through a suitable physical activity [12]. The specific adaptation to motor activity induces also nonspecific adaptation to other stresses [14] and helps the organism of an individual to cope with them. Physical activities bring about

V. Seliger, M. Mácek, O. Skranc, J. Piric, P. Handzo, H. Horák, J. Rous and
Z. Jirka, Department of Physiology, Faculty of Physical Education and Sports,
Charles University, Prague, Czechoslovakia.

also a decrease of blood pressure, body fat, cholesterol, etc. Morbidity and work absenteeism diminish. On the contrary, the working capacity increases as well as resistance to stresses. Finally, in consequence of this also, the work productivity increases [18] and active age is extended.

There are many scientists who are interested in physical fitness problems, who try also to define the term physical fitness. Bucher [7] regards fitness as a quality including mental, moral, emotional, social, cultural and physical fitness. Astrand and Rodahl [5] characterize fitness as determined by energy output, neuromuscular function and psychological factors. In Czechoslovakia we regard fitness as a complex of prerequisites of the organism to react in an optimal way to different stimuli coming from the environment. Physical fitness is then a complex of prerequisites for optimal reactions of the organism to very demanding motor activities and to environmental stimuli. Very frequently we restrict physical fitness to the fitness of circulatory and respiratory systems of the organism. These systems indicate very sensibly the level of motor activity and the resulting adaptation of the organism as a whole. From the introduced reasons it is necessary to take into consideration several criteria in an evaluation of physical fitness. A complex evaluation of physical fitness is regarded as a proper approach.

Methods

Methods selected for the investigation of physical fitness of populations are almost in accordance with the requirements and instructions of the coordinator of the section Human Adaptability IBP [25] and of the coordinator of the program Physical Fitness of Inhabitants [1]. For the conditions in Czechoslovakia two editions of a methodical handbook were published [19, 20], and every year instructions were edited which had to insure a perfect methodical unification [21]. A great help for the investigation was the possibility to provide all institutes with uniform apparatus from special investment funds for associated workshops. All the apparatus, including analyzing instruments, had been tested every year before the investigations were started.

The selection of population was made in a double sampling within the range of 30 km of the sites of the 11 institutes, and the number of persons followed was restricted to 120 persons per one year and per one institute. As a rule four to five persons were invited for examination in the morning hours and the entire investigation ended during forenoon. The experiments were made in the same way and at a same time in one age group in all workshops always during a period from September to December, starting with the 12-year-old age group in the autumn 1968 and ending with the 55-year-old group in 1974. On the whole, 3,700 persons of average population were investigated from which 1,070 persons were given maximum workloads.

On the whole 30 anthropometric indices were measured and also 11 skinfolds for the determination of the percentage of fat in the body. In the work tests on the bicycle ergometer the investigated persons were pedaling up to their maximum at 3 submaximum and 1 maximum workloads. The measurements of pulse rate, pulmonary ventilation, breathing frequency, blood pressure and analysis of the expired air were made at rest and at the end of every workload. This has provided the whole 50 basic data and enabled also computation of other functional values, such as oxygen uptake, carbon dioxide expenditure, pulse oxygen and others. The followed functional indices were elaborated for individual loads and the dynamics of their progress was estimated in dependence on physical exertion and age.

Results and Discussion

Somatometric Characteristic

The progress of the development of the body height in the followed groups is characteristic. The rise of the curve of boys is steeper from 13 to 14 years, and after the age of 15 up to 18 years the growth of body height in girls is expressively slower. In both sexes the heights reach their maximum in men of 23 years and in women 18 years of age. A slow decrease in values of body height comes until the highest followed age.

The growth of body weights during the growing periods corresponds to some extent to the values of body heights. Girls aged 12 and 13 years exceeded the boys in weight slightly. Around the 14th year the value curves cross and the boys exceed the girls. The difference grows significantly until the age of 25 years when the differences in weights between men and women attain the maximum. The difference diminishes after the age of 25 years, above all in consequence of the growing values of weights of women.

The body fat percentage showed evidence that girls as early as 11 years of age differ from boys very significantly in higher values of body fat. During the growing period we can see a small decrease of body fat in both sexes up to the age of 19 to 21 years of age. In adults it is then possible to observe, after the age of 27 years, a gradual rise of values and after 49 years of age a slight decrease.

It may be concluded that the observed samples of inhabitants are very close in the basic physical signs to all samples so far described and regarded as Czechoslovak norms [23], as well as to the values of investigations made by other authors with samples living in similar social conditions [22, 27, 28].

Work Test on the Bicycle Ergometer

Maximal Heart Rate

The values of maximum heart rate show in the growing age a small increase in boys from 11 to 17 years of age (196 beats/min) and in girls a graduated decrease of values from 11 years of age (198 beats/min). The values are identical in both sexes from the age of 19 to 31 years (196-192 beats/min). Afterwards, we can see small differences in maximum heart rates. The values are lower in men than in women. Our average values are somewhat higher in adults then presented by Astrand and Christensen [4] and Robinson [17], and they are close to the values introduced by Buskirk [8] and Hollmann [10].

Work Capacity at the Heart Rate 170 (W 170)

The absolute values of W 170 are higher in men than in women. They increase from the age of 11 years up to 29 years in men (194 W) and remain the same up to 59 years of age. In women we can observe a small increase during the whole lifespan (up to 129 W). The relative values, W 170 per kg of body weight, increase from 11 years (2.2 in boys, 1.7 W/kg in girls) up to 16 to 17 years of age (2.7 in boys and 1.8 W/kg in girls). This increase is followed by a small decrease in men (up to 2.2 W/kg) and contrary to that the same values are observed in women (1.7 W/kg). The values are lower in women than in men. The results correspond to the values observed by Macnab et al [16] and the Canadian study of CAHPER [9].

Blood Pressure

In the values of systolic and diastolic blood pressure when measured at a maximal load an increase is observable growing with age. In general, the values are lower than presented by Luft [15].

Pulmonary Ventilation

The values of pulmonary ventilation found at the maximal workload are lower in women than in men. An increase coming with age can be observed from the groups of 11 years of age (50 l/min boys and 44 l/min girls) up to the age 23 years (109 l/min men, 83 l/min women). From the age of 27 years a small decrease can be observed in both sexes. The results are very similar to the values presented by Luft [15], Astrand [3], Andersen and Hermansen [2] and Binkhorst et al [6].

Maximal Aerobic Power

The rate of maximum oxygen uptake is generally regarded as an index of physical fitness, embracing the function of several organs and systems, from which the cardiopulmonary system is regarded as the most important. In absolute values of maximum oxygen uptake during the work capacity experiment we can observe a continuous increase up to the age group of 21 years in both sexes. Five years later a small decrease begins in values of maximal aerobic power. The maximal observed values are found in the adult, 3.3 l/min in men and 2.2 l/min in women. The relative values are in the growing age nearly the same, 51-48 ml/kg/min in boys and 39-38 ml/kg/min in girls. From 16 years of age we can observe a continuous decrease of observed values in both sexes. Our results correspond to the results of Robinson [17], Hollmann [10], Astrand and Christensen [4], Knuttgen [13] and Ikai et al [11].

Conclusions

Concluding the research we can summarize the results of our investigation of physical fitness of average inhabitants of Czechoslovakia. We are of the opinion that the results of our work may become the norms of the present state of physical fitness of the average population and at the same time a theoretical basis for the efforts to increase physical fitness of the population as an important factor of the prevention of diseases of civilization.

References

1. Andersen, K.L.: IBP Handbook. Measurement of Maximal Oxygen Uptake and Related Respiratory and Circulatory Functions. Bergen:University of Bergen, 1967.
2. Andersen, K.L. and Hermansen, L.: Aerobic work capacity in middle aged Norwegian men. J. Appl. Physiol. 20:432, 1965.
3. Astrand, I.: Aerobic work capacity in men and women with special reference to age. Acta Physiol. Scand. Suppl. 49, 1960.
4. Astrand, P.O. and Christensen, E.H.: Aerobic work capacity. In Dickens, F., Neil, E. and Widdas, W.F. (eds.): Oxygen in the Animal Organism. New York:Pergamon Press, 1964.

5. Astrand, P.O. and Rodahl, K.: Textbook of Work Physiology. New York:McGraw-Hill, 1970.
6. Binkhorst, R.A., Pool, J., van Leeuwen, P. and Bouhuys, A.: Maximum oxygen uptake in healthy nonathletic males. Int. Z. Angew. Physiol. 22:10, 1966.
7. Bucher, C.A.: Foundations of Physical Education. St. Louis:Mosby, 1960.
8. Buskirk, E. and Taylor, H.L.: Maximal oxygen intake and its relation to body composition with special reference to chronic physical activity and obesity. J. Appl. Physiol. 11:72, 1957.
9. CAHPER fitness — performance test manual for boys and girls 7 to 17 years of age. Can. Assoc. Health, Phys. Ed. Recreation, 1966.
10. Hollmann, W.: Höchst — und Dauerleistungsfähigkeit des Sportlers. Munchen:Johann Ambrosius Barth, 1963.
11. Ikai, M. and Kitigawa, K.: Maximum oxygen uptake of Japanese related to sex and age. Med. Sci. Sports 4:127, 1972.
12. Karvonen, M.J.: Körperliche Tätigkeit, Cholesterinstoffwechsel und Arteriosklerose. Schweiz. Z. Sportmed. 9:90, 1961.
13. Knuttgen, H.: Aerobic capacity of adolescents. J. Appl. Physiol. 22:655, 1967.
14. Kraus, B. and Raab, W.: Hypokinetic Disease. Springfield, 1961.
15. Luft, U.C.: Pulmonary function, body composition and physical fitness of 415 airline pilots in relation to age. In Seliger, V. (ed.): Physical Fitness. Proc. Satel. Sympos., Prague 1973, p. 237.
16. Macnab, R.B.J., Conger, P.R. and Taylor, P.S.: Differences in maximal and submaximal work capacity in men and women. J. Appl. Physiol. 27:644, 1969.
17. Robinson, S.: Experimental studies of physical fitness in relation to age. Arbeitsphysiol. 10:251, 1938.
18. Rozenblat, V.V.: Problema utomlenija. Moskva 1961.
19. Seliger, V. (ed.): Metody výzkumu fyzické zdatnosti obyvatelstva. 1.vyd. (Methods of Physical Fitness Examinations of Inhabitants, ed. 1.) Universita Karlova, Praha. 1968.
20. Seliger, V. (ed.): Metody a dílčí výsledky výzkumu fyzické zdatnosti obyvatelstva. 2.vyd. (Methods and Partial Results of Physical Fitness of Inhabitants, ed. 2.) Praha:Universita Karlova, 1970.
21. Seliger, V.: Our experience from the methodic training of the laboratories for the research of physical fitness of the inhabitants within the framework of IBP. In Mácek, M. (ed.): Proceedings of the Second Symposium of Pediatric Group of Working Physiology. Praha:Universita Karlova, 1970.
22. Shephard, R.J., Weese, C.H. and Meriman, J.E.: Prediction of maximal oxygen intake from anthropometric data. Int. Z. Angew. Physiol. 29:119, 1971.
23. Suchý, J.: A System of Control of Development Trends. Antrop. Congress 1969, Praha:Academia, 1971, p. 145.
24. Weiner, J.S.: IBP Handbook No. 1. A Guide to the Human Adaptability Proposals, ed. 2. Oxford and Edinburgh:Blackwell Sci. Publ. 1969.
25. Weiner, J.S. and Lourie, J.A.: IBP Handbook No. 9. Human Biology. Oxford and Edinburgh:Blackwell Sci. Publ., 1969.
26. WHO Report of Scientific Group: Optimum Physical Performance Capacity in Adults. WHO Tech. Rep. Ser. No. 436, Geneva, 1969.

27. Wolański, N.: Rozvoj biologiczny czlovieka. Pan. Wyd. Naukove, Warszawa 1970.
28. Yanev, B. Sterev, P., Boev, P. et al: Physical development and fitness of the Bulgarian people from the birth up to the age of twenty-six. Sofia:Bulgariak Academy of Science Press, 1965.

L'activité physique de loisirs et sa relation avec le bien-être physique et mental et avec les handicaps chez les personnes agées

M. Jenicek, T. Rousseau et M. Bellefleur

Une étude transversale, faite à l'été 1974, nous a permis d'évaluer le bien-être physique, mental et les handicaps des citoyens âges de Ville Saint-Laurent, grâce à des entrevues avec les sujets eux-mêmes [7]. Plusieurs indicateurs de santé ont été mis en relation avec une série de variables indépendantes (Tableau I).

Le problème particulier, sujet de cette communication, a été l'évaluation de l'activité physique non-professionnelle des sujets et sa

Tableau I. Etude sur l'état de santé des personnes agées. Ville de Saint-Laurent, 1974

Aperçu des variables

Variables indépendantes:	Variables dépendantes:
âge,	logement
sexe,	activités – travail
religion,	loisirs
identité culturelle	alimentation – type
race, ethnie, langue	régularité
mobilité géographique	état de santé – physique
situation familliale	mentale
occupation du père	globale
fratrie	dépendance et handicaps
statut socio-économique	
isolement – état civil, années	besoins – finances
de solitude	type d'aide requis
milieu de vie – urbain vs. rural	possibilité de communication
secteur de la ville	

M. Jenicek, T. Rousseau et M. Bellefleur, Département de médecine sociale et préventive, section Epidémiologie, Faculté de médecine, Université de Montréal, Service de santé, Ville Saint-Laurent, Québec, Canada.

relation avec les différentes mesures de la santé. Dans cette étape de l'étude, nous avons essayé de répondre aux trois questions et objectifs suivants.

1. Evaluer de façon appropriée l'activité physique des personnes âgées à l'aide d'une étude épidémiologique de la population générale. Nous avons tenu compte du fait qu'une évaluation de l'activité physique, selon sa régularité, son type et le degré de supervision requis, devait donner une information satisfaisante. Les tests classiques et les évaluations quantitatives ne sont pas possibles étant donné l'âge des sujets et le caractère du travail porte-à-porte.

2. Le type d'activité physique devrait être en relation avec la santé physique, mentale et sociale des sujects. Si l'étude confirme cette hypothèse, peut-on se servir de l'activité physique de loisirs comme un indice du bien-être de l'individu?

3. Est-ce que le type d'activité physique varie en fonction de divers caractères épidémiologiques des personnes et du milieu?

Le matériel et les méthodes

Un total de 510 hommes et 569 femmes, âgés de 60, 65, 70, 75 et 80 ans au moment de l'entrevue, ont participé à l'étude. Ne connaissant pas la variabilité des fonctions mesurées selon l'âge (ceci étant un des buts de l'étude), nous avons donné la préférence à des strates d'âge précises par rapport à l'échantillon aléatoire de tous les sujets au delà de 60 ans. La population suivie est blanche, à prédominance canadienne-française, catholique, d'origine urbaine, d'une strate socio-économique moyenne, avec une formation du niveau secondaire ou plus.

Tous les sujets ont été visités à domicile par une infirmière et ont répondu à un questionnaire pré-codé au cours de l'entrevue.

Aux fins des objectifs mentionnés, nous avons suivi plus particulièrement les variables suivantes:

1. L'activité physique a été répartie selon son caractère, sa régularité et le degré de supervision requis, en sept catégories décrites au Tableau II. Le caractère subjectif de la classification selon cette échelle ordinale se prête au traitement par l'analyse des ridits selon la méthodologie de Bross, éprouvée déjà dans des conditions comparables dans les études épidémiologiques relatives aux accidents, à la pression sanguine, etc. [4, 9]. Chaque sujet se voit attribuer une valeur du ridit correspondant à la moitié de la proportion des sujets dans sa catégorie, plus la proportion des sujets se trouvant dans les catégories précédant la catégorie du sujet. Le ridit moyen peut être

**Tableau II. Catégories d'activité physique
d'après la régularité et le degré
de supervision des loisirs.**

1. Aucune activité physique
2. Promenades occasionnelles
3. Promenades régulières (journalières)
4. Activités sportives non organisées* et irrégulières
5. Activités sportives non organisées* et régulières
6. Activités sportives organisées* et régulières
7. Sport de compétition*

*Activité organisée = programme spécial, supervisé par moniteur qualifié.

ensuite calculé pour chaque strate de sujets et ses limites de confiance peuvent être soumises à l'analyse comparative.

2. La santé physique a été évaluée selon l'échelle de Belloc et coll [3] répartissant les sujets en sept catégories décrites au Tableau III.

3. La santé mentale a été évaluée par l'indice de Berkman [2], qui vise à classer les sujets par pointage dans sept catégories établies en fonction des tendances dépressives, phobiques et de l'isolement, et en fonction des signes de participation sociale, de motivation et de satisfaction.

Les deux indices de santé mentionnés ont été soumis aussi à l'analyse de ridits.

4. La santé globale a été mesurée par l'indice de Grogono et Woodgate [6] qui englobe le bien-être physique, mental et social comme l'illustre le Tableau IV.

5. L'incapacité et les handicaps des sujets ont été déterminés par la méthode rapide de Linn [10]. La classification basée sur 16 catégories est décrite au Tableau V.

**Tableau III. Catégories de santé physique
(indice de Belloc, Breslow et Hochstim [3])**

1. *Handicap majeur:* dépendance pendant au moins six mois de l'année
2. *Handicap mineur:* réduction des activités durant six mois et plus.
3. *Conditions chroniques majeures:* aucun handicap , mais au moins deux troubles au cours des derniers 12 mois. Ex.: asthme, hypertension.
4. *Conditions chroniques mineures:* aucun handicap, mais un seul trouble chronique au cours des 12 derniers mois.
5. *Etat symptomatique.*
6. *Aucune plainte, sentiment de force.*
7. *Aucune plainte, sentiment de faiblesse.*

Tableau IV. Indice de bien-être physique, mental et social
(Santé globale selon Grogono et Woodgate [6])

1. Travail
2. Loisirs et récréation
3. Malaises, douleurs physiques, souffrances
4. Tristesse et malheur
5. Communication avec les autres
6. Sommeil
7. Inependance des autres
8. Plaisirs de table
9. Défécation et miction
10. Vie sexuelle

Fonction normale = 1 point,
    pertubée = ½ point,
    abolie = 0 point.
Indice de santé = somme des points / 10

Tableau V. Mesure de l'incapacité et de la dépendance selon Linn

1. Alimentation
2. Diète
3. Médicaments
4. Langage
5. Audition
6. Vision
7. Marche
8. Bain
9. Habillement
10. Incontinence
11. Rasage ou toilette
12. Surveillance (re: sécurité)
13. Alitement
14. Confusion mentale
15. Manque de coopération
16. Dépression

Fonction normale = 1 point,
Fonction modifié ou aide occasionnelle requise = 2 points.
Fonction abolie = 3 points,
Indice de l'incapacité = somme des points.

La relation entre les divers indices a été testée par l'analyse de corrélation des rangs de Spearman pour les observations pouvant occuper le même rang. Nous avons aussi tenu à déterminer le coefficient de concordance de Kendall pour le même type d'observations [5].

Les résultants et les commentaires qui s'y rattachent peuvent être résumés comme suit:

Dans l'ensemble des observations, les hommes sont plus actifs que les femmes et l'activité physique décroît avec l'âge chez les deux sexes comme on pouvait s'y attendre (Tableau VI).

Le Tableau VII réprésente la répartition des sujets d'après les différentes catégories d'âge. La proportion des sujets occupant les deux premières catégories (pas d'activité physique, sauf promenades occasionnelles) est importante; elle est de l'ordre d'un tiers des sujets.

L'activité physique devient restreinte aussitôt que les sujets abandonnent le travail (au delà de 65 ans).

A l'âge de 60 ans, l'activité physique est la plus intense chez ceux qui ont les occupations supérieures et elle décroît avec le statut occupationnel. Ces différences disparaîssent dès l'âge de la retraite (Tableau VIII).

Nous n'avons pas trouvé d'autres différences du point du vue de l'activité physique qui seraient liées aux caractères des personnes et à l'environnement tels que perçus dans l'étude.

Chez les femmes, l'activité physique est en corrélation avec tous les indices de santé aux différents niveaux d'âge. Par contre, chez les

Tableau VI. R des sujets des diverses tranches d'âge et de sexe, pour leur activité physique

Age	n	R	Intervalle de confiance (p <0.05)
Hommes			
60 ans	197	0.55	0.51*-0.59
65 ans	151	0.46	0.42 -0.51†
70 ans	97	0.50	0.44 -0.56
75 ans	48	0.42	0.34 -0.50
80 ans	13	0.40	0.24 -0.56
TOTAL	506	0.53	0.51 -0.56
Femmes			
60 ans	202	0.62	0.58 -0.66
65 ans	127	0.48	0.42 -0.53
70 ans	121	0.47	0.42 -0.53
75 ans	59	0.34	0.26 -0.41
80 ans	49	0.34	0.26 -0.43
TOTAL	558	0.47	0.45 -0.50

*valeur sans approximation: 0.512
†valeur sans approximation: 0.511

Tableau VII. Distribution des sujets des diverses tranches d'âge et de sexe dans les sept catégories d'activité physique

Age		Catégories de l'activité physique						
HOMMES		1	2	3	4	5	6	7
60 ans (n = 197)	%:	6.60	19.80	36.55	19.80	9.64	5.58	2.03
65 ans (n = 151)	%:	17.22	20.53	36.42	11.92	10.60	1.99	1.32
70 ans (n = 97)	%:	7.22	18.56	50.52	17.53	4.12	2.06	0.00
80 ans (n = 13)	%:	15.38	23.08	53.85	0.00	7.69	0.00	0.00
FEMMES								
60 ans (n = 202)	%:	6.93	15.35	44.06	16.34	9.90	6.44	.99
65 ans (n = 127)	%:	11.02	32.28	43.31	5.51	7.09	.79	0.00
70 ans (n = 121)	%:	16.53	23.97	46.28	5.79	6.61	.83	0.00
75 ans (n = 59)	%:	27.12	37.29	33.90	0.00	1.69	0.00	0.00
80 ans (n = 49)	%:	26.53	36.73	34.69	0.00	2.04	0.00	0.00

Tableau VIII. $\bar{R}$ de l'activité physique des hommes de 60 ans, selon leur scolarité

Niveau de scolarité	n	$\bar{R}$	Intervalle de confiance (p <0.05)
5 ans et moins	21	0.33	0.21 -0.46*
entre 6 et 10 ans	92	0.47	0.41 -0.53
entre 11 et 15 ans	64	0.57	0.50 -0.61
16 ans et plus	20	0.59	0.46†-0.72

*valeur sans approximation: 0.459
†valeur sans approximation: 0.465

hommes, l'activité physique ne correspond pas au degré d'incapacité et à la santé mentale, à part quelques exceptions (Tableaux IX et X).

Jusqu'à présent, les résultats ont montré que le type d'activité physique peut dépendre de la santé physique et de la santé globale (mesurées par indices choisis), mais est relativement indépendant de la santé mentale et des handicaps. Le type d'activité physique est-il

Tableau IX. Matrices de corrélation de Spearman entre les 4 indices de santé et l'activité physique, pour l'ensemble des sujets, les hommes et les femmes

Activité physique	vs:	Linn	Belloc	Berkman	Grogono
Hommes	rho =	0.1742	0.2488	0.2029	0.2637
(n = 485)	t =	3.8887*	5.6463*	4.5532*	6.0076*
Femmes	rho =	0.2698	0.3869	0.2982	0.3661
(n = 540)	t =	6.4991*	9.7333*	7.2455*	9.1262*
Tous les sujets	rho =	0.2361	0.3286	0.2574	0.3316
(n = 1025)	t =	7.7697*	11.1264*	8.5207*	11.2428*

Légende: rho = coefficient de corrélation de Spearman
t = valeur calculée pour vérifier la signification de "rho"
* = "rho" significatif avec $p \leqslant 0.001$

Tableau X. Matrices de corrélation de Spearman entre les 4 indices de santé et l'activité physique, dans les diverses catégories d'âge et de sexe

Activité physique	vs:	Linn	Belloc	Berkman	Grogono
Hommes (n = 485)					
60 ans	rho =	0.0950	0.1608	0.1548	0.2031
(n = 191)	t =	1.3123	2.2395*	2.1539*	2.8518†
65 ans	rho =	0.0763	0.2155	0.2855	0.3177
(n = 146)	t =	0.9177	2.6482†	3.5753†	4.0207‡
70 ans	rho =	0.3410	0.3620	0.1828	0.3061
(n = 94)	t =	3.4795‡	3.7246‡	1.7833	3.0845†
75 ans	rho =	0.1552	0.3117	0.0928	0.0664
(n = 42)	t =	0.9934	2.0749*	0.5896	0.4212
80 ans	rho =	0.3566	0.2220	0.4598	0.3024
(n = 12)	t =	1.2072	0.7201	1.6373	1.0034
Femmes (n = 540)					
60 ans	rho =	0.1533	0.2898	0.2907	0.2679
(n = 197)	t =	2.1664*	4.2288‡	4.2426‡	3.8833‡
65 ans	rho =	0.2287	0.4501	0.2750	0.3294
(n = 125)	t =	2.6058*	5.5894‡	3.1721†	3.8689‡
70 ans	rho =	0.2607	0.3051	0.1876	0.2256
(n = 119)	t =	2.9213†	3.4660‡	2.0661*	2.5053*
75 ans	rho =	0.4803	0.3181	0.3876	0.4389
(n = 56)	t =	4.0243‡	2.4660*	3.0902†	3.5894‡
80 ans	rho =	0.3106	0.2666	0.4109	0.3613
(n = 43)	t =	2.0922*	1.7715	2.8860†	2.4810†

Légende: rho = coefficient de corrélation de Spearman
t = valeur calculée pour vérifier la signification de "rho"
* = "rho" significatif avec $p \leqslant 0.05$
† = "rho" significativ avec $p \leqslant 0.01$
‡ = "rho" significatif avec $p \leqslant 0.001$

choisi de façon compensatoire, avec un degré considérable de liberté?

Le Tableaux XI montre la concordance entre les quatre indices de santé et d'activité physique. Elle est significative chez les deux sexes, à tous les niveaux d'âge, sans être idéale (W = 1.0).

En répondant aux trois objectifs et questions de cette communication, nous pouvons émettre les *conclusions* suivantes:

1. La méthode d'évaluation de l'activité physique est simple et elle paraît pour le moment facile, reproductible et appropriée pour déceler les variations en fonction des divers caractères épidémiologiques décrits (surtout l'âge, le sexe et le niveau de scolarité).

2. La corrélation et la concordance entre les diverses mesures de santé et l'activité physique confirment plutôt que d'éclairer la confusion actuelle lorsqu'il s'agit du choix de mesures de santé adéquates. Toutes les méthodes mesurent le même état de santé hypothétique et global. Le type d'activité physique se dissocie de certains indicateurs (santé mentale et incapacité surtout). Toutefois, pour que cette fonction puisse servir comme indice de santé ou comme autre variable dépendante, il est nécessaire de la valider par

Tableau XI. Coefficients de concordance de Kendall (W) entre les 4 indices de santé et l'activité physique

Hommes			*Femmes*		
60 ans	W =	0.3973	60 ans	W =	0.4697
(n = 191)	χ^2 =	377.4167†	(n = 197)	χ^2 =	460.3537†
65 ans	W =	0.4538	65 ans	W =	0.4781
(n = 146)	χ^2 =	329.0111†	(n = 125)	χ^2 =	296.4388†
70 ans	W =	0.4677	70 ans	W =	0.4920
(n = 94)	χ^2 =	217.4946†	(n = 119)	χ^2 =	290.2815†
75 ans	W =	0.4466	75 ans	W =	0.5077
(n = 42)	χ^2 =	91.5540†	(n = 56)	χ^2 =	139.6278
80 ans	W =	0.4783	80 ans	W =	0.4678
(n = 12)	χ^2 =	26.3040*	(n = 43)	χ^2 =	98.2447†
Tous les hommes			Toutes les femmes		
(n = 485)	W =	0.4461	(n = 540)	W =	0.5081
	χ^2 =	1079.5638†		χ^2 =	1369.4302†

	Tous les sujets	W =	0.4865
	(n = 1025)	χ^2 =	2491.0357†

Légende: W = coefficient de concordance de Kendall
χ^2 = valeur calculée pour vérifier la signification de W
* = significatif avec $p \leqslant 0.01$
† = significatif avec $p \leqslant 0.001$

rapport aux méthodes physiologiques d'évaluation de l'activité physique, à l'état clinique des sujets et à leur classement selon d'autres indices de santé opérationnels, tels qu'utilisés dans l'administration des soins [1, 11].

3. La variation de l'activité physique dans les collectivités moins homogènes au point de vue épidémiologique devrait être étudiée aussi dans un avenir rapproché.

Les études épidémiologiques à grande échelle et dans la population générale exigeront une attention accrue au niveau du développement de méthodes de mesure simples mais valables, qui soient susceptibles de compléter les informations obtenues par les méthodes traditionnelles. La perception de l'état de santé de l'individu et de la population toute entière à l'aide d'une vaste gamme de méthodes non corrélées est l'idéal à rechercher dans les études futures.

Références

1. Ahumada, J., Guzman, A.A., Duran, H. et al: Health Planning. Washington: Pan Amer. Health Org., Scient. Publ. No. 111, April 1965.
2. Berkman, P.L.: Measurement of mental health in a general population survey. Am. J. Epidemiol. 94:105-111, 1971.
3. Belloc, N.B., Breslow, L. and Hochstim, J.R.: Measurement of physical health in a general population survey. Am. J. Epidemiol. 93:328-336, 1971.
4. Bross, I.D.J.: How to use ridit analysis. Biometrics 14:18-38, 1958.
5. Ferguson, G.A.: Statistical Analysis in Psychology & Education, ed. 3. New York:McGraw-Hill, 1971.
6. Grogono, A.W. and Woodgate, D.J.: Index for measuring health. Lancet, pp. 1024-1026, Nov. 6, 1971.
7. Jenicek, M., Rousseau, T. and Bellefleur, M.: Etude pilote de l'état de santé des citoyens seniors de la Ville de St-Laurent. Rapport général. Ville de Saint-Laurent, Septembre 1975.
8. Kantor S. and Winkelstein, W., Jr.: The rationale and use of ridit analysis in empidemiologic studies of blood pressure. Am. J. Epidemiol. 90:201-213, 1969.
9. Kantor S., Winkelstein, W., Jr. and Ibrahim, M.A.: A note on the interpretation of the ridit as a quantile rank. Am. J. Epidemiol. 87:609-615, 1969.
10. Linn, M.S.: A rapid disability rating scale. J. Am. Geriat. Soc. 15:211-214, 1967.
11. Michael, J.M., Spatafore, G. and Williams, E.R.: A basic information system for health planning. Pub. Health Rep. 83:21-28, 1968.

Studies on Aging, Physical Fitness and Health

E. Heikkinen

Introduction

The lifestyle of the elderly and factors which influence the quality of life have become increasingly important scientific objects during recent years. Reasons for this development can be found in the changes of the age structure of populations in industrialized countries and in the simultaneous increase of chronic, degenerative diseases which are in a complicated way connected with aging processes [3]. Gradually also, research on gerontological and geriatric problems has accelerated to its present exponential growth. A great number of cross-sectional studies have been carried out among people aged 65 and over [11, 13]. These studies have described the health status, the need and the use of medical, social and cultural services in different age groups among the elderly.

On the other hand, very few longitudinal or intervention studies have been done among the elderly. Available evidence indicates that social and psychological factors are at least as important as medical and physiological factors in predicting the quality of life and longevity among old people [4, 10]. The intervention studies suggest that the course of diseases can be altered by proper dietary habits even at old age [5]. Also, the trainability of old people has appeared to be better than usually assumed [1, 9, 14].

Because people aged 65 and over constitute a heterogenous group, the present investigations were undertaken to examine various problems of recently retired persons and, during a follow-up period, to investigate factors which are related to changes in the physical fitness, health status and living habits.

General Disposition of the Studies

In this short presentation a general overview of the studies is given and some apparent results are described, particularly those relevant to physical exercise.

E. Heikkinen, Department of Public Health Sciences, University of Tampere, Tampere, Finland.

The original cohort (Fig. 1), one whole age class, consisted of 428 persons aged 66 years living in a town of 70,000 in Central Finland. Of these, 92% were interviewed in 1972. About two years later a part of the subjects participated in health and fitness examinations which also contained variables of biological aging. In 1974 a trainability study was carried out among 26 healthy volunteers from the original cohort. Some results of the studies have been published elsewhere [2, 6, 12].

Results and Discussion

About one half of the 66-year-olds considered themselves healthy (49% of men and 45% of women). Most of the subjects were sufficiently physically fit for outdoor activities (Table I); 97.5% of them could move independently out of doors. Most of the subjects

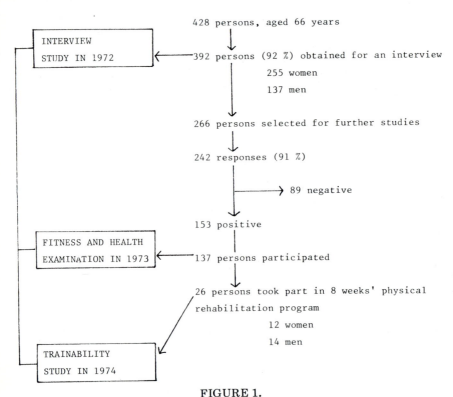

FIGURE 1.

Table I. The Ability To Move Out of Doors Among the 66-Year-Olds

	(%)
1. Not able	1.3
2. Able with the help of others	0.5
3. Able with the help of various auxiliary means	0.8
4. Able with a walking stick	5.9
5. Able with some difficulties without any auxiliary means	11.9
6. Able without any difficulties	80.4

were interested in physical activity but only a few were accustomed to engaging in strenuous physical exercise. Slow walking was the most usual form of a habitual physical training. About 19% of women and 37% of men were interested in sports which cause breathlessness and sweating.

On the basis of medical examination the 68-year-old persons were divided into different categories of bearable physical stress (Fig. 2). It appeared that nearly 20% of the subjects had serious chronic

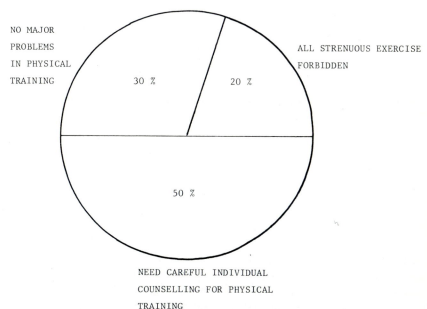

CAPABILITY OF 66-YEAR-OLD PERSONS
FOR PHYSICAL TRAINING

NO MAJOR PROBLEMS IN PHYSICAL TRAINING

ALL STRENUOUS EXERCISE FORBIDDEN

30 %

20 %

50 %

NEED CAREFUL INDIVIDUAL COUNSELLING FOR PHYSICAL TRAINING

FIGURE 2.

diseases which inhibit nearly all physical exercise, and many of them had difficulties in the activities of normal daily life. On the other hand, about one third was evaluated fit enough for even strenuous physical exercises. About one half of the 68-year-olds would need careful individual examinations and instructions for physical training.

Diseases (about 55%) and disabilities (about 32%) were the most important self-assessed restrictions for physical training among the 66-year-olds. Then followed lack of interest, lack of programmed training, lack of skills and lack of suitable company.

In order to evaluate the effects of physical exercise on aging processes we have attempted to develop methods for measuring biological aging in man. The principle is to choose variables which have high correlation coefficients with chronological age [7]. The behavior of some of the parameters among 460 Finnish men appears in Figure 3 which also shows how the index of biological age formed by combining the results of various measurements increases about 1% yearly with advancing age.

The variables of biological aging were measured before and after an eight-week physical training program in which 14 men and 12 women aged 69 years participated. The training program consisted of five one-hour training bouts in a week and included walking-jogging, ball games, gymnastics and swimming. Significant improvement (Table II) was noticed in various physiological functions. The subjects also felt that the training program was psychologically stimulating and increased their self-confidence.

It seems that no major differences exist in the relative trainability of the elderly if the results are calculated on the percentage basis from the pretraining values. Physical training can improve several functions which are gradually decreased with the passage of time. In that meaning physical training may retard some of the aging processes.

Our other studies indicate, however, that the rate of aging itself is not influenced by habitual physical training even though it is practiced for decades (unpublished results). The endurance athletes who have been in "lifelong" habitual physical training received better values compared to their sedentary controls in tests which are directly influenced by physical training. In other parameters like simple reaction time, thresholds for vibratory and auditory perceptions and vital capacity, no major differences were noticed between physically active and inactive men.

Preliminary analyses of the longitudinal data after a four-year follow-up period among the retired persons suggest that predictors of

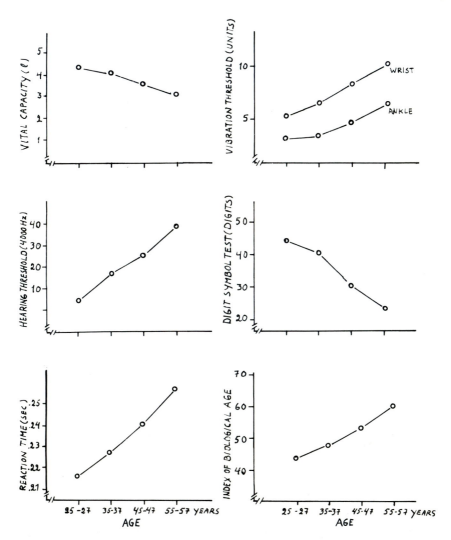

FIG. 3. Changes in selected functions and the index of biological age with aging among 460 Finnish men aged 25 to 57 years.

the development of health and physical fitness among the elderly can be found from the totality of their living situation consisting of various social, biological, medical and cultural determinants. Important categories in that connection seem to be education and previous occupation which are related with present social activities and maintenance of fitness and health.

Table II. Summary of Most Important Changes in Physical Fitness
Among 69-Year-Old Persons During 8-Weeks Physical Rehabilitation Program

$\dot{V}O_2$ max (ml/kg/min)
Men	30.0 → 32.9
Women	28.1 → 31.2

Vital capacity (liter)
Men	3.85 → 3.99
Women	2.37 → 2.61

Balance (Number of successful steps on narrow bridge)
Men	14.1 → 15.2
Women	7.6 → 9.0

Enzyme activities in musculus vastus lateralis (micromoles/gm/min)
MDH	Men	115.4 → 120.7
	Women	91.4 → 100.3
LDH	Men	122.5 → 120.2
	Women	102.2 → 90.1

References

1. Adams, G.M. and deVries, H.A.: Physiological effects of an exercise training regimen upon women aged 52 to 79. J. Gerontol. 28:50, 1973.
2. Aunola, S., Käyhty-Seppänen, B., Heikkinen, E. et al: Functional capability of 68-year-old people in the town of Jyväskylä. Z. Alternsforsch. 31:439, 1976.
3. Brocklehurst, J.C.: Textbook of Geriatric Medicine & Gerontology. Edinburgh and London:Churchill Livingstone, 1973.
4. Chebotarev, D.: Fight against old age. Gerontologist 11:359, 1971.
5. Cheraskin, E. and Ringsdorf, W.M.: Clinical findings before and after dietary counsel. Geriatrics 27:121, 1972.
6. Heikkinen, E., Käyhty-Seppänen, B. and Pohjolainen, P.: Health situation and related social conditions among 66-year-old Finnish men. Scand. J. Soc. Med. 4:71, 1976.
7. Heikkinen, E., Kiiskinen, A., Käyhty, B. et al: Assessment of biological age. Gerontologia 20:33, 1974.
8. Lawrence, P.S.: Patterns of health and illness in older people. Bull. NY Acad Med. 49:1100, 1973.
9. Liesen, H., Heikkinen, E., Suominen, H. and Michel, D.: Der Effekt eines zwölfwöchigen Ausdauerstrainings auf die Leistungsfähigkeit und den Muskelstoffwechsel bei untrainierten Männern des 6. und 7. Lebensjahrzehnts. Sportarzt Sportmed. 26:26, 1975.
10. Palmore, E. and Jeffers, F.C. (eds.): Prediction of Life Span, Recent Findings. Lexington, Mass.:D. C. Heath and Co., 1971.
11. Shanas, E. et al: Old People in Three Industrial Societies. New York:Atherton Press, 1968.

12. Suominen, H., Heikkinen, E. and Parkatti, T.: Effect of eight weeks' physical training on muscle and connective tissue of the m. vastus lateralis in 69-year-old men and women. J. Gerontol. 32:33, 1977.
13. Woodruff, D.S. and Birren, J.E.: Aging. Scientific Perspectives and Social Issues. New York:D. van Nostrand Company, 1975.
14. deVries, H.A.: Physiological effects of an exercise training regimen upon men aged 52 to 88. J. Gerontol. 25:325, 1970.

Author Index  Auteurs

AUTHOR INDEX/AUTEURS

Subject Index Sujets

| A listing of the **COMPLETE SERIES** from the International Congress of Physical Activity Sciences Meeting | **SERIE COMPLETE** des ouvrages du Congrès international des sciences de l'activité physique |

NOTICE

By decision of the Scientific Commission, *French* and *English* were adopted as the two official languages of the International Congress of Physical Activity Sciences – 1976.

In these Proceedings, the communications appear *in the language in which they were presented* for French and English and *in English* as concerns the papers which were delivered in either German, Russian or Spanish. Abstracts in the two official languages accompany each paper included in Books 1 and 2 and the seminar presentations in the other books of the series.

AVERTISSEMENT

Les langues *anglaise* et *française* furent adoptées par la Commission scientifique comme langues officielles du Congrès international des sciences de l'activité physique – 1976. De ce fait, les communications apparaissent au présent rapport officiel *dans la langue où elles ont été présentées* pour ce qui est de l'anglais et du français, et dans la langue *anglaise* pour ce qui est des communications qui furent faites dans les langues allemande, russe et espagnole.

Des résumés dans chacune des deux langues officielles accompagnent chacune des communications qui paraissent aux Volumes 1 et 2 ainsi que les présentations faites par les conférenciers invités dans les autres volumes de la série.